AF361614

Kentuckians and Pearl Harbor

Kentuckians and Pearl Harbor
STORIES FROM THE DAY OF INFAMY

Berry Craig

south limestone

Published by South Limestone Books
An imprint of the University Press of Kentucky

Copyright © 2020 by The University Press of Kentucky
All rights reserved.

Editorial and Sales Offices: The University Press of Kentucky
663 South Limestone Street, Lexington, Kentucky 40508-4008
www.kentuckypress.com

Unless otherwise noted, photographs are by the author.

Library of Congress Cataloging-in-Publication Data

Names: Craig, Berry, author.
Title: Kentuckians and Pearl Harbor : stories from the day of infamy /
    Berry Craig.
Description: [Lexington, Kentucky] : South Limestone, [2020] | Includes
    bibliographical references and index.
Identifiers: LCCN 2020032976 | ISBN 9781949669275 (hardcover) | ISBN
    9781949669282 (pdf) | ISBN 9781949669299 (epub)
Subjects: LCSH: Pearl Harbor (Hawaii), Attack on, 1941. | World War,
    1939–1945—Kentucky.
Classification: LCC D767.92 .C727 2020 | DDC 940.54/266930922769—dc23
LC record available at https://lccn.loc.gov/2020032976

This book is printed on acid-free paper meeting
the requirements of the American National Standard
for Permanence in Paper for Printed Library Materials.

Manufactured in the United States of America.

To my father, the late Motor Machinist's Mate
First Class Berry F. Craig Jr., US Navy,
and my father-in-law, the late Master Sergeant
Robert P. Hocker Jr., US Army,
both of whom enlisted after Pearl Harbor
and came home with battle stars
on their Asiatic and Pacific campaign ribbons.

Contents

Illustrations follow page 135

Introduction

"Nearly every American alive at the time can describe how he first heard the news," Walter Lord wrote in the foreword to *Day of Infamy,* his minute-by-minute account of the Pearl Harbor attack. "He marked the moment carefully, carving out a sort of mental souvenir, for instinctively he knew how much his life would be changed by what was happening in Hawaii." No Americans remembered December 7, 1941, with more precision than those who survived the surprise Japanese air raid that plunged the United States into World War II. Caught in the deadly rain of bombs, torpedoes, and strafing fire, they "went through successive stages of shock, fear, and anger," Lord added.[1]

Gunner's Mate Second Class James Allard Vessels of Paducah experienced all three emotions aboard the *Arizona.* The super-dreadnought became the most iconic of the warships sunk on the date President Franklin D. Roosevelt said would "live in infamy." Vessels returned to Pearl Harbor for the thirtieth anniversary of the attack. Nineteen years earlier, a memorial had been built over the rusty, bomb-blasted, fire-blackened, and submerged hull of the battleship, which still seeps fuel oil even today. The gleaming white structure straddles but does not touch the *Arizona.* Inscribed on an inside wall are the names of 1,177 crewmen—officers, sailors, and marines—who perished. Most are still entombed in the ship's remains. Reading the roll of the dead, Vessels found a name he was looking for, Gunner's Mate Third Class Ross Worth Lightfoot. He was Vessels's partner in a card game they never finished.[2]

The air-raid alarm sounded around 7:55 A.M., just before "morning colors," when the Stars and Stripes was to be ceremonially run up the stern flagstaff. The ship's acclaimed band was set to play "The Star Spangled Banner." The band's director, Frederick William McKinney, and its drummer, Emmett Isaac Lynch, were Kentuckians. They joined the scramble for battle stations. Under fire, Vessels hurriedly climbed to a machine-gun platform high atop the mainmast; the musicians scurried deep below decks to help pass ammunition up to the gunners. At 8:06, a bomb blew up the *Arizona*. Vessels's lofty perch saved his life; every member of the band died.[3]

The *Arizona* was close to the end of "Battleship Row," a procession of capital ships moored next to Ford Island in the middle of Pearl Harbor. The *California* was first in line. Torpedoes and bombs sank that battlewagon dubbed the *Prune Barge* for the seemingly endless supply of dried fruit sent from the Golden State. Almost one hundred of its crew died, Fireman First Class Jim Hamlin supposedly among them. From Harlan, Hamlin was, however, alive. He was one of several men from the Bluegrass State whose families received telegrams reporting that their loved ones had been killed or were missing in action. Most of the wires correcting the mistakes arrived before Christmas, thus transforming Yuletide mourning and grief into joy and thankfulness.[4]

Sundays were usually a day off—"liberty" to sailors and marines—for most of those in uniform in Hawaii. Joe Sanders, from Mayfield, and a shipmate from the light cruiser *St. Louis* planned to rent a camera in Honolulu and take pictures in the lush green hills above Hawaii's capital city. Japanese airmen canceled the photo shoot.[5]

The planners of the Japanese attack knew that success depended on air superiority. So, while most of the planes targeted the Pacific Fleet, others flew off to destroy army, navy, and marine air bases and their planes on the ground. The soldier Calvin Leisure of Ohio County had just finished guard duty at Wheeler Army Airfield, which adjoined Schofield Army Barracks north of Pearl Harbor. He was looking forward to breakfast but never made it through the chow line. Everybody scattered when the enemy airmen pounced, firing cannons and machine guns and dropping bombs on the unsuspecting Americans. Leisure grabbed his M-1 rifle and fought back from a golf course sand trap. John Wood, a marine from Glasgow, managed to finish his morning meal before he spotted strange-looking airplanes flying toward Pearl Harbor. He, too, was at war, though President Franklin D. Roosevelt did not formally declare it so until December 8.[6]

One of the first antiaircraft projectiles aimed at the Japanese warplanes might have been the sailor J. C. Riley's brand-new baseball bat.

A shipmate on the destroyer *Case* said that he hurled the Louisville Slugger at some low-flying aircraft. From Benton in Marshall County, Riley confessed that he did not remember the toss but did recall losing his bat somehow.[7]

The army private Herman Horn of Frankfort, the state capital, never knew what became of his breakfast—an apple and a bottle of milk. He deposited it in his tent next to his cot, dozed off, and woke up again to the din of airplane engines, explosions, and gunfire. He forsook his sustenance when he and the rest of his outfit were herded into trucks that sped off to shore batteries and antiaircraft guns at Fort Barrette, near Pearl Harbor. They dodged strafing enemy planes on the way. "I often wondered where my apple and my milk went," he said.[8]

Explosions startled the soldier Charles Hocker at Schofield Barracks. He dismissed the noise, figuring planes were dropping harmless smoke bombs in a training exercise. Also an Ohio Countian, he realized his potentially fatal mistake when he saw aircraft painted with round, bright red rising-sun insignia dropping real bombs and shooting real cannon and machine-gun rounds. "They killed a lot of my buddies," said Hocker, who suffered a slight leg wound.[9]

The attack caught the sailor Clarence Meece of Somerset with his trousers down, literally. He was in a "head"—toilet to landlubbers—on the light cruiser *Raleigh* when a Japanese torpedo found its mark. "It raised the ship up about a foot and me about a foot higher than that," he recalled.[10]

The sailor Perry Calhoun of Eddyville was expecting trouble—finding an empty wash rack for drying his duds in a navy barracks on Ford Island. The Sabbath was his wash day. He was gathering up clothes when bombs began tumbling down. Some of his pals grabbed obsolete World War I–vintage bolt-action Springfield rifles and started shooting at the foe. Calhoun claimed they downed a plane.[11]

The attack sprang from a half dozen aircraft carriers. The Japanese air armada consisted of 350 fighters, dive-bombers, horizontal-bombers, and torpedo-bombers. Japan calculated that America's mighty Pacific Fleet—especially the eight battleships and three carriers—was the direst threat to its growing Asian empire. After the fleet had been destroyed, Asia would be Japan's fiefdom, or so Japanese military and political leaders calculated.

All the Japanese targets were on Oahu. Besides Pearl Harbor, the main ones were Hickam and Wheeler Army Airfields and naval air stations at Kaneohe Bay and on Ford Island in Pearl Harbor. There were Kentuckians at both army air bases, but most Bluegrass State men in uniform in Hawaii were sailors. Still others were marines, soldiers, and airmen. Some, too, were civilians, many of them the wives and children of servicemen.

Though Kentucky is landlocked and many miles from the sea, it has a surprisingly long nautical tradition. Several Kentucky riflemen served essentially as marine sharpshooters in Commodore Oliver Hazard Perry's fleet in the War of 1812 Battle of Lake Erie. (Hazard is the seat of Perry County.) Lawrenceburg's Kavanaugh Academy—"the Annapolis of Kentucky"—prepped scores of eager young men for the US Naval Academy in the early twentieth century. Admiral Hugh Rodman, a Frankfort native, commanded the Pacific Fleet after World War I.[12]

Given the evidence of their letters home before December 7, Kentuckians seemed mostly happy in Hawaii. "I strongly urge anyone considering signing up to do so without delay for it's a great life and the KP's are too far apart to worry me," the army air force private Elliott C. Mitchell Jr. declared in a letter published in the *Paducah Sun-Democrat,* his hometown paper. Another Kentucky man, probably a sailor, believed America was bound to join World War II, which started in Europe on September 1, 1939. But, when Uncle Sam did jump in, "there will be nothing to fear here," he bragged in a letter published in the *Louisville Courier-Journal,* the state's largest paper. He claimed the Japanese were too scared to attack Oahu because of the fleet, "two large flying fields here," and "army camps all around the island." Hawaii, he added, was "about 6,000 miles from Japan—farther than you are from Europe": "Japan could never bomb this place unless she sent airplane carriers out and it would be too long a trip to make without refueling, and an airplane carrier could never get within 1,000 miles of this place."[13] Like his name, the sailor's fate is apparently forgotten. But "Remember Pearl Harbor!" went down in history as a famous American war cry and the name of a popular song.

It was 12:55 p.m. in western Kentucky when the attack began, an hour later in central and eastern Kentucky. Jim Hamlin was on his ship forty-five hundred miles from Harlan, in eastern Kentucky. He remembered: "A fellow hollered, 'The Japs are bombing us!'" Another guy replied: "I didn't even know they were mad at us."[14] Probably most Kentuckians were similarly stunned. They, like the anonymous *Courier-Journal* letter writer and many other Americans, might have expected the United States to join the war sooner or later, but in Europe alongside the British and the Soviets fighting Nazi Germany and Fascist Italy. America had been supplying Great Britain and the Soviet Union with a mountain of military aid. In December 1941, they were the only countries left to battle the German dictator Adolf Hitler and the Italian strongman Benito Mussolini, brothers in arms bent on conquering and divvying up most of Europe.

In 1941, the television era was a decade or more away. Radio broke the news of Pearl Harbor, the Sunday morning newspapers having been out for hours.

The attack was over by 10:00 A.M., Hawaii time, 2:00 or 3:00 P.M. depending on where one lived in Kentucky. In homes, churches, businesses, other public places, and parked vehicles, thousands of men, women, and children, angry, anxious, fearful, sorrowful, and bewildered, gathered around radios tuned to the news. For the rest of their lives, few forgot where they were and what they were doing on the day Pearl Harbor was attacked.

The *Sun-Democrat* leaned Democratic on its editorial pages. But it and the rest of the state press—no matter how fiercely Republican or Democratic—reflected the state motto "United We Stand, Divided We Fall" and lost no time endorsing war against Japan—and Germany and Italy, to boot. "War has chosen us!" exclaimed the *Louisville Courier Journal,* the state's largest paper. "Japan's attack on the United States is part of the world treachery, the world revolution, which the Nazis have created. . . . America will now unite to beat Japan. America must now unite to finish the job by beating Germany, the source of all our woe."[15] Some editorials were measured, considering the topic at issue. Others shamelessly pandered to racism and xenophobia. In almost all papers, the Japanese were *Japs,* a mild epithet compared to other slurs that showed up in print.

In any event, many Americans had never heard of Pearl Harbor and probably could not have found Hawaii on a globe or in a world atlas. Others knew the islands from either *National Geographic* magazine and books or movie newsreels. Hawaii was a tropical paradise synonymous with "hula dancers, ukuleles and pineapples." Faraway Hawaii was "famed in song and story" and known as a vacation playground for the rich and famous, including film stars. Probably most Kentuckians had forgotten that the big navy base made the news in state papers in November 1938 when the navy aviation cadet J. W. Beam, evidently of the famous Bardstown whiskey distilling family, lost his life in a plane crash.[16]

But Kentucky residents who kept up with the news knew trouble with Japan was brewing. The Japanese seemed determined to carve out a vast Asian empire and, in the process, drive the Americans and the Europeans out of the Far East. President Franklin D. Roosevelt aimed to check Japan. He had won a third term in another landslide in 1940. But most Americans—even FDR's most ardent fans—were still disinclined toward warring with anybody; the country became deeply isolationist after World War I. Hence, the president tried economic pressure, which failed to stop Japan. Meanwhile, American sailors were in harm's way in the Atlantic. US and British merchant ships were transporting guns, tanks, airplanes, and tons of other war materiel to Britain and the Soviet Union. Prowling the Atlantic shipping lanes, German submarine wolf packs were sinking the cargo vessels at an alarming rate. US and British warships were teaming up to protect the vulnerable convoys. On Halloween, a Nazi sub sank the American destroyer *Reuben James* near Iceland; close to one hundred men were lost. The kaiser's U-boats had torpedoed the United States into World War I against Germany. It looked like Hitler's would do likewise in 1941.

After Pearl Harbor, most Americans—even fervent war opponents—were all in for getting even with Japan and licking the Germans and Italians, too. Scores of young men enlisted on December 8 when President Roosevelt declared war on Japan, which had declared war on the United States and the United Kingdom right after the Pearl Harbor attack. (Germany and Italy declared war on the United States three days later.) Before the president asked Congress for a war declaration, Kentucky papers reported that Senator Albert B. Chandler, a Democrat from Versailles, planned to vote for war. An army reserve officer, he also aimed to volunteer for active duty. "We will be able to take care of the situation and in a typical American way," "Happy" boasted. He ended up keeping his seat. Kentucky's senior senator, Majority Leader Alben Barkley, also supported FDR's war declaration. But the *Paducah Democrat* predicted a lengthy war.[17]

Like the *Courier-Journal* editorial, Barkley hinted that Hitler had had a hand in Pearl Harbor, a view common in the United States. "This concept was absolutely false," wrote the historians Gordon M. Prange, Donald M. Goldstein, and Katherine V. Dillon. The Japanese, they added, "planned and carried out the attack entirely on their own." Nonetheless, Barkley maintained that Japan did not act alone: "Not only is this war being made upon us by Japan . . . it is being made upon us by those who control Japan, those who have dictated to Japan, those who have prodded Japan to engage in this unspeakable treachery and duplicity which has brought this tragedy upon the two nations."[18]

In the days after Pearl Harbor, state papers were filled with news stories presaging a rapidly rising tsunami of Bluegrass State volunteers for military service. (The tidal wave included my two uncles from Mayfield and my father-in-law from Arlington, the latter in Carlisle County. All three joined the army. My father, a native Tennessean from Knoxville, enlisted in the navy in 1942 after he turned eighteen.) The staff writer H. L. Nations told *Courier-Journal* readers that the Louisville resident Clarence A. Combs Jr. was a sailor aboard the battleship *Oklahoma,* which the Japanese attackers had "set afire." Clarence's big brother, Russell Arnold, twenty-five, had come home after serving six years on the capital ship. He wished "he had been there for the action" and vowed to reenlist soon. His little brother, Charles Arnold, promised to follow his siblings into service. "I'm worried," admitted their mother, Georgia Combs. "They're shooting at my son." Smashed by torpedoes, the *Oklahoma* capsized. Combs survived, but more than four hundred of his shipmates did not.[19]

Few Pearl Harbor survivors are alive in Kentucky or anywhere else today. All the men I interviewed between 1976 and 2007 are dead. For his book, published in 1957, Lord talked to or corresponded with 577 men and women—Americans, including Hawaiians, and Japanese. For many years after World War II, the media ran stories about Pearl Harbor, almost always on or near the anniversary of the attack. More often than not, those stories featured local survivors and appeared on the front pages of newspapers and led the evening television news. But, with the passing of time and of survivors, Pearl Harbor anniversaries became less newsworthy to newspaper editors and television news producers. Today, while most of the media run wire service or network news stories on December 7, the stories seldom make the front page or lead a news broadcast.

Pearl Harbor gets some ink in Kentucky history books. In their *New History of Kentucky,* Lowell H. Harrison and James C. Klotter mentioned navy Chaplain Howell Forgy and his link to "Praise the Lord and Pass the Ammunition!" And they noted that Admiral Husband E. Kimmel, "the unfortunate commander of the naval forces" at Pearl Harbor, was from Henderson. They quoted an *Arizona* sailor from Louisville who remembered: "The whole harbor was on fire. . . . I went into a state of shock."[20]

This book will not focus on the never-ending debate over whether Kimmel and Lieutenant General William Short, the army commander in Hawaii, really were to blame—or were innocent scapegoats—for America's greatest military disaster. Nor will it take up the absurd claims by the president's detractors that FDR knew the attack was coming and let it happen so he could drag the United States into World War II and help the British. Prange, Goldstein, and Dillon provide what I think is the best summary of what really happened: "Out of the smoke arising from honest debate and sincere scholarship, as well as the miasma exuding from the swamp of buckpassing, political opportunism, and name-calling, two facts emerged: first, the Japanese planned and executed the attack entirely on their own, with no urging, tempting, or backstairs assistance from Roosevelt, Hitler, or anyone else; second, the success of the operation resulted as much from superior Japanese efforts and performance as from American miscalculations and blunders."[21]

This book does not tell the Pearl Harbor story from the perspectives of admirals, generals or politicians. Nor is it a comprehensive account of the attack. Other books ably fill those bills—from Lord's *Day of Infamy* to Prange, Goldstein, and Dillon's works and Craig Nelson's more recent account.[22] This book aims to break new ground by telling the untold, forgotten, or little-known stories of ordinary Kentuckians, military and civilian, on the most extraordinary day in their lives. It concludes with home-front reaction to one of the most pivotal events in American history.

History records that, in 1941 America, segregation and race discrimination were the law in the South and border states like Kentucky and the social order almost everywhere else in the country. Yet "the surge of patriotism prompted by Pearl Harbor transcended the racial divide," wrote Chris Dixon. "African Americans reacted to the Japanese attack with a sense of vengeance that seemingly left no doubt regarding their commitment to their nation and its war against Japan." At the same time, Pearl Harbor was "a powerful referent point to denounce racism everywhere, as the white supremacy underpinning both American racism and the colonial enterprise was challenged in myriad ways during the Pacific War."[23] This duality was reflected in a December 20, 1941, editorial in the *Louisville Leader,* one of the state's two leading black newspapers.[24]

When Pearl Harbor was bombed, there were precious few opportunities for African Americans to escape racial discrimination by joining the military. Blacks could not serve in the marines until 1942. A year before, the marine commandant, Major General Thomas Holcomb, said that letting "Negroes" into the Corps would amount to a "definite loss of efficiency." He added: "If it were a question of having a Marine Corps of 5,000 whites or 250,000 Negroes, I would rather have the whites."[25] The army and navy had a small number of blacks. African American soldiers served in support units commanded by white officers. Typically, they were cooks, truck drivers, and laborers. In the navy, blacks could serve aboard ships but only as cooks and mess attendants. I was able to find only one black Kentuckian who was on Oahu during the attack. The army cook Luby Saxon of Graves County was at Schofield Barracks. I have also included the story of Private Robert H. Brooks of Scott County. It was first reported that he died at Pearl Harbor, but he was killed on December 8 during the Japanese attack on the Philippines.

In writing this book, I never forgot my editors' admonitions when I was a rookie reporter long ago: "Quote, quote, quote—let your subjects tell their stories in their words." I followed their counsel as much as possible.

Lord extensively quoted his sources as he deftly guided readers back and forth between American defenders and Japanese attackers in a chronological account of the attack from start to finish. Lord was a lawyer and popular historian. My background as a journalist led me to a different approach in writing my book. I opted for a series of vignettes grouped in chapters. For example, one chapter is about Kentucky sailors on the *Arizona* and *Oklahoma* and another about airmen at Hickam and Wheeler Airfields. There are also chapters about civilians on Oahu and about the Kentucky home front.

Europe had been at war for more than two years when the Japanese bombed Pearl Harbor. But the sailors, soldiers, airmen, and marines—and the handful of coastguardsmen—in Hawaii enlisted or were drafted when America was at peace. Some joined for adventure or to escape the routine of farm-, factory-, or other work. Others just wanted a reliable job. The Depression was still hanging on; military service was steady work, "three hots and a flop," meaning breakfast, lunch, and supper and a comfortable-enough bunk in a barracks or on a ship. "I was 26 years old when I went in the Navy [in 1940]," Hamlin said. "That was during hard times. I was too old to sponge off my daddy and too young to get a job." He signed up in Louisville, where he said the recruiting office was crowded with other volunteers. "On the application blank, it said, 'Why do you want to join the Navy?' I wrote on there, 'So I can get something to eat.'" He added: "A dollar-a-day job was pretty good pay back in those times. . . . The Navy paid $21 a month." A chief petty officer stood up and read aloud Hamlin's reason for enlisting. "Everybody laughed," he recalled. "I said, 'Go ahead and laugh. That's why you're all up here.'"[26]

This book is based on interviews that I conducted, interviews conducted by others, and printed sources, including newspaper stories, many of them contemporary, unpublished memoirs, and official military records. I also heeded the Pulitzer Prize–winning biographer Robert Caro, who told Hillel Italie of the Associated Press (AP): "One of my mantras is Go There, wherever there is, to infuse myself in the culture and geography of a place." He usually goes "there" with his wife, Ina, as his chief research helper. Melinda, my spouse and main research aide, went with me to Hawaii, where we met Daniel Martinez, the chief historian at the Pearl Harbor National Memorial. A few steps from his office, visitors catch small, white-painted navy motorboats to the USS *Arizona* Memorial. Martinez kindly consented to an interview and took us to places usually off-limits to visitors, notably the USS *Utah* Memorial, which is on navy turf on the opposite side of Ford Island from the

Arizona Memorial. The obsolete 1911-vintage battlewagon had been turned ingloriously into a target ship. Hit by two Japanese torpedoes, the *Utah* rolled on its side and sank in shallow water; sixty-four of its crewmen died. Martinez pointed out that the *Utah*, *Arizona*, and *Oklahoma* Memorials, the latter on Ford Island near the USS *Missouri*, are owned and operated by the National Park Service. "Also, the park service has parcels of land to support the memorials' use," he said.[27]

Like Melinda and me, Martinez is a baby boomer and the son of a World War II veteran. (His grandfather worked at the navy's Red Hill Underground Fuel Storage Facility at Pearl Harbor when the Japanese attacked.) "I think that the challenge the park service has here is making sure that people that have no idea about this story immerse themselves in it by going into the museum, which is very user-friendly with oral histories playing in there," he said.[28]

It was an emotional trip for us; at times, we were unashamedly moved to tears. Melinda's father, the late Robert P. Hocker Jr., was stationed at Schofield Barracks. In 1944, he shipped out to the Philippines, Iwo Jima, and Okinawa as a master sergeant in army intelligence. We rented a convertible and headed for the Twenty-Fifth Infantry Division Museum at Schofield Barracks. We drove past buildings used in the filming of *From Here to Eternity*, which won an Academy Award as the best movie of 1953. We also took in Halona Beach Cove—dubbed "Eternity Cove"—where the bathing-suited Burt Lancaster and Deborah Kerr were famously filmed prone on the sand in a steamy—for the time—surf-soaked embrace.

My father, the late Berry Craig Jr., was a sailor at Pearl Harbor before his LCI (landing craft infantry) gunboat departed in 1944 for the Marshall Islands campaign. We thought of him when we parked and looked down on the Halona Blow Hole, where the sea rushes in through a lava tube and the water shoots skyward like a mini–Old Faithful. One of my father's shipmates got too close, and the spray blew his hat into the ocean.

Melinda and I, too, visited the Royal Hawaiian Hotel, the storied "Pink Palace of the Pacific," which the navy leased as a rest and recuperation center for sailors in World War II. My ex-motor machinists mate first class father frequented the still posh resort hotel when he was on liberty.

Like most Pearl Harbor veterans, most Hawaiians who witnessed the attack are gone. But stories are passed from generation to generation. On our trip to see Martinez, we chatted about the attack with our thirtysomething Uber driver. He said that, when the raid started, his Honolulu grandmother took his father outside to "see the pretty fireworks": "He was a baby, and she held him in her arms. She didn't know what was happening. Nobody did."

We found irony everywhere on Oahu. Our United Airlines flight from Los Angeles landed at Senator Daniel K. Inouye International Airport adjacent to Pearl Harbor and Hickam Airfield, now Joint Base Pearl Harbor–Hickam. Inouye's father was a Japanese immigrant; his maternal grandparents had emigrated from Japan. At first, Japanese Americans were suspected of disloyalty and not permitted to join the army. (Such strictures were not applied to German and Italian Americans.) When the ban was lifted in 1943, Inouye enlisted. He fought in Italy, made lieutenant, lost an arm, and earned a Medal of Honor. A Democrat, he was a congressman before serving in the Senate. He died in 2012 at age eighty-seven.

On our way to the gate, we taxied past US-made Japan Airlines and Japanese ANA passenger jets. In Honolulu, many signs are in Japanese and English; Americans and Japanese mingle and throng streets, hotels, restaurants, bars and stores, buses and trolleys.

On the hiking trail to Kaena Point, we chatted amiably in English with a Japanese couple who seemed to be in their sixties, our age. We wondered whether their fathers fought our fathers and whether they wondered the same thing about us. We saw many Japanese visitors at Pearl Harbor. Martinez said exhibits at the museum were specially designed to tell the story of Pearl Harbor though the words of attackers and defenders, "both sides": "That was pretty edgy at the time we did that because many but not all people really didn't care about the Japanese side."[29]

Except for the *Utah* and the *Arizona*, the wreckage of war has long been cleared away from Pearl Harbor. But a sign outside the Pearl Harbor Aviation Museum on Ford Island reminds visitors that they are on "a battlefield, as surely as hallowed ground as Yorktown, Gettysburg, Château-Thierry, the beaches of Normandy, the waters of the Mekong Delta, the sands of Afghanistan, and a host of other distant places, both well-known and long forgotten." Punctuating that message are jagged holes Japanese bullets and bombs made in the wire-reinforced windows of a hangar that shelters some of the museum's planes. The old airfield runway, crumbling in spots and choked with weeds, is similarly scarred. So are disused seaplane ramps. Martinez pointed to unfilled pockmarks and patched holes where the newer concrete is a lighter shade than the old. "Here, the voice of history beckons us to pause, to yield to thought and introspection . . . to ponder the heavy price exacted by a determined enemy," the sign also says. Such entreaties are not needed at the *Arizona* and *Utah* Memorials and the National Memorial Cemetery of the Pacific (dubbed "the Punchbowl" because it is in the crater of that ancient volcano). They speak for themselves.

Lord's book, which I first read in high school in the mid-1960s, piqued my interest in the day of infamy. Shortly after I became a reporter and feature writer for the *Paducah Sun-Democrat* in August 1976, the late Dr. James W. Hammack, one of my history professors at nearby Murray State University, gave me a list of Pearl Harbor survivors in Kentucky. I interviewed eleven of them in Paducah, Mayfield, and other western Kentucky communities. I left the paper—which had become the *Sun*—in 1989 to teach history at Paducah Community College, now West Kentucky Community and Technical College. I retired in 2013. For most of my tenure, I freelanced for the AP, writing "Kentucky Backroads," a column mainly pegged to Kentucky history and folklore. I interviewed a few more survivors for the AP, the last one in 2007. I also interviewed Kentucky civilians about where they were and what they were doing on December 7, 1941.

Pearl Harbor Day is personal to me. I was born on December 7, 1949, in Mayfield, where Melinda and I live. When I wrote for the Paducah paper, I authored a column telling how December 7 twice interrupted my father's career plans. On December 7, 1941, he had his sights set on playing minor league baseball the next year. A seventeen-year-old, left-handed pitcher and Knoxville, Tennessee, high school junior, he had already inked a minor league contract with the old St. Louis Browns (now the Baltimore Orioles). After he turned eighteen in 1942, he quit school (he went back after the war and graduated in 1946) and volunteered for the navy. A shoulder injury ended his baseball career with the Class D Mayfield Clothiers 1947. He enrolled at Murray State on the GI Bill in the fall of 1949 but quit after one semester to support my mother and me and, later, my brother, Tim, who was born in 1955. He never went back to college.

The column paid an unexpected dividend. It turned up one of my father's LCI shipmates. (Daddy returned to Pearl Harbor on a minesweeper just before the war ended in 1945.) The late Benny Storm of Metropolis, Illinois, near Paducah, read what I wrote and phoned me. Though he and my father lived only forty miles from each other, they had not seen each other since World War II. My father, Storm, a shipmate from Arkansas named Plunkett, and their wives promptly met for a reunion lunch at Leroy and Lita's truck stop in Paducah. They are all deceased.

Daddy lived to be ninety-one. I never heard him disparage the Japanese. None of the Pearl Harbor survivors I interviewed did either. The enemy sank two ships from under Hamlin, who was aboard the USS *Chicago* when the cruiser was lost in the 1943 Battle of Rennell Island. "[The Japanese] were just following orders like we were," he said. "I don't hate them, and I hope they don't hate me either."[30] J. C. Riley even proposed a get-together some day between the Pearl Harbor attackers and defenders. "Yes, sir, I'd really like to see that," he told me.[31]

At least in October 2019, Pearl Harbor was still making the news in Kentucky. "I never met a Kentuckian who wasn't either thinking about going home or actually going home," said Chandler, who was a former Kentucky governor. Nearly seventy-eight years after the Pearl Harbor attack, Corbin's Ulis Claude Steely grabbed headlines on the television news.[32]

Machinist's Mate Steely died on the battleship *Oklahoma*. DNA testing on his remains identified him. His remains were placed in a shiny, silver-colored casket and flown stateside to Atlanta and on to Lexington. A hearse took Steely home to Corbin, where he was buried with military honors in the cemetery at Grace on the Hill Church, where his father had been the pastor. We're a rural community," said Mayor Suzie Razmus. "Family is everything to us. Home is everything to us."[33]

1

America and Japan

"Face-to-Face Like Duelists at the Salute"

FDR's eleventh-hour message to Emperor Hirohito "in the midst of darkening war clouds in the Far East" merited a front-page banner headline in the December 7, 1941, *Louisville Courier-Journal.* The paper provided no details about what the president wrote. But it reported that the December 6 letter "was viewed as possibly a step of last resort to avert an open break with Japan, since it was considered unlikely that Mr. Roosevelt would communicate directly with the emperor unless virtually all hope had been abandoned of a satisfactory adjustment of Japanese-American difficulties through the usual diplomatic channels."[1]

But Hawaii was in the local news before the first Japanese warplanes appeared over Oahu. Coincidentally, the morning paper published a letter from a Falls City sailor at Pearl Harbor and a staff writer's Hawaii travelogue. Radioman Third Class Herbert R. Purdum of the destroyer *Fanning* wanted his dad, the Salvation Army major Harry L. Purdum, to do him a favor: tell everybody back home to quit worrying about military morale in Hawaii and "take care of their own."[2]

Young Purdum, a Louisville Male High School grad, edited the *Fanning Forum,* the ship's newspaper. "We don't need any encouragement but from all the discussions I've heard lately, the civilians do," he advised his parent. Luckily for young Purdum, the *Fanning* was a long way from port on December 7. The "tin can" was steaming back across the Pacific Ocean, helping escort the aircraft carrier *Enterprise,* which had ferried marine planes and pilots to US-held Wake Island in case trouble brewed with the Japanese. The task force was due back at Pearl Harbor at 7:30 A.M. on the seventh, but heavy seas slowed the refueling

15

of the carrier's destroyer screen. At 6:15, the ships were still about two hundred miles west of Oahu.[3]

Purdum's story made page 12; the *Courier-Journal* printed the travelogue on page 35. Nobody who read the story knew it would be at least four years before tourists from Louisville or anyplace else could take Tom Ochiltree up on his invitation to visit the territory of Hawaii, 4,370 miles west of the Bluegrass State's largest city.[4]

Ochiltree described what he claimed was a typical passenger ship departure, which inexplicably "always is about 43 minutes late in casting off." Hawaiians "stack flower leis around your neck clear up to your ears when you depart and shake your hand or kiss you, as the case may be." Homeward-bound holidaymakers toss "bright colored paper streamers" to locals ashore. The Royal Hawaiian Band belts out music that "cuts you all up inside; the way 'My Old Kentucky Home' does someone from the Bronx," he deadpanned. "By the time these native musicians and singers get around to 'Aloha Oe' everyone is having a real good cry."[5]

As the vessel shoves off, Hawaiian boys dive into the harbor from the ship or from the dock while appreciative travelers toss coins to them, according to Ochiltree. Speedboats trail the vessel as the last lads to go ashore "do beautiful swan dives from the top deck." Passengers drop their leis into the Pacific as the ship rounds Diamond Head, the extinct volcano almost everybody recognized from picture postcards, geography books, and newsreels. "Over they go, ginger, carnation, tuberose, gardenia and orchid necklaces—enough to make a mainland florist weep. The wake of the ship carries these flowers back toward the islands, a sign that the visitor will return some day," Ochiltree noted. He explained that the arrival of cruise ships is about "the same except that the shore boats bring people out with their presents of flowers."[6]

The scribe marveled that Hawaii was the only place on earth "where a volcanic eruption is the signal for people to go on a holiday": "It's like the opening of the baseball season in Brooklyn." Explosions were interrupting the Sabbath peace in Hawaii about the time Louisville residents were finishing Sunday lunch. The blasts were humanmade, not natural; the danger was coming, not from deep inside the bowels of the earth, but from a clear blue sky. The peril was not deadly lava. A lethal rain of bombs, torpedoes, and strafing fire was falling on thousands of unsuspecting and bewildered servicemen and -women at Pearl Harbor and army, army air force, and marine bases and camps nearby and elsewhere on Oahu.[7]

Almost every sailor, soldier, or marine—and many army air force men—arrived in Hawaii by ship, usually landing in Honolulu Harbor, where the Aloha Tower loomed as the tallest building on the islands. Those who left from the East Coast traveled Albert Owen Rowe's route. But the Louisvillian's ocean voyage to Schofield Barracks, Hawaii's main army base, was anything but a holiday cruise. "Rode the U.S. Army Transport Leonard Wood from New York to San Francisco," the twenty-one-year-old Male High graduate wrote home in a letter the *Courier-Journal* published in mid-March 1941. "I was so far down in the hold I didn't see daylight for a week. Got so seasick I lay in my bunk three days straight. Too sick to move or eat." Rowe did not spare the gory details of a malady shared by many landlubbers on the high seas: "Did you ever vomit when you hadn't eaten for over three days? It was the worst physical experience I've ever known. You start getting better after the fourth day."[8]

Assigned to the Eighth Field Artillery's Regimental Headquarters Battery, Rowe had soldiered in Albany and Plattsburgh, New York, where he joked that he "was doing all right": "private hotel room, maid service, 9 o'clock reveille, dollar forty per day for meals, etc." He claimed he "got tired eating in restaurants": "Same as when I was working at Thompson's at 4th and Walnut in '36."[9]

Rowe confessed: "The sudden change from knee-deep snow in Plattsburgh to 105 in the shade in Panama gave me acute spring fever." He spent two days and two nights in the Canal Zone, where he picked up some souvenirs and local currency and observed that "four out of five doors is a saloon." He explained the canal's geographic oddity: "[Its] Pacific side . . . is twenty-seven miles east of the Atlantic side. In other words you go east to get west down there." He said that traffic flowed left, British style, making it hard for an American "to dodge traffic when all cars drove on the wrong side of the street": "You always look the wrong way. And the bus drivers cuss you out."[10]

Rowe said it took the *Wood* eight days to reach San Francisco, where he was billeted at Fort McDowell on Angel Island. He was switched to the transport *U. S. Grant* for the Oahu leg. Before heading for Hawaii, the ship "stopped at Alcatraz to pick up laundry done by the convicts." Evidently, he had conquered his seasickness. He said the *Grant* was "smaller and slower and rocks more than the Wood but . . . feeds better." He did not say how long it took to reach Hawaii, but he did say that the *Grant* docked at Honolulu at 10:00 p.m.: "Noticed the time by the Aloha Tower clock." He rode a train past Pearl Harbor, observing the Pacific Fleet "lighted up": "Myriad lights of red and white against a background of midnight blue spread out as far as the eye can see." He said he was "stooging in the supply office here": "Got enough material about Oahu and Hawaii to make a book." He cautioned that US military personnel were prohibited from saying anything about statehood, that the local weather was like Louisville weather in June, and that his outfit was athletic—"everybody but me boxes, runs, plays tennis, etc." He preferred to "get in a lot of flying time—on my bunk."[11]

Rowe liked what he had seen of Hawaii, noting that "all classes, creeds and colors are mixed here," adding that he might enroll in the University of Hawaii should he "get the time, money and opportunity." Meanwhile, he was basking under a tropical sun, reading and studying, when he was off duty. He suspected the home folks were freezing in late winter: "This time last winter, I was sleeping in a tent, with the snow six inches deep and the temperature deeper—12 below."[12]

An editor's note that appeared with the letter said that Rowe "was the 'perfect recruit' signed up by the Army two years ago in Louisville." The soldier-to-be "gave the correct answer to every question asked by the enlistment office and attained a rating of 97.25 percent." Too, recruiters claimed that he "was the most nearly physically perfect applicant here in the last twenty years."[13]

At Wheeler Army Airfield, next to Schofield Barracks, Private Elliott C. "Bim" Mitchell Jr. of Paducah was so pleased with army life that he wrote his hometown recruiter, Sergeant P. A. Wymore. Wymore had signed Mitchell up in October 1939. Mitchell, twenty-three, advised the sergeant that he was with the Eighteenth Air Base Squadron and learning aerial photography.[14]

"The teaching staff is excellent and I am already able to turn out very creditable work," Mitchell penned. "Conditions are ideal for this work and I am most satisfied with the way things have worked out so far." Besides enjoying military schooling, he was having "a wonderful time doing other things," including instructing pilots in instrument flying in the Link Trainer.[15]

Mitchell swore army chow beat home cooking, a revelation his mother might not have appreciated: "For variety and excellence the food here can't be surpassed. I have gained 20 pounds on it and feel fit as a fiddle." He was happy with his army dentist, adding: "It was certainly a pleasure to get such excellent work and not have to worry about paying for it the first of the month."[16]

Mitchell found the Hawaiian weather agreeable, too: "I have acquired a swell coat of tan at the beach." He cited other pleasant diversions from army routine, including swimming, baseball, boxing, bowling, and movies besides "other sports." He concluded: "Yes sir, taking everything into consideration I am doing all right, not only learning to do things I wish but also aiding materially in protecting our country. It's a shame that everyone can't have the same advantages I am enjoying and I strongly urge anyone considering signing up to do so without delay for it's a great life and the KP's are too far apart to worry me."[17]

It seems likely that Mitchell knew Sergeant Leslie Zeiss of Paducah, who was also at Wheeler Airfield. He, too, wrote his hometown paper. The *Sun-Democrat* published his letter with a tongue-in-cheek editor's note: "[Zeiss] has either being doing a lot of research work about his new environment or has been reading some guide books." Anyway, the sergeant advised: "Hawaii is the land where they play football without shoes. . . . Aloha means hello, love and goodbye (Hollywood has a word—marriage—which means practically the same thing). . . . [R]ain is called liquid sunshine."[18]

Waves, Zeiss added, "roll for over a mile at Waikiki beach": "Gardenias are bought for a nickel a bunch. . . . [T]he temperature averages 75 degrees day and night the year round. . . . [T]here is no word for weather, which never changes." Hawaii was snake free, Santa Claus showed up in an outrigger canoe, schoolgirls wore orchids in their hair, and there were no billboards. He said the locals pronounced *w* as *v* and ran "toward instead of away from a volcanic eruption." Everybody was treated to the sight of "several rainbows practically every day."[19]

On November 5, the day Hirohito endorsed the Pearl Harbor attack plan, another Kentuckian wrote home that the United States would invariably fight in the war. But he added that Japan was afraid to strike Hawaii. The *Louisville Courier-Journal* published part of the lengthy missive on December 21 "to show that they were even wrong in Hawaii."

The letter's unnamed author boasted: "We are about 6,000 miles from Japan—farther than you are from Europe, and Japan could never bomb this place unless she sent airplane carriers out and it would be too long a trip to make without refueling, and an airplane carrier could never get within 1,000 miles of this place."[20]

He described Pearl Harbor as "a wonderful sight" with "so many battleships that it is impossible to count them": "Submarines, etc., then these two large flying fields here and army camps all around the island." He said: "[Military aircraft] are on constant patrol duty and so are the ships. Japan knows all of this, I suppose, and that is why they are afraid of us." He recounted lying on Waikiki Beach at night and watching "searchlights pick out planes in the sky": "I think every mountain on the island must have a searchlight on it." He wished he could reveal "how well fortified this place really is": "Then no one would worry about us out here. I think it is the ships in the Atlantic that will see the action."[21]

Tom Ochiltree was not so sanguine; four months before the *Courier-Journal* published his tongue-in-cheek travelogue, it printed the staffer's sober assessment of Hawaii should war break out there. Conflict involving the United States would turn the islands' economy upside down, he predicted in a story that ran on August 3, 1941: "Despite their perfect climate, the islands are not self-sufficient." He said Hawaii had nearly no diversified farming. The economy was based on growing pineapples, sugarcane, and cattle: "If war should come, the military authorities will force the plantation owners to plow up their lands and plant general food crops. The fields to be so used have already been designated."[22]

In his travel story, Ochiltree had detailed passenger ship arrivals and departures. He said that island papers no longer reported comings and goings of naval vessels. But he wrote that it was hardly a military secret that Oahu was one of the world's most heavily fortified locales: "This summer Pearl Harbor was jammed with units of the fleet, with battleships moored side by side like rowboats at an amusement park lake. It is possible to see squadrons of planes wing their way out to sea over Waikiki any afternoon while just off that famous beach the battleships and cruisers can be seen."[23]

With the possibility, if not the likelihood, of war between the United States and Japan increasing, "there are no two people on the islands who seem to agree regarding the loyalty of the [local] Japanese population," Ochiltree wrote. "But somehow your sympathies go out to these people when you hear Japanese schoolchildren, during recitation in their history classes, refer at great length to 'our forefathers who landed on Plymouth Rock.'" Deteriorating relations between Washington and Tokyo had "produced as a by-product the complex problem of how to deal safely and fairly with the Americanized Japanese of the Hawaiian Islands."[24] (Overwhelmingly, "the Americanized Japanese" proved their loyalty to the United States even though dozens of them were put into internment camps. Nonetheless, many young men—notably, as we have seen, longtime Hawaii Democratic senator Daniel Inouye—volunteered for military service.)

Ochiltree said he detected "a new feeling of unrest in the air" against the Japanese Americans: "You sense it at a baseball game when a Japanese team is playing a Navy or a Chinese nine. During the various pageants and parades, the applause for the Japanese performers is somehow colder than that given to any other Oriental or Polynesian group. Usually the Japanese floats are the largest and most elaborate and their ball team wins more than its share of games, but that makes no difference."[25]

Ochiltree said that, more than any other ethnic group, Japanese Americans had decorated their shops with US flags and put up signs with an "'It's Great to Be an American' theme." He promised: "Without exception, all the Japanese with whom I talked during a visit to the islands this summer made a point to impress me with their loyalty to this country. Those born on the islands are American citizens—a fact which they also make clear."[26]

Most Hawaiians lived on Oahu, though it is not the largest island. That distinction goes to Hawaii, "the Big Island." Pearl Harbor is on the south side of Oahu and west of Honolulu, Hawaii's capital. The ancient Hawaiians, who were Polynesians, called the bay Wai Momi, "Waters of Pearl," for its pearl-yielding oysters.[27]

Captain James Cook and his British navy sailors were the first Europeans to visit Hawaii. The storied explorer showed up with two ships in January 1778, nearly two years after George III's querulous American colonies opted to part company with Mother Britain on less than amicable terms. Cook dubbed the archipelago the Sandwich Islands for

John Montague, the earl of Sandwich and first lord of the British Admiralty.[28]

Cook's expedition returned home without him in 1779; he had been killed in a clash with Hawaiians. Cook's sailors recounted his grisly demise but also told fantastic tales "of an archipelago of tropical islands, bursting with fruit and erotically swaying *hula* dancers," wrote Julia Flynn Siler. The stories brought more European visitors: "Some were drawn by the lure of trade and opportunity. Others were searching for an unspoiled paradise." The Hawaiians got the worst of it. "Over the next hundred years, Cook's fellow travelers . . . would wreak a kind of vengeance, as 90 percent of the archipelago's population died of European diseases," according to Craig Nelson.[29]

In 1810, Hawaii became a united kingdom under Kamehameha I. A decade later, the first American missionaries arrived. Profit ultimately trumped piety. Some of the immigrants got rich growing sugarcane. Others prospered as merchants or suppliers and repairers of whaling ships and vessels engaged in the growing transpacific trade with China. More Americans migrated, hoping to cash in, too. At the same time, the navy saw military potential in Hawaii. After ships switched from sail to steam power, Hawaii became a vital coaling station in the growing transpacific trade. Though still a minority, Americans ultimately dominated nineteenth-century Hawaii's economy, society, and government.

American sugar kings grew even wealthier thanks to the US-Hawaiian Reciprocity Treaty of 1875. The pact permitted both Hawaiian- and American-processed sugar to be traded between the two countries duty-free. In Hawaii, sugar production soared, as did the country's foreign trade. A massive expansion of sugar cultivation led to a huge demand for labor. As a result, hundreds of immigrant workers, most of them Asians, arrived in the islands. "Both of these events occurred in an environment in which colonialism and imperialism became an ever more frequent characteristic of the behavior of powerful nations," Tom Coffman has written. Also under the agreement, King Kalakaua promised not to hand over any Hawaiian port, harbor, or territory to any country other than the United States. "Thus lay the earliest official roots of America's claim on Pearl Harbor," Siler wrote.[30]

King Kamehameha III had in 1840 transformed Hawaii into a constitutional monarchy with an elected legislature. In 1887, Americans, aided by well-armed white paramilitary soldiers, pressured Kalakaua into accepting a new constitution that left him virtually powerless. The charter included stiff property and income requirements for voting and serving in the legislature. The restrictions disenfranchised almost all native Hawaiians. "Among those who believed that the king had been forced to sign, the document became known as the 'Bayonet Constitution,'" wrote Siler.[31]

After 1887, the sugar kings and their allies looked forward to increasing wealth and political power. Yet boom times were tied to Hawaiian sugar's favored status in the US market. The McKinley tariff bill of 1890 soured Hawaii's sweet sugar deal. It permitted sugar from other countries to enter the United States duty-free starting in 1891. The tariff was a hard blow to Hawaii's economy because, by the 1890s, the kingdom had become perilously dependent on sugar cultivation. The sugar kings concluded that only annexation by the United States could save them from inevitable financial ruin.[32]

In 1891, Queen Liliuokalani ascended the throne. An ardent nationalist, she demanded a new constitution that would restore crown control, curb American influence, and restore political power to native Hawaiians. The sugar kings would have none of it. In 1893, they backed a coup, aided by marines, that overthrew the queen. The Americans declared themselves a republic under President Sanford Dole, a sugar millionaire who was in on the coup. Annexation was a dream delayed, however; President Grover Cleveland, a Democrat, was skeptical. The dream came true in 1898 when the United States annexed Hawaii during the Spanish-American War. The president at the time was William McKinley, a Republican imperialist.[33]

The United States envisioned the new territory of Hawaii as a significant acquisition militarily and economically. General John M. Schofield, who had traipsed all over the islands, told the House of Representatives that Pearl Harbor was ideal for a modern navy. The old Yankee general said that the Pearl Harbor's finger-like inlets—Americans called them *lochs,* Gaelic for *lakes*—and surrounding shoreland could comfortably accommodate dozens of warships. There was also plenty of room for docks, maintenance facilities, and coal stocks. Schofield warned that, if the United States did not bag Hawaii, the Spanish or the Japanese possibly would.[34]

Even so, there was a big problem at the harbor mouth. A coral reef prevented the entrance of large ships. In 1902, work crews began dredging, deepening and widening the entrance. Congress gave its blessing to Naval Station Pearl Harbor in 1908. Three years later, the armored cruiser *California* easily steamed through the entrance and dropped anchor in the inner harbor. Thirty years later, Japanese bombs and aerial torpedoes sank the battleship *California* not far from where the old cruiser was moored.[35]

By the time the navy opened the Pearl Harbor base, the Americans, Germans, and Japanese were challenging the centuries-old world powers, Great Britain, France, and Spain. In the treaty that ended the Spanish-American War—"the Splendid Little War" to the triumphant Yankees—once-mighty Spain had to give the upstart Americans Guam, the Philippines, and Puerto Rico. The Spanish also agreed to grant independence to Cuba (which America dominated). Elsewhere in the Pacific, the Stars and Stripes flew over American Samoa and Howland and Baker Islands.[36]

In the decade after the Americans humiliated the Spanish, the Japanese embarrassed another old European power, imperial Russia, in the Russo-Japanese War of 1904–1905. Theodore Roosevelt mediated an end to the conflict and won a Nobel Peace Prize for his trouble. But the Treaty of Portsmouth galled the Japanese because it did not give them the reparations payments and Manchurian territory in China they had demanded.[37]

Nonetheless, Japan sided with the Allied powers, including Russia, when World War I began in Europe in 1914. Japan's navy helped protect the Indian and Pacific Oceans and Hawaii against German warships and commerce raiders. Japan felt slighted again in the 1919 Treaty of Versailles, which officially ended the war. (An armistice stopped the fighting on November 11, 1918.) During the war, the Japanese had captured German possessions in the Mariana, Caroline, and Marshall Islands and reduced Germany's sphere of influence in China. The pact allowed them to keep it all. But they wanted—and failed to get—a treaty provision guaranteeing nonwhite nations equality with white nations.

Japan felt snubbed again in the 1921–1922 Washington Naval Conference. Japanese naval expansion worried the United States and Great Britain. America suspected that Japan had long-term designs on

Hawaii, the Philippines, and Guam; likewise, the British considered the Japanese a potential threat to their Asian colonies. At the same time, the Americans and the British feared Japan as a danger to their considerable economic interests in China.

The conference produced a treaty that set a ratio of battleship and aircraft carrier tonnage that favored the United States and Britain over Japan. Many Japanese officials considered the deal proof that "the Anglo-Saxons" would never treat them as equals. "As far as I'm concerned, war with America starts now. We'll get our revenge over this, by God!" Japan's chief naval advisor angrily warned after the treaty was signed.[38]

The treaty's repercussions echoed down to December 7, 1941. The day following the air raid, Japan's home minister claimed the attack was born in 1922: "Ever since the ten:six ratio was imposed by the Washington treaty, we have endured unspeakable drills . . . and today we must say these drills produced a wonderful result." An architect of the attack declared that the treaty forced his country to develop new naval technologies to overcome the pact's limitations. In turn, the new technology helped ensure victory at Pearl Harbor. Previously, Japanese naval aviation tactics had emphasized aerial torpedo attacks. "We introduced dive-bombing and found it to be highly destructive and superior as a method of surprise attack," he explained. "It also enabled us to put more stress than previously on the offensive potential of carrier planes."[39]

A 1922 US Supreme Court decision further angered Japan. Borne by a nativist tide surging across white America, the high court ruled that Japanese immigrants were ineligible for citizenship. In 1923, the justices upheld a ban on Japanese owning real estate in the United States. "Japanese immigrant farmers were [in that year] producing 10 percent of California's produce on 1 percent of its farmland," according to Nelson. In 1924, a nativist Congress forbade further immigration from Japan. No fewer than fifteen Tokyo newspapers fumed against America's "insulting behavior." Shortly afterward, Japanese army and navy brass branded the United States "enemy number one."[40]

Simultaneously, the Japanese saw themselves hemmed in by European powers. The British had Hong Kong, the Malay Peninsula, and Singapore; Britain and France held sway in parts of Shanghai. Germany still controlled China's Shantung Province. The East Indies were Dutch, Indochina was French, and the Soviet Union was encroaching on Manchuria. Japan's "enemy number one" had Hawaii, the Philippines, Guam, and Midway in the central and western Pacific. Published in 1925, a novel titled *The Great Pacific War* described simultaneous Japanese attacks on the U.S. Pacific Fleet, Guam, and the Philippines. Written by Hector C. Bywater, a British newspaper correspondent, the book "predicted exactly what would happen in the closing weeks of 1941," though there is no evidence it influenced Japanese military strategy. But English-speaking Japanese admiral Isoroku Yamamoto, one of the Pearl Harbor attack's main planners, happened to be a naval attaché in Washington when the novel was published in English and later translated into Japanese.[41]

At any rate, there is no doubt that a book by an American admiral profoundly affected the thinking of Yamamoto and other Japanese navy brass hats: Alfred Thayer Mahan's *The Influence of Sea Power upon History, 1660–1783*. Published in 1890, it was a book that could be judged by its cover. Mahan argued that great powers had great navies and that victory at sea hinged on using modern warships to vanquish the enemy's fleet in a decisive battle. Afterward, the enemy's ports and coast would be vulnerable to blockade and even invasion. Though he called for America to annex Hawaii to thwart Japan's expansionism, the Japanese navy leadership was among his biggest boosters. After all, Japan won wars against Russia and China via "decisive Mahanian battles," Nelson pointed out.[42]

While Yamamoto was stateside, he also became a disciple of Billy Mitchell, an army brigadier general who preached the gospel of airpower with near missionary zeal. Military success on land and sea hinged on control of the skies, he argued. In 1921, Mitchell persuaded Congress to let him prove it by bombing the *Ostfriesland,* a captured World War I German battleship. The dreadnought sank in twenty minutes. Skeptics scoffed that it was a sitting duck, stock-still at anchor, and that Mitchell's airmen did not have to face antiaircraft fire. Nonetheless, the general had bragged he could sink a battleship, and he did. Ultimately, his outspokenness got him demoted and court-martialed. He resigned from the army and died in 1936. Yamamoto considered him anything but disgraced. (History vindicated Mitchell, who is considered the inspiration for the army air force and, later, the independent US Air Force.) Yamamoto and Japan's naval air commander "essentially came to believe that the navy should turn itself into a floating air force," Nelson wrote. (On April 18, 1942, a little over four months after Pearl Harbor, a force of sixteen B-25 medium bombers led by Lieutenant Colonel James H. Doolittle took off from an aircraft carrier and bombed Tokyo. The army air force officially named the twin-engine plane the "Mitchell" in honor of the general Yamamoto admired.)[43]

At least since the turn of the twentieth century, Tokyo, Washington, and the European powers had jockeyed for economic dominance over weak and divided China. The Americans demanded an "Open Door" policy, meaning they, too, should have a fair chance to get rich off the Chinese. The Japanese wanted the Far East for themselves. "The very presence in Asia of the United States, along with the European powers, was a constant irritation to Japanese pride," wrote Gordon W. Prange, Donald M. Goldstein, and Katherine V. Dillon. "The press lost no occasion to assure such intruders that Japan would slam the Open Door in their faces." On September 3, 1940, the influential Tokyo *Yomiuri* editorialized: "Japan must remove all elements in East Asia which will interfere with its plans. Britain, the United States, France and the Netherlands must be forced out of the Far East. Asia is the territory of the Asiatics."[44]

Like America, Japan had rapidly industrialized. At first, the Americans rooted for the Japanese, considering them "in a measure as their protégés." Japan embraced more than a few elements of American popular culture; baseball became its national pastime, too. Eventually, however, the Americans concluded that "the 'plucky little Japs' were not only brave and clever but dangerous and a bit on the devious side," according to Prange, Goldstein and Dillon.[45]

The United States was blessed with abundant raw materials essential to industrialization—particularly coal, oil, natural gas, iron ore, and copper. Japan was virtually devoid of petroleum and such essential minerals. So the Japanese looked elsewhere to find them. Japan already dominated Korea and southern Manchuria, the latter in northeastern China. In 1931, the Japanese invaded Manchuria and established Manchukuo, a puppet state. The territory was rich in coal, but it also contained significant copper and iron ore deposits. China and Japan were members of the League of Nations, the post–World War I international body that was supposed to deter aggressors through collective security.

If diplomacy failed to deter an aggressor, economic sanctions were to be applied. If that was insufficient, military action was supposed to follow. When the league criticized Japanese aggression in Manchuria, Japan withdrew from membership, and the league did nothing to punish it.

The United States further angered Japan by refusing to recognize an independent Manchukuo and by backing Generalissimo Chiang Kai-shek's Nationalist regime in China. In 1937, the Japanese invaded northern China, widening the rift with America. President Woodrow Wilson, a Democrat, championed the league, but Republican senators prevented American membership. President Roosevelt, a Democrat and internationalist like Wilson, stepped up his condemnation of Tokyo's aggression. "This moral denunciation only hardened the resolve of the average Japanese," John Toland wrote. "Why should there be a Monroe Doctrine in the Americas and an Open Door principle in Asia?" Japan viewed its conquest of "bandit-infested Manchuria" as paralleling America's military adventurism on its own doorstep in the Caribbean basin and Latin America to safeguard US business interests and main-tain Washington's hegemony south of the border. Likewise, the Japa-nese asked: "Why was it perfectly acceptable for England and Holland to occupy India, Hong Kong, Singapore and the East Indies, but a crime for Japan to follow their example? Why should America, which had grabbed its lands from Indians by trickery, liquor and massacre, be so outraged when Japan did the same in China?"[46]

Meanwhile, events halfway around the world affected Japan's time-table of conquest in Asia. World War II began in Europe on September 1, 1939. France fell to Nazi Germany in June 1940 and established a col-laborationist government at Vichy. At the same time, the Japanese army had been advancing against Chiang's Nationalist and Mao Zedong's Communist military forces. The two enemies had agreed to an uneasy alliance to stop the invaders. In September 1940, capitalizing on France's defeat, the Japanese swept into northern French Indochina. Also in Sep-tember, Japan signed the Tripartite Pact with Nazi Germany and fascist Italy. The agreement committed the governments to "assist one another with all political, economic and military means when one of the three Contracting Parties is attacked by a power at present not involved in the European War or in the Sino-Japanese conflict." The concordat was obviously aimed at the United States; a convenient 1939 nonaggression pact bound the archenemies Germany and the Soviet Union for the time being.[47]

Roosevelt replied to Japanese aggression with ever-tightening economic sanctions. America was still deeply isolationist and in no mood for war even after Japanese warplanes sank the US gunboat *Panay* in the Yangtze River off Nanjing, China, in 1937. Three crewmen were killed and forty-three wounded. The United States claimed that the attack was deliberate, which it probably was, but the Japanese insisted it was a mistake. The incident was settled after the Japanese apologized and paid an indemnity.

In 1938, the United States put Japan under a "moral embargo." In January 1940, Congress ended the 1911 Treaty of Commerce and Navigation, which enabled the president to start shutting off exports of potential war materiel to Japan. In May, the United States exerted some military pressure by shifting the Pacific Fleet from San Diego to Pearl Harbor. In July, the Americans upped the economic ante by embargoing aviation gasoline and high-grade scrap iron and steel subject to Uncle Sam's licensing and control. In September, FDR stopped shipments of all scrap iron and steel to Japan. By the end of the year, petroleum was the only war materiel still flowing there.[48]

While the US embargo hurt Japan's economy, the Japanese saw America as an even greater military threat. "Japan considered America's huge naval expansion program aimed directly at it," Prange, Goldstein, and Dillon wrote. "Since the stationing of a large segment of the Fleet at Pearl Harbor . . . the United States Navy had stood athwart Japan's path—a navy which Japanese admirals thought capable of menacing their nation's very existence." Ever since Commodore Matthew Perry led his quartet of warships into Tokyo Bay in 1853, Japan and the United States "had enjoyed a unique history of friendship and mutually profitable trade": "Yet now they stood face-to-face like two duelists at the salute. The Japanese had a name for this ugly situation: Taiheiyo-no-gan ('Cancer of the Pacific')."[49]

Nonetheless, Japan first opted for diplomacy, sincere or otherwise. In November 1940, Tokyo sent a new ambassador to Washington, Admiral Kichisaburo Nomura. He had American friends and acquaintances, including the president. They met when he was a naval attaché and FDR was assistant secretary of the navy. Joseph Grew, America's ambassador to Japan, had friends in Tokyo, too: "Seldom have two nations at official loggerheads been represented by two such men of mutual goodwill as Grew and Nomura—two physicians who would make every effort to help cure the 'Cancer of the Pacific.'" Japanese diplomats were still in Washington, ostensibly trying to stave off war, when the first bombs and torpedoes fell on Hawaii.[50]

Though Japan soundly defeated Russia in 1905 and viewed America with increasing disdain, Tokyo was not sanguine about fighting a two-front war against the Soviet Union and the United States in 1941. Likewise, Joseph Stalin, the Soviet dictator, did not wish to have to commit significant forces to a conflict with Japan in the Far East. He knew war with Germany was inevitable. The August 1939 nonaggression pact he signed with Hitler was a case of two tyrants desperate to buy time to bolster their military machines against each other. So, in April 1941, Japan and the Soviet Union signed a nonaggression pact. Between 1932 and 1939, Soviet and Japanese troops had fought an undeclared border war in Mongolia, a Soviet puppet state, and Manchukuo. In 1939, a Soviet-Mongolian force decisively defeated the Japanese at the Battle of Khalkhyn Gol, which helped convince Tokyo to stop fighting Moscow.

In July 1941, a month after Hitler invaded the Soviet Union, Japanese forces pushed into southern Indochina, which they planned to use as a staging area for capturing the oil-rich Dutch East Indies. Roosevelt froze Japanese assets in America and ultimately acquiesced in a plan devised by Treasury secretary Henry J. Morgenthau Jr. and Assistant Secretary of State Dean Acheson that imposed an oil embargo on Japan. Negotiations between Nomura and US secretary of state Cordell Hull failed to bear fruit, and both nations inched closer to war. In October, General Hideki Tojo became prime minister, replacing Fumimaro Konoe, who did not share the militarists' enthusiasm for fighting America. Tojo steered Japan squarely toward war with the United States; on November 5, Emperor Hirohito approved plans to attack Pearl Harbor. Eleven days later, the attack force started for its rendezvous in Hitokappu Bay in the Kuril Islands of northern Japan. Admiral Chuichi Nagumo, the commander, was told to abandon the attempt if Tokyo informed him that talks with the Americans were somehow successful.[51]

Throughout history, naval battles had been fought ship to ship, gun to gun. "In World War I the battleship still reigned queen of the sea, as she had, in changing forms, since the age of Drake, and Battle Line fought with tactics inherited from the age of sail," Rear Admiral Samuel Eliot Morrison wrote. The queen was about to be dethroned by "the aircraft carrier task group, for which completely new tactics had to be devised." Carriers were invented in the 1920s and greatly improved in the subsequent decade. So were carrier aircraft—fighters, torpedo-bombers and dive-bombers: "The performance of these vessels and their planes brought about a new conception of the aircraft carrier's place in naval warfare." At first, carrier-based planes were to provide air cover for their battleship fleets and for hunting and tracking the enemy's capital ships: "Now roles were reversed; the carrier became the nucleus of a striking force capable of projecting firepower deep into enemy-held waters, and the proud battlewagon, when not employed in shore bombardment, joined the protective screen to the carrier."[52]

But there were double precedents for destroying an enemy fleet with an unexpected air raid, one theoretical, the other actual. In 1938, the USS *Saratoga* carried out a successful "surprise attack" on Pearl Harbor. It was only practice, but Yamamoto likely took notice. He certainly was impressed with what the British carrier *Illustrious* accomplished in real wartime conditions in 1940. On the night of November 11–12, twenty-one British Fairey Swordfish torpedo-bombers roared off the flattop and jumped the unsuspecting Italian fleet in the harbor at Taranto, Italy. They struck in two waves, dropping torpedoes and bombs. The British lost only a pair of planes and four men—two killed and two captured. "The Fascists lost thirty-two men and three battleships, nearly half of its capital fleet, and had to sail to Naples to avoid another devastating assault, giving the British the upper hand in Mediterranean naval power," Nelson wrote.[53]

British success at Taranto must have encouraged the Japanese naval air brass even more. The Swordfish—dubbed "the Stringbag"—was a slow, lumbering, obsolete single-engine, two-seater, open-cockpit, fabric-covered biplane. The Japanese admirals knew their fast, agile metal monoplanes were among the most advanced carrier aircraft in the world. The Pearl Harbor attack force would consist of Nakajima B5N2 Type 97 torpedo/horizontal-bombers, Aichi D3A1 Type 99 dive-bombers, and Mitsubishi A6M2 Type 0 fighters. The Americans dubbed the B5N2s "Kates," the D3A1s "Vals," and the A6M2s "Zeros." The Kates had a pilot, a center observer-bombardier, and a rear gunner–radio operator. Vals carried a pilot and a rear gunner–radio operator. The Zero was a single-seat fighter. The Kates and Vals also had forward-firing machine guns. Zero firepower included machine guns and a pair of twenty-millimeter cannons. The Japanese planned to employ these planes to deliver a knockout punch against the Pacific Fleet. While aircraft rained down destruction from the sky, five eighty-foot "midget" submarines would be launched from full-size submarines. The midget submarines were to slip into Pearl Harbor before the air attack and wreak further havoc with their torpedoes. On November 26, under strict radio silence, the Japanese headed across the Pacific toward Pearl Harbor. That same day, Hull gave the Japanese diplomats in Washington the framework of a "proposed basis for agreement." The note was an "alternative to war" and not an ultimatum.[54]

Meanwhile, back in Japan, Yamamoto was overseeing the planning of, preparation for, and training for the top secret attack, code-named Operation Z. He did not share Tojo's zeal for war against the Americans, but he dutifully did all he could to make the raid a success. However, in January 1941, he warned a prominent saber rattler: "Should hostilities break out between Japan and the United States, it would not be enough that we take Guam and the Philippines, nor even Hawaii and San Francisco. To make victory certain, we would have to march into Washington and dictate the terms of peace in the White House. I wonder if our politicians, among whom armchair arguments about war are being glibly bandied about in the name of state politics, have confidence as to the final outcome and are prepared to make the necessary sacrifices." Tojo and the militarists publicized the quote but without the key last sentence. The idea was to give the impression that the admiral would humiliatingly impose peace terms on the Americans in the presidential mansion.[55]

The torpedo and high-level bomber attack groups had practiced at Kagoshima Bay on Kyushu Island in southern Japan. Strikingly similar to Pearl Harbor, the bay is on the island's southern side, has a narrow mouth, and extends inland with an islet in the middle.[56]

The Japanese also warmed up for their prime target, Battleship Row, which consisted of seven battleships moored along the eastern side of the pool-table flat, 441-acre Ford Island. The bows of all the battleships faced the harbor entrance to facilitate a quicker departure. Moored by itself, the *California*, the Battle Force flagship, led the patrician procession. Next came a plebian interloper, the fleet oiler *Neosho*. Astern of the *Neosho* lay the paired *Oklahoma* (outboard) and *Maryland*. Behind them were the conjoined *West Virginia* (outboard) and *Tennessee*. Trailing the twinned battlewagons was the *Arizona*, anchored inboard of another yeoman, the repair ship *Vestal*. The *Nevada*, anchored by itself, brought up the rear. The proud *Pennsylvania*, the Pacific Fleet flagship, was drydocked for repairs over in the Pearl Harbor Navy Yard.

In the attack's first wave, Kates, each carrying a torpedo, were to sink the outboard battleships. Other Kates were to fly over high and horizontally bomb the inboard battleships. Also, dive-bombing Vals were expected to help send Battleship Row to the bottom of Pearl Harbor and destroy Ford Island's aircraft facilities, hangars, patrol planes, and antiaircraft batteries. Success required overcoming twin technical hurdles: the harbor is too shallow for conventional aerial torpedoes to do their deadly work, and battleship deck armor is too thick for conventional bombs to penetrate. So the Japanese devised a shallow water–running torpedo and converted heavy sixteen-inch naval shells into aerial armor-piercing bombs.

Most of all, Japanese victory at Pearl Harbor depended on surprise. That seemed a mission impossible, or close to it. The armada, known to the Japanese navy as the Kido Butai (Carrier Striking Force) would have to steam undetected to the doorstep of Oahu. The most direct route from Hitokappu Bay to Oahu is about thirty-four hundred miles in a southeasterly direction across the central Pacific. But that course would cross major shipping lanes and invite discovery. So the Japanese plotted a forty-two-hundred-mile trip across the northern Pacific, which they knew would be almost devoid of ships. The approach of winter brought thick fog, dense clouds, storms, and bone-chilling, icy weather. Navigation and midocean refueling would be difficult, but so would detection. The weather was indeed foul and the seas heavy. Several sailors were washed overboard; refueling was anything but easy and routine. But the fleet stayed on schedule and had no need to follow an order to turn back if the Americans or their friends at sea or in the air sighted the task force before December 6 or if a peace accord could be reached. The Japanese encountered no aircraft and only one Japanese freighter. Continuing peace talks in Washington were fruitless, with the Americans concluding that Tokyo wanted war all along.[57]

Yet it was still possible for the Americans to discover the armada as it closed in on Oahu. US air and sea patrols from Pearl Harbor could have found and fought the Japanese on the high seas. If American radar picked up the approaching enemy planes, they would be vulnerable to American fighters and antiaircraft guns ashore and on ships.

So the attack was an enormous gamble, but the Japanese believed that, if it paid off, the United States would be powerless to retaliate for months, maybe even years. Perhaps like the Russians in 1904, the Americas would sue for peace after suffering such a one-sided defeat. Meanwhile, Japan would widen its Asian empire. It would conquer all of China, drive the British and the Dutch out of Asia, seize Guam, Wake, and the Philippines from the Americans, and create an impenetrable defense perimeter around its vast empire using some of the islands it got from Germany after World War I. Thus, an American invasion from Hawaii or anyplace else would almost certainly be doomed to failure. Japan confidently called its empire-to-be the "Greater East Asia Co-Prosperity Sphere." Tokyo planned to establish puppet governments throughout the vast region and keep them in line with Japanese occupation troops who would ruthlessly suppress any opposition to rule from Tokyo. At the same time, the conquered peoples would have to provide Japan the labor and natural resources it needed to hold absolute sway in Asia. Hitler boasted his Third Reich would last a millennium; the Japanese figured all Asia would be theirs to rule for many years to come, too.

In any event, Nagumo's sailors were spoiling for a fight. They were bombarded endlessly with anti-American propaganda. They were told the Americans duped Japan in the Treaty of Portsmouth, cheated it at the Washington Naval Conference, and dishonored it by cutting off Japanese immigration. They knew white American racists and xenophobes ranted against the "Yellow Peril," meaning Japanese and Chinese. (The Japanese considered the Americans and the Chinese inferior.) Evidently, it did not occur to the Japanese political and military leaders that "to attack an unsuspecting people, when your government was still negotiating, and in defiance of the Hague Convention of 1907 which Japan had ratified, was dirty ball," Morrison wrote. Nonetheless:

"Treaties, for the Japanese government of that time, were to be honored or broken according to the Emperor's presumed interest."[58] On December 5, Hull concluded that Nomura and his diplomatic entourage were "not playing in the open," that "what they say is equivocal and has two meanings." Hull was sure that "they don't intend to make any honorable agreement with us."[59]

The next day, FDR dispatched his conciliatory cable to Hirohito. Its ultimately revealed contents included an entreaty to avert "tragic possibilities" and maintain "the long period of unbroken peace and friendship" between the United States and Japan. The two nations had prospered "through the virtues of their peoples and the wisdom of their rulers." They, too, had "substantially helped humanity." The president concluded: "I address myself to Your Majesty at this moment in the fervent hope that Your Majesty may, as I am doing, give thought in this definite emergency to ways of dispelling the dark clouds. I am confident that both of us, for the sake of the peoples not only of our own great countries but for the sake of humanity in neighboring territories, have a sacred duty to restore traditional amity and prevent further death and destruction in the world." The ultimate consequences of December 7 would be the deaths of more than three million Japanese soldiers, sailors, airmen, marines, and civilians and the devastation of Japan's major cities from the air, including the atomic bombing of Hiroshima and Nagasaki. No bombs fell on American cities; 116,600 Americans died fighting Japan, all of them far from home.[60]

2

"We Are Too Big, Too Powerful, and Too Strong"

The Japanese carriers—*Akagi, Hiryū, Kaga, Sōryū, Shōkaku,* and *Zuikaku*—were 220 miles north of Oahu on December 7 when they turned into the wind at 5:50 A.M. and launched the first wave of fighters and bombers into a still dark sky. A second wave of planes followed at 7:15. Nagumo's half dozen flattops had plenty of protection—two battleships, a pair of heavy cruisers, a light cruiser, nine destroyers, three submarines, and eight tankers. Twenty-eight submarines—eleven carrying small airplanes and five transporting midget submarines—were his advance force.[1]

All told, 350 aircraft would attack Oahu. The first wave numbered 183 planes, the second 167. The force included horizontal-bombers, torpedo-bombers, dive-bombers, and fighters. Thirty-nine more were assigned to combat air patrols, and an additional 40 were kept in reserve. It looked like the armada had achieved surprise, but Nagumo did not know for sure until he heard from Commander Mitsuo Fuchida, the first wave leader. Nagumo was especially anxious to neutralize the American air bases, whose fighters posed the greatest threat to his planes. So part of his air fleet was to bomb and strafe Wheeler and Hickam Airfields plus the smaller air bases on Ford Island and at Kaneohe and Ewa Mooring Mast field, a marine base. But the main target was Pearl Harbor.[2]

Meanwhile, before 7:00 A.M., the destroyer *Ward* attacked a submarine in the defensive sea zone outside the entrance to Pearl Harbor and reported the action to the harbor control post. The lieutenant in charge phoned the chief of staff, who wanted confirmation from the *Ward* but passed the message to Kimmel and Admiral C. C. Bloch, also a Kentuckian, who commanded the Hawaii-headquartered Fourteenth

Naval District. Bloch and Kimmel opted to wait for word from the destroyer.[3]

At 7:02 A.M., army radar operators at the Opana Point mobile radar station on Oahu's north shore detected a mass of airplanes 137 miles out and contacted the Army Aircraft Warning Information Center at Fort Shafter in Honolulu. The duty officer dismissed the contacts as perhaps army B-17 bombers expected from California and instructed the operator not to "worry about it." At 7:53, Fuchida, twelve thousand feet above Oahu aboard his command plane, a Kate, radioed Nagumo the coded message he was anxious to hear, "Tora! Tora! Tora!" (meaning that surprise had been achieved). He "could see no movement or alarm," Martinez said. "Pearl Harbor, the Gibraltar of the Pacific, was tranquil and at rest."[4]

More than 180 vessels were in Pearl Harbor. Not since July 4 had all eight battlewagons been in port together. Vice Admiral William S. Pye, commander of the battleships, was unworried that his capital ships might make easy targets for air attackers. "The Japanese will not go to war with the United States," he boasted on December 6. "We are too big, too powerful, and too strong."[5] Short and Kimmel seemed to share Pye's confidence, if not his cockiness. "With twenty-twenty hindsight, it is mystifying to read again and again of how insistent military officers in Hawaii were before December 7 that nothing was a threat to them, yet this was a broadly held sentiment in the United States before the shock of Pearl Harbor," the historian Craig Nelson wrote. Anyway, the huge battleships bristled with the biggest guns in the fleet, but the carriers *Enterprise, Lexington,* and *Saratoga* were Yamamoto's biggest game. He especially feared their long-range striking power; after all, he figured to smash Pearl Harbor with swarms of carrier-based bombers and fighters.[6]

Battleship Row represented the naval might that Admiral Mahan had urged on his country. The great ships presented "a thrilling line of masts and funnels." Keeping them company were their lessers—cruisers, destroyers, tenders, repair ships, and other nondescript craft at anchor all around the sprawling, busy harbor.[7]

Oahu's air defense force included 394 army, navy, and marine aircraft—fighters, bombers, scouting and observation planes, and other types, many of them obsolete or under repair. Most critically, only 108 fighters—93 army and 15 navy—were available to intercept an intruder.

The best of the lot were the army Curtiss P-40 "Warhawks" and navy Grumman F4F "Wildcats," both rugged, lethal machines in the hands of capable pilots. Even so, Nagumo's speedier and more maneuverable Zero fighters had a clear edge over the other American machines— mostly outdated army Curtiss P-36 "Hawks" and lumbering navy and marine Brewster F2A "Buffaloes."[8]

As Pacific Fleet commander, the Henderson-born Kimmel was boss of everything navy and marine in Hawaii, no matter whether in the air, ashore, or afloat. He was named commander on January 9, 1941. "Hubby" Kimmel succeeded his old friend Admiral James O. Richardson, who had too stridently opposed moving the fleet from California to Hawaii. The shift was supposed to make Tokyo think twice about trying to grab British and Dutch colonies in Southeast Asia. Richardson said the move to Pearl Harbor was folly on multiple counts. He argued that, if the United States ended up fighting Japan, warships in Hawaii would have to return to California to bring their crews up to battle strength. He also felt that West Coast supply, repair, and training facilities were superior to those at Pearl Harbor. And he maintained that extended absences from their families stateside were hurting morale among his sailors and marines. In addition, he claimed that, because the Japanese believed the US fleet to be unprepared for war anyway, its presence at Pearl Harbor would not scare them. His carping landed him in hot water with FDR and the navy brass, so he was sacked. The fleet stayed in Hawaii, to boot.[9]

Kimmel was to take over on or about February 1. Obviously, Washington thought highly of him. No matter, his appointment reportedly "came as a complete surprise"; Kimmel's aide thought his chief would faint at the news.[10]

Born in 1882, Kimmel was from a military family. His father, the Missourian Manning M. Kimmel, was a West Pointer who fought on both sides in the Civil War, switching from Yankee blue to Rebel gray. Major Kimmel settled in Henderson after America's bloodiest conflict. Naturally, Bluegrass State papers played up Admiral Kimmel's prestigious appointment. The *Owensboro Inquirer* reported that his Henderson friends said Kimmel really wanted to be a soldier like his dad. He settled for the Naval Academy in 1900 only after "a lack of vacancies in the cadet corps" kept him out of West Point. The Kentuckian "plunged into life at Annapolis as if to prove to the military academy that it had missed a good man." He graduated in 1904 and "began a swift rise in naval ranks that continued until his current appointment," the paper said. On the way up, he briefly served as an aide to Franklin D. Roosevelt, then assistant secretary of the navy.[11]

During World War I, Kimmel was a liaison officer to the Royal Navy. He also served on the staff of his fellow Kentuckian Rear Admiral Hugh Rodman while Rodman commanded US battleships with the British Grand Fleet. After the war, Kimmel attended the Naval War College, commanded destroyers, and was the executive officer of the battleship *Arkansas* and the skipper of the battleship *New York*. Kimmel made rear admiral in 1937 while he was budget officer in the Navy Department in Washington. He returned to sea duty and held two assignments in the Pacific before advancing to fleet commander. His last post was commander, Cruisers Battle Force.[12]

Kimmel married into another military family. His wife was Dorothy Kincaid, the daughter of Rear Admiral Thomas W. Kinkaid and sister of Admiral Thomas C. Kinkaid. But the teenage Kimmel seemed an unlikely salt; he nearly died in a sailboat accident, according to his brothers. "Hubby" and four of his buddies shoved off into the Ohio River, which flows past Henderson. Kimmel's little vessel capsized under the old Louisville and Nashville Railroad bridge near town, dumping the quintet in the deep, muddy water. A fisherman rescued them, and somebody saved the boat. "But Kimmel's ardor for sailing was so dampened that soon a sign went up on the boat, 'This Boat for Sale Very Cheap H. E. Kimmel,'" the *Inquirer* advised.[13]

On January 26, the *Louisville Courier-Journal* published a sketch of the new fleet commander that provided more details of the apparently near-fatal boating mishap. Evidently, after setting sail about 3:30 P.M. on the fateful day in 1895 or 1896, the lads tacked upstream to the Henderson waterworks, then turned to drift back with the strong current. At the Louisville and Nashville span, "a gust of wind hit the boat and the boys threw their combined weight to one side." The "sloop yacht" flipped over, and "they found themselves swimming for their lives." The reporter confirmed that an angler saved the them and that, "after some sober reflection, the dampened ardor of the sailors turned to downright apathy." Hence, young Kimmel put his boat on the market.[14]

"[Kimmel] had no idea of turning to the water for a career," the *Courier-Journal* said. "He did, of course, think of serving his country, for that was a Kimmel tradition." The reporter cited not only his father but also his maternal grandfather, Herman Husband. Though a Quaker, Husband supported the Regulators, hard-pressed farmers who staged a populist rebellion in the Carolina backwoods before the Revolutionary War. Evidently, Grandpa Husband was the subject of a new biography that portrayed him as "a type of modern John the Baptist, making straight the path for the patriots who later took the next step that became the War of the Revolution."[15]

The reporter agreed that Kimmel did not jump at the Annapolis appointment: "The boat episode and the chilly water made him hesitate. But again his mind went back to his ancestors." Kimmel pondered a family picture of his great-grandfather John Husband, an early nineteenth-century flatboat man who had hauled cargo from Pittsburgh to Henderson. He even moored the scow where his great-grandson's boat flipped over. The reporter added that Henderson dwellers convinced John to stay and open a store.[16]

Kimmel's navy career naturally kept him away from home for long spells. The *Courier-Journal* story told about the time the admiral was reunited with his five-year-old son, Ned. The lad had not seen his dad for two years. When he returned, Ned sized him up critically and whispered in his mother's ear: "Is THIS all the Daddy that I've got?"[17]

Kimmel was nearly fifty-nine when he ceremoniously took command of the fleet aboard the *Pennsylvania* on February 1. "Hubby" was a well-built five feet, ten inches tall and weighed 180 pounds, according to the historians Gordon Prange, Donald Goldstein, and Katherine Dillon: "Virile, with a clean look that carried the tang of the sea, Kimmel seemed the living embodiment of 'NAVY.'"[18]

The historian Steve Twomey similarly described the new commander: "If a civilian had been told to conjure the visage, carriage, and career of an admiral in 1941, Husband Edward Kimmel would have materialized. He owned the part. . . . As an ensign, a commander, a captain, and an admiral, Kimmel had sailed almost every sea the planet offered and stepped on every continent, or at least the ones that were not all ice." Though he survived the Pearl Harbor attack unscathed, the admiral had shed blood for his country: "In 1914, as he stood on the deck of a warship sent to protect American lives during Mexico's revolution, a bullet—fired from ashore by someone unknown—had struck a railing and splintered, the shards wounding him in an arm and both legs." No matter, he stuck to his post. "In a photo, dollops of blood stain the right sleeve of his white uniform," Twomey wrote. "He looks untroubled."[19]

Walter Lord described Kimmel as "hard, sharp, and utterly frank," a navy lifer who "worked himself to the bone" and "looked and acted uncomfortable in easygoing surroundings." Kimmel even frowned on the navy's new khaki uniforms, harrumphing that they diminished "the dignity and military point of view of the wearer."[20]

Kimmel earned ink in the *Owensboro Messenger* on May 18, 1941. "President Roosevelt . . . dipped deep down into the Navy pool of rear admirals and passed over 46 higher ranking men to pick Husband Edward Kimmel as Commander-in-Chief of the U.S. Fleet," wrote a Newspaper Enterprises Association wire service reporter. He described Kimmel, Admiral Ernest J. King, the commander of the Atlantic Fleet, and Admiral Thomas C. Hart, the commander of the Asiatic Fleet, as "three cold steel, fighting men": "The Navy's stripping for action."[21]

Kimmel was an ordnance expert and "a keen strategist," according to the reporter. "There is little nonsense about him." Maybe not, but he had a wry sense of humor: "He seems to enjoy frightening junior officers nearly out of their wits by calling them to the bridge, and discussing the day's orders with brows gathered like storm signals, blue eyes staring. Then he breaks into a wide grin as he dismisses them. They get to know it is a form of hazing intended as good clean fun, but more than one of them has been tempted to make a dive for it before the grin came."[22]

Kimmel's friends explained his decisiveness by declaring: "He knows what he wants." Yet: "Others who have felt its blunt edge say he is 'brusque, aggressive.'" Nonetheless, "officers and men alike who have served with him concede the fairness of his decisions." Though Kimmel was born in Kentucky, his "life at sea and in strange ports has left little in his voice and manner to identify him as a Southerner." The reporter wrapped up his story by noting that, because Kimmel was also Pacific Fleet commander, he would see active duty at sea should the United

States go to war before he retired in five years, speculating: "Perhaps the most brilliant chapter of his career is yet to be written in the log."[23]

"An officer or non-commissioned officer who shall suffer himself to be surprised . . . must not expect to be forgiven," warned British major general James Wolfe, who famously surprised and defeated the marquis de Montcalm at Quebec and captured the strategic city from the French in the French and Indian War. Wolfe was fatally wounded, as was Montcalm. Kimmel allegedly wanted to die at Pearl Harbor. The army and navy brass failed to react "with alacrity to what the *Ward* had seen and done," Twomey wrote. "Everyone remained in the vice grip of peace." He concluded: "What would have unfolded if the response in these last minutes had been faster is, of course, unknowable." Even so, there might have been enough time "to sound general quarters on all ships and be waiting with all antiaircraft guns loaded and all eyes skyward."[24]

No sooner did the attack start than Kimmel knew his career was ruined, or so the story went. The attack also spoiled his golf outing with Short. Still at home when the air raid began, the admiral stepped outside into his yard and spied "aircraft . . . descending, climbing, darting, red balls visible on every wing," Twomey wrote. Kimmel went to his office, where he helplessly view the carnage, suspecting he would at least be demoted. Hence, he tore off his four-star, full-admiral shoulder boards and replaced them with two-star, rear-admiral ones. Supposedly, too, a spent bullet struck him in the chest and fell harmlessly to the floor. "I wish it had killed me," he reputedly said when he picked it up, according to Nelson.[25]

Back in July, Kimmel had been happy to make the news. An AP story portrayed him as a brass hat with a heart. Dressed in civilian clothes, the admiral went into a Honolulu store to buy trousers, according to the story that ran nationwide. The clerk handed him a pair he seemed to like, and he ducked into a changing room to try them on. Meanwhile, two navy petty officers in uniform came in seeking suits, socks, ties, and other items of clothing. The clerk got so busy with them that he forgot his other customer. So: "He dashed to the alcove and found the man holding up the trousers." They were too big and needed to be altered: "The clerk said the house tailor was busy with the petty officers; would the customer mind waiting?"[26]

Kimmel smiled and said: "The Navy comes first. You know, national defense." After a while, the clerk returned with the alterations complete. "Will you charge it?" the customer requested. "The name is Kimmel." The astonished clerk exclaimed: "Admiral Husband E. Kimmel!" The customer grinned again and replied: "That's right."[27]

While Kimmel was clothes shopping, Yamamoto was refining his plans for the Pearl Harbor attack. The two had much in common, according to Prange, Goldstein, and Dillon. Both were from small towns; both graduated in 1904 from their country's naval academy. Furthermore: "Each was a bundle of driving energy; each had a strong will and fierce devotion to his profession. Each made his presence keenly felt wherever he went, and when either wanted his way, he could lean hard."[28]

The American public was in a hard-leaning mood after Pearl Harbor. John and Jane Q Citizen demanded answers. The people knew from a week of newspaper and radio reports that the attack was a calamity perhaps unparalleled in US history. But it would be a while longer before they knew how massive the disaster was.

All told, 1,998 navy personnel were dead, and another 710 were wounded. Marine casualties were put at 109 killed, 69 wounded. The army lost 233, with 364 wounded. The civilian toll was 49 dead, 35 wounded.[29]

Twenty-one ships were sunk or significantly damaged. Battleship Row was gone. The *Nevada* was aground, the *Arizona*, the *Oklahoma*, the *West Virginia*, and the *California* were sunk. The *Tennessee* and the *Maryland* were damaged. So was the *Pennsylvania*, which had been in dry dock. Rounding out the roster of sunken ships were the mine layer *Oglala* and the destroyers *Cassin* and *Downes*. Damaged but still afloat were the cruisers *Helena, Honolulu,* and *Raleigh,* the destroyer *Shaw,* the seaplane tender *Curtiss,* and *Vestal,* a repair ship. A black-and-white photo of the *Shaw* exploding in a giant fireball is one of the most famous images from World War II. The photographer was a Kentuckian, twenty-nine-year-old Apprentice Seaman Lucien J. Bodkin Jr. of Bardwell, the Carlisle County seat. Bodkin was assigned to Fleet Air Photographic Squadron (VD) 1 and took the photo from the ground.[30]

Aircraft losses were put at 171; most of the planes were destroyed on the ground. The attackers destroyed 74 army aircraft at Bellows, Hickam, and Wheeler Airfields. The navy lost 54 planes at Ford Island

and Kaneohe Naval Air Stations; 10 planes from the *Enterprise* were downed by friendly and enemy fire. The Japanese wrecked 33 marine planes at Ewa Mooring Mast field.[31]

Victory cost the Japanese 29 planes, five midget submarines and 64 men. A large I-class submarine that was part of the attack force was sunk later with the loss of 121 men.[32]

Kimmel and Short were relieved on December 17, via "one of the most drastic shake-ups in U.S. military and naval history," according to the *Louisville Courier-Journal*. Rear Admiral Chester W. Nimitz replaced Kimmel; Lieutenant General Delos C. Emmons succeeded Short. The next day, FDR appointed a five-member panel to find out what happened at Pearl Harbor and why. It was called the Roberts Commission after its chair, the Supreme Court justice Owen J. Roberts. Major General Frank B. McCoy was to represent the army, Brigadier General Joseph T. McNarney the army air force. On the navy side sat Admiral William H. Standley and Rear Admiral Joseph M. Reeves. Both were retired.[33]

The commission was not a court-martial. Its job was fact-finding—examining evidence and hearing testimony, including from Kimmel and Short. The press seemed to have faith in the panel. The *Louisville Courier-Journal* was confident the commissioners would calmly, carefully, expertly, and responsibly discover "why the Army and Navy at Hawaii were not on the alert against the surprise attack": "The assurance exists now that exact justice will be meted out, and this assurance gives us no room for self-righteous recriminations based on hindsight."[34]

The panel began its hearings in Hawaii on December 22, working out of Fort Shafter, army headquarters. Roosevelt received the commissioners' report on January 24. It focused on Kimmel and Short, not subordinate admirals and generals. It said: "In the light of the warnings and direction to take appropriate action transmitted to both commanders between November 27 and December 7, and the obligation under the system of coordination then in effect for joint cooperative action on their part, it was a dereliction of duty on the part of each of them not to consult and confer with each other respecting the meaning and intent of the warnings and the appropriate means of defense required by the imminence of hostilities." The conclusion? "The Japanese attack was a complete surprise to the commanders, and they failed to make suitable dispositions to meet such an attack. Each failed to properly evaluate the seriousness of the situation. These errors of judgment were the effective causes for the success of the attack."[35]

Thus, for Kimmel and Short, public shame now followed defeat, demotion, and removal from command. The Kentuckian was dropped from admiral to rear admiral. Short also was shorn of two stars, falling from general to major general. "Possibly only an individual who, like these two officers, had given decades of stainless service to his country could understand just what the scalding verdict meant to them," Prange, Goldstein, and Dillon wrote. "Duty was the cornerstone of their lives." Both demanded a chance to clear themselves via court-martial; neither got one. The Kentucky congressman Andrew Jackson May, a Prestonsburg Democrat, evidently considered the Roberts Commission verdict ample proof of their awful guilt. He said Kimmel and Short should face a firing squad; neither did, and both soon retired.[36]

May, who chaired the House Military Affairs Committee, raised eyebrows and hackles when, in an April 6, 1942, Army Day speech at Pikeville, he told the crowd that after Short and Kimmel "come up for court martial I'm in favor of holding a shooting match." He turned to reporters and added: "You can quote me on that, and if it gets back to Washington, that will be all right too." The lawmaker poured it on, charging that Short and Kimmel "had received repeated and ample warnings to take every precaution because war was imminent" and that "they had not heeded these warnings." (In June 1946, a joint congressional investigation headed by Senate majority leader Barkley found that Short and Kimmel had erred in judgment but had not been derelict in their duty.)[37]

Eight days later, May backpedaled, telling the House that his remarks "had been 'misinterpreted' because they were not published in full." He acknowledged that "the quotations were 'substantially correct'" but "incomplete." He declared "that he was 'not in the habit of wanting men executed without a trial.'" He "wouldn't even consent to the killing of a dog without a fair trial." He declared that, in his speech to his constituents, he proposed that, if, "after a full, fair and complete court-martial hearing, this admiral and general were found guilty of negligence resulting in the death of 3,000 or 3,400 men [2,403 were killed], then there ought to be a shooting match."[38]

May's crawfishing came too late to stave off criticism. Even state papers that leaned Democratic editorially—notably the *Louisville Courier-Journal*—were unimpressed, unfavorably comparing May to the president for whom he was named: "Andrew Jackson, who was never a mild man, told some friends at the end of his service as President that he was leaving the White House with two principal regrets—that he had never had an opportunity to shoot Henry Clay or hang John C. Calhoun." The editorial added: "It is impossible to imagine the old soldier, violent as he sometimes was, talking like Andrew Jackson May at Pikeville on Army Day. . . . This war is not going to be won by picking on scapegoats, much less by shooting Americans without trial." It concluded: "Our advice to Mr. May would be that Hitler and Hirohito are ample targets for his oratorical gunplay."[39]

The Democratic *Danville Advocate-Messenger* editorialized that May "made a fool of himself with an ugly remark": "Kimmel and Short are the 'goats' in the surprise attack on Pearl Harbor, but they were like everyone else in the U.S.—from the President on down. The Japs just 'put one over on us' and that's all there is to it." Henry Ward, the *Paducah Sun-Democrat* city editor, knew what it was like to be misquoted in the press. He had been the Democratic House majority leader in the most recent session of the General Assembly. "But I wouldn't be surprised if May did propose shooting Kimmel and Short without further ado," he wrote in his column. "He's that type."[40]

May took his lumps in *Courier-Journal* letters to the editor. "Well, sir, if we must shoot General Short and Admiral Kimmel, I think the best way to do that would be to shoot a Congressman or Senator on either side of them," proposed Bill Lovelace of Berea. "But I think, if we do have to do any shooting, we should shoot ten Congressmen and Senators and let the general and admiral go to Washington to take the ten vacant places, for I think that the general's and the admiral's heads would be worth more than ten of some heads that are in Washington."[41]

Guy Hatfield Jr. of Richmond preferred spilling the foe's blood: "Let's not shoot Admiral Kimmel, let's direct our shooting toward the real enemy. Kentucky's Admiral Kimmel wasn't the only person caught with his guard down, there were 130,000,000 other unsuspecting Americans." Henry L. Muir of Bardstown sent the *Courier-Journal* a copy of a letter he wrote to May. The paper reprinted it. It read in part: "Have you never made a grave mistake? Don't you know that Kimmel and Short are heartbroken, that their life ambitions as protectors of America have been blasted, that they are just as good Americans as you or I and that either of them would willingly and gladly give his life for his country[?] Have a heart, man, have a heart."[42]

Jessie Jane Caskey of Lebanon suggested that Kimmel and Short deserved a second chance: "How terrible must be the punishment of mental anguish they are undergoing daily. . . . They have spent their lives being fitted as leaders in war. We need them now. Let them redeem that mistake which others, too, were to blame for." David Banks of Henderson, Kimmel's hometown, also said he wrote May defending the admiral and Short: "They have already been cruelly, and, for all you or I know, unjustly humiliated. Maybe it was somehow necessary as a matter of policy to sacrifice these two men, but even if such a policy could be understood, there could be no pride in it for any American. In any case, the very least that Admiral Kimmel and General Short have a right to expect of the public is that judgment shall be suspended until all the facts can be known."[43]

"Woman at the Window" knew that the military had "spent time, money and pains" educating and training the two commanders: "Surely in our far-flung naval and air setup there must be some spot where these men could contribute to our war effort without too much harm being done in case they should slightly oversleep on a Sunday morning—or something." She could not understand why Kimmel and Short "should now be retired with pay while their hard-pressed country is in the midst of war."[44]

While the *Courier-Journal* maligned May, it was evenhanded in assessing the Roberts Commission's verdict. "No further punishment, whatever its character, can be a tenth as severe as what [Kimmel and Short] . . . have already received," it editorialized. "That fact should make against vindictiveness in our thinking of their cases." The paper opposed "self-righteous condemnation" because Kimmel's and Short's "complacency was part of a contagion pretty general in America at the time, and by no means yet altogether abated."[45]

Even so, the *Courier-Journal* did not exonerate the admiral or the general: "It was their duty to be immune from such contagion. But they have paid and will pay the penalty, while some of their loudest critics at the moment were doing their best within a month before Pearl Harbor to lull the people into the belief that the Neutrality Act would keep us out of war."[46]

Kimmel doubtless would have appreciated the *Madisonville Messenger's* Roberts Commission report editorial. It mentioned neither him nor Short and blamed the Pearl Harbor debacle largely on "the subconscious acceptance of isolationist complacency": "The concept that collapsed at Pearl Harbor was the isolationist notion that the proper American foreign policy was to start from the premise that we were impregnable and then wait for a hostile navy or air force to prove it."[47]

Kimmel must have experienced more than a twinge of schadenfreude in 1947 when May was convicted of taking bribes from munitions suppliers during the war and bundled off to federal prison. Three years before, his loose lips led another round of bad press and, worse, it was alleged, to the spilling of American blood. After a visit to Pearl Harbor, he returned stateside and, at a press conference, told reporters that US submarines had been so successful sinking Japanese ships and getting away because Japanese navy sub hunters were not setting their depth charges to explode deep enough. It is not clear whether the Japanese readjusted their depth charges because of May's heedless remarks. But Vice Admiral Charles Lockwood, the commander of the US Pacific submarine fleet, later estimated that, however unintentional, the leak of secret information directly caused the loss of ten submarines and eight hundred crewmen.[48]

Meanwhile, Kimmel had gone home to Henderson, arriving there on February 27, 1942. Eleven days before, Secretary of War Frank Knox had accepted the admiral's request to retire, effective March 1. On March 4, the AP reported that Kimmel was "remaining quietly in seclusion" with his siblings S. H. and Lambert Kimmel. The brothers were shielding him from reporters, answering, "We do not know," when newspaper scribes asked where Kimmel planned to go after leaving Henderson. He was expected to stay about a week in the family home, a dwelling "of colonial type" on about an acre of land and "situated back some 100 feet from Green street and surrounded by large trees and shrubbery."[49]

3

The *Arizona* and the *Oklahoma*

Though the Pacific Fleet's three carriers were elsewhere, Pearl Harbor was a rich target for the attackers. "What a windfall for us! No matter how careful the planning, a more favorable situation could not have been imagined," Fuchida said after the war.[1]

Fuchida's pilots bore in on Battleship Row. The Kate crews had clear shots at the *California*, the *Oklahoma*, the *West Virginia*, and the *Nevada*. No torpedo nets protected them. The navy brass believed such safeguards to be unnecessary because the harbor was too shallow for conventional torpedoes to be effective. The Americans were, of course, unaware that the Japanese aerial torpedoes were specially designed for operating in shallow water. "I was struck with the shortsightedness of the United States in being so generally unprepared and in not using torpedo nets," Fuchida also said.[2]

Likewise, battleship decks and superstructures were more than stout enough to survive strikes from conventional bombs dropped from single-engine carrier aircraft, or so the admirals thought. The Americans knew nothing of the enemy's special armor-piercing bombs. When the last of Fuchida's planes flew away to their carriers, only the *Tennessee* and the *Maryland* were still afloat, but they were damaged. The bombed and torpedoed *Nevada* was aground after trying to escape. The concrete dry dock helped saved the *Pennsylvania*, though the battleship was bombed. Fuchida recalled peering from his Kate and seeing the havoc his fliers were wreaking below: "I also thought of our long hard training in Kagoshima Bay and the efforts of those who had labored to accomplish a seemingly impossible task. A warm feeling came with the realization that the reward of those efforts was unfolded here before my eyes." Coldness ultimately followed. The Americans sank four of the six attack carriers at the Battle of Midway in June 1942. Many of the aviators victorious at Pearl Harbor died in the crushing Japanese defeat. Sooner or later, all the battleships at Pearl Harbor, save the *Arizona* and the *Oklahoma,* were repaired and modernized and returned to fight the Japanese.[3]

The *Arizona*

Though the *Arizona* was moored inboard of the *Vestal,* first reports claimed a torpedo struck the battleship early in the air raid. Evidently, horizontal-bombers alone destroyed the super-dreadnought. Several bombs fell on it, damaging its aft and midship sections. About 8:10 a.m., a 1,763-pound naval shell turned into a bomb fell from a five-plane formation of high-flying Kates, crashing through the forward deck, and igniting powder magazines and aviation gasoline stored for the ship's scout planes. The explosion triggered "a chain reaction that turned the ship itself into a bomb," Nelson wrote. The blast produced an enormous fireball and heaved the 32,600-ton *Arizona*'s bow nearly fifty feet in the air. The ship virtually broke in half, and, when the battlewagon crashed back to the water, the impact churned a twelve- to fifteen-foot wave that slapped against the Ford Island shoreline. "[The ship's] enormous superstructure [was] enveloped in vicious and immense oil-black clouds, her forward compartments flooding with both water and oil," added Nelson. It took the *Arizona,* engulfed in flames, just nine minutes to sink: "The souls of 1,177 sailors and marines were lost, more than died in the Spanish-American War and the First World War combined. It was the highest mortality in the sinking of a single vessel in American naval history, and of human beings killed by a single explosion in the history of war . . . until Hiroshima." The ship was a complete loss. All but 334 of the 1,511 crewmen on board died, including Rear Admiral Isaac C. Kidd, the commander of Battleship Division One, and the *Arizona*'s skipper, Captain Franklin Van Valkenburgh.[4]

Some of the *Arizona*'s officers and men survived because they were ashore on liberty. Fireman Third Class Herbert Buehl and his buddy Kenny Keniston, of the same rank, were enjoying the first day of weekend liberty with Keniston's brother Don, a seaman second class. But, instead of hunting down a hotel in Honolulu, the trio decided to spend Saturday night aboard ship, then maybe hit town again on Sunday. "We weren't making that kind of money," remembered Buehl, a Wisconsin native who retired to Jeffersontown near Louisville. Had they bedded down in town, the Kenistons would have lived, and Buehl would have escaped a terrifying brush with death by suffocation and drowning.[5]

Before returning to the *Arizona*, the three sailors took in a movie and had a "very delicious meal" in a "very fine restaurant." They ordered strawberry shortcake for dessert. Afterward, they walked off dinner by taking "in some of the sights that were available." Hungry again around 11:00 P.M., they gobbled waffles and syrup, then boarded a late launch, overcrowded with sailors returning to their ships.[6]

When the general quarters alarm sounded, Herbert and Kenny were talking over what to do for the rest of Sunday after Kenny got back from Catholic church services on the *Nevada*. "While we were standing there, [a] chief petty officer come running down through the corridor and said, 'The Japanese are attacking. Close your battle ports and man your battle stations,'" Buehl said. "And so for a minute, we just kind of froze. But the first class electrician's mate that was there said, 'Well, if it's so, we might as well do it.'" Buehl and Keniston shut the ports, then parted—Keniston to lose his life and Buehl to near death. "I never even said good-bye to my friends. We just—everybody was quiet."[7]

Buehl's battle station "was about four decks down, by the number 3 gun, and also the radio shack . . . our control center." The first man who arrived was supposed to put on a headset and contact the engine room. Buehl was first, but he could not raise anyone: "So I stood there with the headsets on for a few minutes, and whether it was a bomb or a torpedo that hit the ship, I don't know, but it knocked the lights out."[8]

Buehl decided to investigate. He took off the earphones and went to an open doorway that was at the top of a ladder leading to the passageway between the bases of the number 3 and number 4 gun turrets: "And I just stood there because I hadn't been given any permission to leave my battle station, and as I stood there, there was this terrific explosion." He said it felt "just like a tornado had gone through the ship": "It just pushed me from the top of the ladder to the bottom. And I have no idea how I got down there."[9]

Lucky for Buehl, he landed on his feet: "So I just took my hands, and I rubbed my body all over and checked my arms and legs to see if I had any broken bones or was bleeding, and I wasn't." He went through another doorway into the passageway and discovered several other sailors. "But by now, the explosion had consumed all the oxygen in the air, and we weren't able to breathe," he said.[10]

Hoping to find air beyond a closed door, Buehl dropped to his knees and opened the four "dogs"—latches on the bottom. The dogs, he explained, made the door watertight: "Thank goodness somebody opened the four on the top, and we're doing all of this without being able to breathe. I mean, we just knew we had to do this, and there was some fellows that were losing it a little bit, but most of us had contained [*sic*] our senses. And when we opened the door up, there was oxygen on the other side, and so we could breathe."[11]

Once through the doorway, the men shut and dogged off the door to preserve what air they had. "I mean, it was all black as pitch," Buehl remembered. One man proposed "to find out who the senior person is here" and agree that he would be in charge. As it turned out, there were three ensigns and four enlisted sailors. One of the officers spoke up and said: "Well, I'll report our condition." Somehow, he found a battle lantern that lit his way up a ladder to the number 3 turret. He escaped through a hatch in the turret overhang.[12]

Topside, the ensign could see that the *Arizona* had blown up. It looked to him like the whole forward section of the ship was gone. "So," Buehl said, "he crawled back in again and came down and told us that we might as well abandon ship because the ship was on fire and there wasn't anything that we could do, and he would be the only one that would be able to tell us that we could abandon ship."[13]

Having escaped asphyxiation, the men faced drowning. "The water had already started to leak into the base of this number 3 gun, and so we all knew that we had to leave," Buehl said. "We crawled up through the number 3 gun, out through this hatch." Buehl grabbed the hatch handle, planning to drop to the deck. But he found himself dangling "maybe ten feet or better up in the air." He managed to swing himself over to a ladder on the outside of the turret and climbed down. His shipmates apparently did likewise.[14]

The men made for the starboard side of the turret—facing Ford Island—figuring the huge steel box would shield them from strafing planes. "Well, we had to have another little consultation there and we decided we're going to take the life raft off of the side of the ship, or this turret, and throw it in the water," Buehl said. They followed the raft into the water but failed to find it in the thick, black gelatinous mass of fuel oil floating on the surface: "This oil was covering all of our body, and so we were getting tired. It just isn't possible to swim because your skin breathes too, and we were just getting so tired." Buehl headed for the *Arizona*'s aft mooring quay, a large white-painted concrete structure with a wooden bumper at the base. (The sixteen quays, two for each battleship, survive.) Two men standing on the bumper grabbed his wrists and pulled him up so he could reach the bumper. "They said, 'Now, you've got to get up the rest of the way yourself because there are other men that we have to pull out of the water,'" Buehl remembered.[15]

Buehl feared that, if he tried to boost himself out, he would slip and fall back in the oily water and drown. "So you get this extra energy and I forced myself up on this bumper," he said. Luck was still with him. Some of his shipmates started one of the *Arizona*'s thirty-foot launches and headed for the quay, where he and other survivors were standing on the bumper. The sailor driving the boat told them to "jump in" but warned: "I'm not stopping because there are Japanese fighters all over the place."[16]

Though Buehl hit a bench, his leap was successful. Still: "Since I was so oily and everything, I just about slipped [to] the other side." He suggested that they should stop and help men struggling in the water. The driver refused and said he was Ford Island bound, nonstop. So Buehl tossed overboard boat hooks and anything that would float to help men struggling in the water.[17]

The boat docked safely, and Buehl found welcome shelter in the basement of a house: "It was like a bomb shelter, 'cause it had a walk-in basement. And we went into this basement, and they told us that they wanted to get some mattresses to lay down for us." But, when the mattresses were brought in, the refugee sailors were told they were for women and children who lived on the island and not to be stained by oil-soaked sailors.[18]

Denied a rest, Buehl went to some officers seated at a table and taking the names of men who had managed to get off the stricken ships. They asked him his name and serial number: "When I was in boot camp, they told me I can forget everything I ever knew, but don't forget that [serial] number, and I never have. It was 300-19-34. And I just assumed it was correct. They never said, 'Well, that doesn't sound right to me.'" He got the number right.[19]

After signing in, one of the officers took Buehl and others to bring back men's clothing from some of the nearby houses. Buehl swapped his ruined white T-shirt, shorts, and socks for civilian duds that "just about fit" him: "[The original owner] was a little bit bigger around the middle at the time than what I was, so it was a little hard for me to keep 'em on. But anyway, I had something to cover me up."[20]

Afterward, the men were sent to hangars to assemble fifty-caliber machine-gun belts for fighter planes from the *Enterprise*, which was on the way back to Pearl Harbor. "And so the rest of the afternoon, that's what I did," Buehl remembered. "I was feeling kind of woozy [by suppertime] from all of this oil and everything." He managed to eat but felt worse afterward. He spent a sleepless night in the hangar and "felt terrible" by Monday morning.[21]

Buehl headed to the island hospital. Again, fortune smiled on him: "One of the fellows that I went to boot camp with was a pharmacist's mate and he knew me." He told Buehl to take off his clothes, climb into bed, and not worry about a shower. His boot camp buddy promised to find a doctor to examine him.[22]

Buehl's luck finally ran out when the doc appeared about fifteen minutes later. He spied the clothes and demanded to know where Buehl got them. "From one of the houses over on Ford Island," he confessed. The doctor replied: "You know, you stole those from me." Fuming, he added, "I've got a good mind to court-martial you," grabbed his clothes, and stormed out.[23]

Buehl's luck returned. "Don't let it bother you, Herb," his buddy assured him. "Tell me what your sizes are and I'll get you shoes and pants and shirt and socks and whatever you need." He also invited him to at least wash the oil out of his hair.[24]

Buehl went to the head but got so dizzy he nearly fell. But help soon arrived. "I think they washed my hair at least about three or four times before they got the oil all out," he said. "And then I took my shower and cleaned up and they helped me with that too, 'cause that oil just sticks to you, you know. It's awfully hard to get off." Feeling better, he put on a pair of new skivvies and climbed back in bed.[25]

Buehl told the friendly pharmacist's mate he was having a hard time breathing: "It just feels like there's a knife being stuck in me when I breathe real hard." The medico produced "a water pipe type of thing": "He put water in the base, and then some sort of brown liquid in the top part of it. And it must have been electric, where he could plug it in so that it would form steam and then I would inhale this. And he said, 'Now, when you inhale this . . . each time, try to breathe a little bit deeper and just keep doing that.'"[26]

Buehl stayed on the pipe until about six o'clock, when somebody yelled: "There's a foreign object in the air and we don't know what it is." Everybody was ordered under the beds. Buehl helped a fellow patient who "was a little worse off" than he was. The "foreign object" turned out to be a weather balloon.[27]

Buehl was feeling better Tuesday morning when he was sent to a receiving center for assignment. By the time he got there, he had broken out in boils—one on his right shoulder, others on his left leg. A chief pharmacist's mate froze and lanced the boils. He told Buehl: "You're never going to have any trouble with boils any more." Buehl said he never did.[28]

The next day, Buehl was supposed to help make a silhouette book of Japanese planes. Before he could get started, he was reassigned to the destroyer *Farragut,* which saw heavy action in the Pacific theater to the end of the war. After the war, he visited Pearl Harbor three times before he was featured in a 1999 Pearl Harbor Day story in the *Louisville Courier-Journal.* He said his first trip back was the worst one: "You just flash back to all the men that were your friends." Most of them were dead, he added: "I was just a snap of a finger away from not making it."[29]

Buehl's shipmate, twenty-year-old Gunner's Mate Second Class James Allard Vessels of Paducah, had been enjoying a friendly game of "Acey-Deucy" with his buddy Ross Worth Lightfoot, a gunner's mate third class, on the antiaircraft deck. The duo had to keep up with the time; all hands aboard ship were expected to join morning colors, the traditional flag-raising ceremony on the fantail when the ship's acclaimed band played the national anthem.[30]

An unexpected explosion on Ford Island broke up the card game. "Lightfoot and I jumped up to see what was going [on] as we couldn't figure [out] what was happening," Vessels said. At first, neither he nor

Lightfoot saw the source of the blast. But they looked aft and spied a torpedo bomber "with this big rising sun painted on the side" and instantly realized "he was a Jap." The shipmates watched helplessly as the torpedo slammed into the *West Virginia*.[31]

Vessels dashed below decks, warning anybody within earshot that the Japanese were attacking. The general quarters alarm sounded, sending him, Lightfoot, and the rest of the men on board scurrying to their battle stations. Vessels's was at the very top of the mainmast, a three-legged steel tower that functioned as the ship's secondary battery control station, air defense station, main battery gun director, searchlight platform, and lookout post. He was part of an antiaircraft-gun crew that manned four fifty-caliber machine guns on a dizzying platform dubbed "the birdbath." About ninety feet above the waterline, it was the loftiest spot on the ship.[32]

Vessels joined a line of sailors and marines clambering up outside ladders, a wearying trek in peacetime. Now, the slog was also terrifying. Vessels and most other *Arizona* crewmen had never been in battle. A sailor bound for the air defense station watched his shipmates reflexively duck to protect themselves "as if they could avoid being hit": "Hell . . . short of jumping off a ladder, there was no way to avoid the rounds and heavy bomb shrapnel flying at us from all directions. Guys were droppin' off the ladders like flies. And we'd just keep movin'." He added that everybody had been trained to take two or three rungs at a time. No matter, each sailor behind another one would yell out: "Come on! Get movin'!"[33]

When Vessels and the rest of the crew got to the birdbath, they discovered that all the ammunition was below in a magazine. He and the other gunners watched helplessly as high-flying Kates, bombing horizontally, joined Vals in working over Battleship Row. He knew their only chance was for somebody to go below for bullets. "Every time a bomb would hit us, it would knock us off of our feet and we'd get back up again and try to get organized to get ready to go back down," he said. "About that time, another one would hit us, and it'd knock us off our feet again."[34]

Next came the biggest shock in their young lives. "The ship blew up," Vessels said, adding: "[The concussion] tore most of our clothes off. But if we hadn't been up in the mainmast, we wouldn't have made it."

Martinez agrees: "They were lucky because the explosion went forward right over the *Tennessee* and *West Virginia* and Ford Island." From their vantage point, Vessels and his shipmates had a bird's-eye view of the Japanese pilots at their lethal work. Battleship Row was a funeral pyre. The *West Virginia,* smashed by as many as seven torpedoes and two bombs, sank upright like the *California.* The *Tennessee,* inboard of the *West Virginia,* was ablaze but not going down. Next to the upside down *Oklahoma,* the *Maryland* was hit but not in danger of sinking. The *Nevada* managed to get under way. But, pummeled by bombs and torpedoes and in danger of sinking and blocking the harbor entrance, it was run aground. Across the harbor in the protective dry dock, the *Pennsylvania's* antiaircraft gunners raised a storm of fire, and the ship was saved. "The Japanese torpedo-bombers came in barely above naval housing on the main island and would have to bank sharply to avoid hitting the *Arizona,*" Vessels said. "The rear gunners tried to machine-gun us, but they couldn't get their guns lowered enough and the bullets whizzed over our heads."[35]

After the fires subsided, Vessels and his shipmates began the long climb down from their lifesaving perch. Sailors in the foremast had no such luck; it collapsed forward into the inferno. Vessels recalled seeing a dead officer on the mainmast's searchlight deck—about halfway down the birdbath and the main deck. The searing heat from the fires had peeled back the soles of his shoes. (After the attack, only the machine guns in the birdbath, the searchlights, the quarterdeck low catapult, and the aft number 3 and 4 turrets were believed salvageable.) On the antiaircraft deck, Vessels saw just one man standing, a sailor so badly burned that he recognized him only because he was tall and because of where he was. It was Ross Worth Lightfoot, whose injuries were fatal.[36]

Vessels said he heard that the bomb that destroyed the *Arizona* went down the smokestack: "Now whether it did or not, I don't know but I do know that when we did come down . . . after it quit burning enough that we could come down, that our stack . . . was completely gone." He helped load wounded men onto a launch and climbed aboard himself for the short trip to Ford Island. He was wounded himself; a bullet from somewhere had found its mark in his right leg. He cut it out himself with his pocketknife.[37]

After the boat reached Ford Island, Vessels climbed out and started helping pull stranded sailors, many of them wounded, from the water, thick with leaking fuel oil that was blazing in patches around the stricken ships. Wearing only shoes and skivvies, he knocked on the door of a house seeking clothing. A woman answered the door and offered him one of her husband's spare uniforms. He was an officer. A grateful Vessels pulled it on anyway and spent the rest of the day returning salutes from fellow enlisted sailors. "We expected an attack by the Japanese army," Vessels said. "We were prepared to go into the hills and fight it out if we had to."[38]

Vessels was also thankful that a special purchase he had made ashore did not go down with the *Arizona*. He had bought an engagement ring and wedding band for his fiancée, who was also his childhood sweetheart. "He had them in his locker for a while, but he thought they might not be real safe there and he had mailed them home to his parents," his daughter, Margaret Vessels Shoulta of Paducah, remembered.[39]

Frances "Anita" Hodge, Vessels's bride-to-be, lived in Fancy Farm, about thirty miles southwest of Paducah. James wanted his folks, Walter and Annie Mae Vessels, to take the rings to Anita's parents, James Elvis and Lula Elizabeth Hodge, for safekeeping. "They made arrangements to come to Fancy Farm," Shoulta said. "They would all go to church together and have dinner afterwards." The get-together was set for December 7.[40]

After the midday meal, Frances tried on her engagement ring, and everybody retired to the parlor and gathered around the radio. "They were listening to music and all of a sudden it came over the radio that Pearl had been bombed," Shoulta said. "It was just devastating." News bulletins said the *Arizona* had been sunk, but neither family knew what happened to James. About two weeks later, Vessels's mother and father got welcome news in the mail—a note from James that said he was OK. He got a short leave to come home in February; wasting no time, he and Anita got married on the twenty-fifth.[41]

Vessels's fellow Kentuckian Ensign Robert Lawrence Leopold never left the *Arizona*. A Louisville native, the young officer was one of about 950 crewmen whose bodies were never recovered. On December 6, he had sent a happy sixty-ninth-birthday telegram to his father, the prominent Falls City attorney Lawrence S. Leopold. A subsequent wire—an official navy one—told Lawrence and Irma Schwabachs Leopold that their son was dead. The cable did not say where, but they knew anyway.[42]

Before he joined the navy, Leopold had been following his father's footsteps. He went to the University of Louisville, earning bachelor's and law degrees, the latter in 1940, when his dad welcomed him into the family practice. But the father-son partnership ended almost as soon as it started when Leopold enlisted in the Naval Reserve on July 10, 1940. After he trained on the USS *Wyoming*, he was named a midshipman on September 16, 1940; an ensign's commission followed on December 12. Two weeks later, he earned a prestige posting to the battleship fleet; he was heading to the *Arizona* as a communications watch officer. His battle station was the communications office, where presumably his life ended. His death got front-page coverage in the *Courier-Journal* on December 13. The story also reported the death of Ensign R. G. White, twenty-one, of Clay City, "who was killed off Guam." The paper published their photographs but provided no details of their deaths.[43]

"[Leopold] attended Male High School, where he was captain of the best drill company of the R.O.T.C.," the paper said. He was a University of Louisville campus leader, too, serving as president of the Liberal Arts Student Council and the Law School Council. He also belonged to the university's honorary College of Cardinals and earned the Student Council citizenship trophy. He was the first member of the city bar to perish in the war. Meeting on December 19 at the Jefferson County Courthouse, the bar association praised Leopold as a "loyal, faithful and generous-spirited citizen." Later, the *Courier-Journal* reported that he was the war's "first known fatality among the membership of the American Bar Association."[44]

White was also a University of Louisville alum. The January 16, 1942, *Cardinal*, the student newspaper, honored White, Leopold, Ensign Herbert Hugo Menges, and Lieutenant Lou Miller. Menges was "killed in action," though the paper did not say how or where. Miller lost his life in an accident at Texas's Duncan Army Airfield. "These are the first names on U. of L.'s roll of honor," the paper said. "Other names, it is a sobering thought, may follow, some of the best of the country's young blood, some of its finest. It is the extreme cost which our country must pay, and which those who go are prepared to pay."[45]

Joseph Dahlem lauded Leopold in a letter to the editor in the *Courier-Journal* on December 21, 1942. He described the ensign as "a very fine young Jewish boy . . . [who] had every opportunity when joining the law offices of his distinguished father [and] . . . a man loved by all who know him." Instead, young Leopold chose "to serve his country." Dahlem said that, "by stabbing us in the back" at Pearl Harbor, the Japanese proved they were "truly a Yellow Race." He apparently meant *cowardly* because he concluded his letter by urging: "Let us resolve to be true Americans and put out of our hearts and minds any trace or thought of racial hatred so that Robert will not have died in vain."[46]

Like so many other parents with a loved one reported killed or missing at Pearl Harbor, the Leopolds were anxious to know how their son died and where his body might be. They at least wanted his remains brought home for burial. A family friend, the wealthy and well-connected Louisville lawyer William Marshall Bullitt, volunteered to help.[47]

On December 20, 1941, he wrote his friend the retired army major general Frank R. McCoy in New York. FDR had appointed McCoy to the Roberts Commission, whose investigations were to include a trip to Oahu. Bullitt hoped that, when the general got to Hawaii, he might "be able to ascertain without too much trouble something about the death, and whether the body was recovered." He explained that young Leopold "had just begun to practice law with his father when . . . he felt the war was approaching; that his duty was to fight [and so he] . . . enlisted in the Navy." Ensign Leopold "bade his parents goodbye Christmas Day [1940]": "They never saw him again."[48]

Bullitt said the Leopolds knew only what the navy telegram said of their son: "They would like to know, if possible, whether his body was recovered, and if so they would like to bring it back to Louisville for burial." Otherwise: "They would be glad to know anything else they can learn concerning his end." Bullitt suspected the general would be swamped "with similar requests."[49]

McCoy, president of the Foreign Policy Association, had already left for Hawaii, his secretary replied in a December 26 letter, and could not be contacted. She said the general's wife had told her "that the Red Cross investigates similar cases." Hence, she suggested that the Leopolds contact the Jefferson County chapter. Meanwhile, Bullitt wrote to another influential friend, Washington attorney Norman H. Davis, chairman of the American Red Cross, which was headquartered in the national capital. He asked Davis to try to get the Honolulu Red Cross to provide details of Leopold's death. "His family have no idea whether his body has been recovered, is irrecoverable, or, if recovered, whether they can do anything toward bringing it back," he explained. He said he contacted McCoy: "But he got away before I knew of Leopold's death and his secretary told me that perhaps you could do something for me."[50]

On January 5, 1942, Davis wrote Bullitt promising to do all he could. But he warned: "It is extremely difficult to obtain such reports now." He also promised to notify him of any news. Four days later, the national Red Cross headquarters forwarded disappointing news to Elsie K. Mantle, the executive secretary of the Jefferson County chapter. The Navy Department had decided to bury the bodies of sailors and marines where they fell in action. "This procedure is necessary because of the difficulty of ocean transportation in war-time," explained A. W. Johnston of the national office. "These men will be buried with full military honors." He regretted "the necessity of conveying this sad news." He added: "If by any chance Ensign Leopold was captured by the Japanese, it might be possible for the International Committee to secure information about him." At the same time, the Red Cross disliked raising "the parents' hopes in this matter, but [knew] . . . how difficult it is to accept the loss of a son in circumstances such as these." He advised Mantle that, should the Leopolds wish to inquire further, she should help them fill out the necessary form. Mantle relayed the information to Bullitt and included the form.[51]

On January 28, McCoy, back in New York, wrote Bullitt, proposing that he "write a personal note to some friend of yours in the [Navy] Department" about Leopold. "You must know [Under Secretary Frank] Forrestal, and a personal letter to him would, I think, be the best approach—or to [Secretary] Frank Knox himself." Leopold's name is enshrined in the Gardens of the Missing, in the Punchbowl.[52]

The ensign's name also appeared in the Louisville media off and on for much of the war. Within days of his death, an Ensign Robert Leopold Fund was established to benefit sailors and their families. In January 1942, a local "Bundles for Bluejackets Ball" raised $3,000 in his name. In February, the city's brand new Bundles for America charity donated $3,200 in his name to the Navy Relief Society. In March, Leopold was honored at a flag-raising ceremony at Memorial Auditorium sponsored by the National Society of Colonial Dames of Kentucky. "The new flag which we have just unfurled is a pledge to Bobby Leopold, and the many others who have died, that we will preserve and defend the kind of government that they believed in and fought for," Brigadier General Stephen G. Henry, the commandant of Fort Knox's Armored Force School, told the crowd. "As for those of us at Fort Knox, this new flag is a pledge from 60,000 soldiers—soldiers who will pass by it in months to come—that Bobby Leopold shall not have died in vain."[53]

In 1943, the navy established a V-12 officer-training program at the University of Louisville and named four barracks for Leopold, White, Menges, and another Louisville grad killed in the war, Lieutenant Bethel Veech Otter, who died on Corregidor in the Philippines in 1942. After the war, the buildings were converted into offices and dormitories but were razed in 1979 to make way for a new chemistry building. Also in 1943, the *Leopold* and the *Menges,* new destroyer escorts, started hunting German submarines in the Atlantic Ocean. Leopold's sister and Menges's mother christened the two warships. Apparently, the navy did not say publicly how Menges died until late in the war or after the war. Admittedly, the truth would have been less than morale lifting on the home front. Menges was a fighter pilot on the *Enterprise.* Panicky American gunners shot him down and killed him when he tried to land on Ford Island on the night of December 7. News reports described him as killed at Pearl Harbor.[54]

After she heard the Pearl Harbor news on the radio, Margaret Ann Dawson Tilford of Louisville decided to phone FDR and marine commandant Thomas Holcomb to find out about her brother, nineteen-year-old Private James Berkley Dawson. He was part of the *Arizona's* marine contingent. Tilford, twenty-three, had no influential friends in Washington. Even so, after she got to work on Monday, she tried to call the White House and the Pentagon but failed to reach the president or the marines' top general. "I was young and naïve," she later recalled. "I don't know what I would have said. I guess I just would have asked them if my brother was alive."[55]

On December 17, a messenger delivered the feared cable to 416 West Breckinridge, the Falls City address of Ella R. Dawson, Margaret and James's mother; their folks were divorced. The wire confirmed that Dawson, a naval officer's aide, was dead. Typical of similar messages, it provided no details. A photograph of Dawson in his dress uniform and an obituary made the *Courier-Journal* on December 18 under the head-line "Gives His Life." The paper said only that he had gone to Male High School, had joined the marines in March, and had "been killed in action in the Pacific."[56]

Margaret and her husband, B. W. Tilford, moved to Paducah, where she told her Pearl Harbor story to the *Paducah Sun*. The paper published it on December 7, 1988. The couple was at her mother's house on the day of infamy. The three were enjoying a symphony program on the radio when Margaret excused herself to take a bath. Ten minutes later, B. W. told her a bulletin said the Japanese had attacked Pearl Harbor.[57]

The trio stayed close to the radio as more bulletins came "fast and furious." A paper carrier delivered a *Courier-Journal* extra that provided more information about the attack. But the news they desperately wanted was not in print.[58]

Tilford said she and her mother "went through 10 days of total agony": "I think we both knew he was dead. Then we got the telegram: 'We regret to inform you. . . .'" Tilford did not say how, but the family ultimately found out that, when the *Arizona* exploded, the blast hurled her brother into the water, where, badly burned, he died.[59]

B. W. joined the army air force in 1942 and was based in Hawaii for six months during the war. Afterward, he and Margaret visited Pearl Harbor and rode out to the *Arizona* Memorial in a small boat crowded with other visitors. "Here were all these people on vacation having a good time—cold beer, joking and laughing," she remembered. "As we pulled up alongside it, you could have heard a pin drop. It was awe-somely reverent. I get goosebumps thinking about it now."[60]

The Pearl Harbor dead were buried in different cemeteries in and around Honolulu. When plans to build the National Memorial Ceme-tery of the Pacific were announced after the war, families were given a choice: the remains of their loved ones could be transferred to the new burial ground or returned home to be reinterred. Tilford recalled: "Mom said they were going to move the body anyway, might as well move him home."[61]

Private Dawson came home in 1947 and was reburied in the Zachary Taylor National Cemetery. "You reflect on his death but it's like it never happened. You reflect especially on holidays," Tilford said.[62]

Yuletide 1941 was joyless at Louise and Stateler Maddox's Owensboro home. The couple knew Stateler's brother, Dean, and uncle, Raymond Maddox, were at Pearl Harbor. Dean, a seaman first class, was on the cruiser *Honolulu;* Raymond, a chief petty officer, was aboard the *Arizona.* Louise and Stateler had heard nothing from either of them. "Christmas was a nightmare at our house," Louise remembered. "It was a very touching, sad time. We didn't set up a Christmas tree. A lot of people didn't. You didn't feel like you wanted to do those things. You wanted to go to church. You wanted to pray."[63]

After Christmas, the family learned that Dean was alive. He had been ashore on liberty. Raymond died on the *Arizona;* his body was never found. Born in 1910, he joined the navy in 1927 after graduating from Owensboro High School. He was considered "one of the snappiest ball players in this section," the *Owensboro Messenger* reported on January 2, 1929. "He has shown the same spirit in the athletic field in the Navy."[64] Before he joined the *Arizona,* Maddox was a starter on the USS *Pennsylvania's* basketball and baseball teams. A standout at second base, he helped the *Pennsy's* nine win "the Iron Man pennant, the trophy competed for by all ships in the Navy." He is memorialized in the Gardens of the Missing.[65]

The Louisvillians Robert and Mary Watkins also desperately hoped to hear from a loved one on the *Arizona*—their twenty-two-year-old son, Fireman Second Class Lenvil Watkins. They prayed for good news but got the worst news on February 8, 1942. A navy telegram said he was dead and that his remains were "still missing after an exhaustive search." The family had moved to the Falls City from Muhlenberg County.[66]

"[Lenvil's safety] was the first think I'd think of in the morning and the last thing I'd think of at night," she said. "I'd look in the mailbox four or five times a day. I tried to tell myself he was safe. I tried to tell myself, 'He'll write. There's a war on and he just can't get time to write.'"[67]

For years, she or a friend had placed a wreath in Lenvil's honor on the World War II memorial shaft on the old Jefferson County courthouse lawn. Robert died in 1963. "I was only 16 when Lenvil was born," Mary said. "He was my oldest and it hurt. It still does, even though it's so long ago. But we have to take these things."[68]

Gunner's Mate Third Class Lambert Ray Tapp also died on the *Arizona,* though the navy assured his folks that he was alive. The Mercer Countians L. A. and Gertrude Tapp, who owned Shakertown Fruit Fram, heard nothing about their twenty-three-year-old son until December 21, when an official telegram came. The wire advised that Lambert Ray was "missing following action in the performance of his duty and in the service of his country." The message did not say when and where, but the Tapps knew he was on the *Arizona.*[69]

But a January 6 telegram provided the Tapps "a very happy new year," according to the *Harrodsburg Herald.* The navy said Lambert Ray was "now reported to be a survivor" and "will doubtless communicate with you at an early date informing you of his welfare and whereabouts." The navy "deeply regretted" any "anxiety caused by the previous message." The Tapps never heard from Lambert Ray. They got another navy telegram on January 9; a Murray Leland Tapp had survived, not their son. Lambert Ray was "now reported missing upon the latest casualty lists." The navy "fully appreciated" the family's "great anxiety" and promised: "Any report as to the fate of your son will be communicated to you promptly when received." Tapp's remains were not recovered; his name and Watkins's are enshrined in the Gardens of the Missing.[70]

The Kentuckians Frederick William Kinney and Emmett Isaac Lynch are also memorialized in the gardens. Kinney was the director of the *Arizona*'s band, twenty-one strong. He and all his musicians died with their ship; most of their bodies were never found. Officially, Pacific Fleet Band Number 22, their musical group was "the only US Navy band which was formed together, trained together, transferred together, reported aboard a ship together, fought together, and died together."[71]

The *Arizona*'s band—and other battleship bands—had been all set for morning colors. The routine never varied. At 7:55 A.M., a blue "prep" flag was hoisted atop the navy yard water tank, a signal for ships to raise their prep flags. On each ship, a crewman stood at the bow with a "jack" flag—the blue, white-starred field from the US flag—while another crewman waited at the stern with the Stars and Stripes. At 8:00 A.M., the prep flags aboard ship were replaced with the jack and the national colors; on the big ships, the band struck up the National Anthem as the crews snapped to attention and saluted.[72]

The annihilation of the *Arizona* band caught the attention of reporters looking for a fresh story angle to feed the public's seemingly insatiable appetite for Pearl Harbor news. In a statement, the navy said that "many a civilian" had asked, "What becomes of the boys in the band when the guns begin to roar?" The fate of the *Arizona*'s band provided "the most dramatic answer." They rushed below to their battle stations, performing their hazardous duties "passing ammunition to the guns above." The statement concluded: "To a man the Arizona's band was killed when the battleship's magazine exploded."[73]

The *Honolulu Advertiser* also honored the slain musicians. "Like every man in the navy, ashore or afloat, the bandsman is a fighter," the paper said. "It makes no difference whether a sailor plays the French horn, or a saxophone or kettle drums." The musicians are ready for action "when 'battle stations' is sounded." Aboard the big ship named for the forty-eighth state, "the band was there to the man, and to the man they went down." Deep below the main deck, as enemy planes attacked "and guns roared, bandsmen labored in one of the most dangerous spots": "When the ship's magazine exploded, they were wiped out. There was none to play them aloha."[74]

In a Newspaper Enterprise Association syndicated wire story, Robert Ruarf told his readers: "On sea duty a Navy musician's chores extend above and beyond the expulsion of wind from a horn. He may hold down a key job in the ship's vital communications center. He can steer a course, shoot a machine gun, bandage a wound or swab a deck—and he can do it just as well as the next guy." Ruarf also wrote that the *Arizona* band took "the fleet championship in a musical battle." Actually, the band made the final four. The championship round was set for December 20. "In honor of the lads who died when the magazine went up," the championship trophy was named for the *Arizona*.[75]

Kinney, who was married, was born in Ashland in 1910. Said to be an accomplished baritone player, he was in his high school band and orchestra. He graduated in 1926 and joined the navy, apparently aiming to make music his military career. Musician First Class Kinney and his fellow musicians joined the *Arizona* in June 1941.[76]

Also married, Musician Second Class Lynch joined the navy in Louisville in 1940, after playing in the city symphony. He was born in 1916 in Tennessee, was orphaned as a boy, and grew up in Louisville's Ormsby Village Children's Home. He majored in music and minored in economics at Georgetown College, graduating in 1939. He joined the navy in 1940; like Kinney, he was a product of the navy music school.[77]

The *Oklahoma*

Several torpedoes hit the *Oklahoma*'s port side, blasting gaping holes in the hull. The capital ship—dubbed the *Okie* by its crew—rapidly rolled on its side, capsized, and sank. More than four hundred crewmen died. Sailors and civilian navy yard workers managed to cut open the bottom of the hull and free several men trapped inside. In 1943, the navy started a massive salvage operation; amazingly, work crews managed to turn the 27,500-ton *Oklahoma* upright, patch the hull, and refloat the warship. It was placed in dry dock later in the year. Recoverable remains were removed. At the same time, plans called for it to be stripped of guns and other usable equipment and repaired enough to make it relatively water-tight. But the navy decided that the 1916-vintage *Oklahoma* was too old and too heavily damaged to return to service. So it was decommissioned in 1944 and sold for scrap in December 1946. In May 1947, it ingloriously sank under tow from Pearl Harbor to California.[78]

Hal Jake Allison, Henry Neal and Opal Allison's twenty-one-year-old son, was a fireman second class on the *Okie*. The Paducah couple knew nothing of the attack until Monday when they listened to FDR's war declaration on the radio. "My son is dead," Opal announced, rising from her chair. Her fearful premonition was correct, though the Allisons received no official word for two weeks. The dreaded navy telegram came on December 21; Hal, who joined the Navy in 1939, was missing in action.[79]

Many other families received similar messages. Devoid of details, the cables left recipients hoping for the best and fearing the worst. Families were urged not to reveal their loved one's ship or duty station to prevent possible aid to the enemy, however inadvertent and unlikely. Some civilians believed, or wanted to believe, that *missing* meant their family member might somehow be alive. "'Missing' means 'probably dead,'" Martinez said. But more than a few mothers, fathers, and wives chose to interpret it as "they haven't found him yet—they're somewhere; maybe they were captured by the Japanese." He cited a letter the mother of a missing *Arizona* crewman wrote to the navy. She said her son could not be dead because she saw a photograph of him in *Life* magazine. "It wasn't him," said Martinez, who has read many such letters. "I thought this is inconceivable; these people have no idea what happened, where Pearl Harbor is or what it is."[80]

Henry Neal and Opal had received a letter from Hal Jake that he wrote at sea on December 5. "He indicated that they would probably make port on Saturday, and that he would write them again at that time," the *Paducah Sun-Democrat* reported on December 22, 1941. "They have had no further news from him since then, until Sunday's message." The couple's worst fears were confirmed on February 12, 1942, when they got another navy telegram explaining: "AFTER EXHAUSTIVE SEARCH IT HAS BEEN FOUND IMPOSSIBLE TO LOCATE YOUR SON . . . AND HE HAS THEREFORE BEEN OFFICIALLY DECLARED TO HAVE LOST HIS LIFE IN THE SERVICE OF HIS COUNTRY AS OF DECEMBER SEVENTH NINETEEN FORTY ONE." Henry Neal immediately contacted his brother, Henry Clay Allison, in Mayfield, who quit his job at Oscar Alexander's grocery and enlisted in the navy that very day. "[Henry Clay] is now somewhere in the Pacific, aboard a U.S. ship and gunning for Japs—he has a good reason," the *Mayfield Messenger* editor Jess Anderson wrote in his column.[81]

The day the Allisons officially learned their son was dead, his shipmate Seaman First Class Frank Webb was back home celebrating life with his parents in Louisville. "They'll never get us again at Pearl Harbor," he vowed to a *Courier-Journal* reporter. Webb said that, when he heard the general quarters alarm, he was getting ready for Sunday worship services. "But church was forgotten in the ensuing four hours," the reporter explained. Webb escaped the doomed *Oklahoma*, swimming two hundred yards to a cruiser. He climbed aboard and helped crew forty-millimeter "pom-pom" antiaircraft guns. The Louisville Male High School graduate survived the "plenty noisy" attack with a burn on his back, which he dismissed as "only a skin burn."[82]

Allison is honored in the Gardens of the Missing. So is his fellow Kentuckian Ensign Lewis Bailey Pride Jr. From Madisonville, Pride also perished on the *Oklahoma,* a "victim of the treacherous Japanese raid which cost the navy ninety-one officers and 2,638 enlisted men," the *Madisonville Messenger* told its readers in a front-page story on December 16, the day Pride's parents, Louis Bailey Sr. and Nell Wade Pride, received word that he was dead. They had been confident their only child, a twenty-three-year-old Annapolis grad, was safe. Second District congressman Beverly M. Vincent, a Brownsville Democrat, had wired them the week before, assuring the Prides that their offspring's "name was not on the list of casualties then in hands of the navy department in Washington."[83]

The official telegram reporting Pride's death said the ensign would "be buried near the scene of action." The wire asked his family not to reveal the name of his ship. "Bravely, Mr. and Mrs. Pride at their home, Snowdown, received the news their only son had given his life for his country," the paper said. Friends and relatives expressed condolences in person or on the phone. The flag at Madisonville High School, Pride's alma mater, was lowered to half-mast. A memorial service convened "at chapel hour."[84]

The paper described Pride, twenty-three, as a "handsome, athletic figure, who stood six feet four inches tall," and "was one of the most popular young men in the naval academy." He was a scholar and a standout on the rowing team. He had been born in Miami, where his father, then a Florida contractor, was helping build a naval air station. The family moved to Madisonville in 1922. Pride graduated from Madisonville High School in 1935, after starring on the football team. He attended Western Kentucky Teachers College and the University of Kentucky before Vincent offered him an appointment to the naval academy in 1937. Set to graduate in June 1941, he received his diploma and commission in February, "the course of the academy having been speeded up because of the world situation," the *Messenger* explained.[85]

The paper reprinted comments from Pride's Annapolis roommates that were published in the 1941 naval academy yearbook. They described him as somebody "always willing to eat, sleep, fight . . . start a party . . . lend you money, always help with a problem, and not borrow your ties." His buddies claimed he was "right straight out of the mountains of 'Kaintucky'": "If you don't believe it, why not ask him." If Pride had replied truthfully, he would have said Madisonville is deep in flatland western Kentucky. No matter, his fellow midshipmen pronounced him "a well-rounded fellow, and 'the pride of the navy.'"[86]

Pride's death also made the *Louisville Courier-Journal,* which remembered him as "one of Madisonville High School's most distinguished sons of the sports world . . . an outstanding lineman on the football team." The paper also cited his prowess on the naval academy rowing team. He made the junior varsity crew in 1938. Then: "In 1939, Pride was held in reserve until the Poughkeepsie Regatta, where he was sent into the crew lineup at stroke oar. This was described as a stroke of strategy characteristic of Crew Coach Buck Walsh." In 1940, Pride rowed at the number 7 spot and helped coach the plebe crew. On March 1, 1941, he was sent to the Pacific Fleet, forsaking a sixty-two-foot, eight-man racing shell for a 583-foot battleship with a crew of nearly fourteen hundred officers and men.[87]

The unidentifiable remains of Pride and others killed at Pearl Harbor were ultimately buried in the Punchbowl. In 2015, advances in DNA identification led the Defense POW/MIA Accounting Agency to exhume and examine remains. DNA comparison with Pride's relatives in 2016 established a match, and, on June 18, 2016, his remains were reburied with full military honors in his family's plot in Madisonville's Oddfellows Cemetery. Rear Admiral W. Michael "Sky" Crane and Lieutenant Governor Jenean Hampton, a Bowling Green Republican, were among the dignitaries present. Back in Honolulu, a small metal rosette was fastened next to his name in the Gardens of the Missing to show that Pride's remains had been identified.[88]

Pride's parents died, one after the other, on the morning of June 6, 1947, coincidentally the third anniversary of the World War II Normandy invasion. "They never fully knew what happened to [Ensign Pride's] . . . earthly remains or if they might actually lay at rest," a *Madisonville Messenger* reporter quoted Crane. "Well, today, I think Mother and Father Pride will be happy to know we were finally able to answer that request. Today, we unite this family here on earth. Yet, back in 1947, I know that a mom, a dad, a son and Father God were united in Heaven. They are just continuing their celebration today, as we celebrate Ensign Pride's homecoming here on earth."[89]

Hampton, an air force veteran, said: "Those who serve our nation, do so at a great cost to themselves. They lose family time, key time with friends, they miss holidays, key moments in their kids' lives—and some give the ultimate sacrifice." The lieutenant governor confessed: "I am rarely without words, but to be invited to attend this celebration—this welcome home—I was truly honored."[90]

The city's Pride Elementary School, at the corner of Pride and Bailey Streets, is named for the ensign. So is the local Veterans of Foreign Wars post. In 1943, the navy launched the *Pride,* a destroyer escort, which helped guard convoys and battle German U-boats in the Atlantic.[91]

It is evidently not known whether Ensign Pride knew Allison or Fireman First Class Samuel Crowder, thirty-five, another Kentuckian whose name was also chiseled in stone in the Gardens of the Missing. DNA identification brought Crowder's remains home, too. In December 2017, he was reburied next to his mother, Charlotte Sullivan Cannon, in Louisville's Resthaven Memorial Park. Papers coast-to-coast ran the story. As of October 2019, at least six other *Oklahoma* sailors from Kentucky had been identified via DNA matching for individual burial: Seaman First Class Millard Burk Jr., nineteen, Shelby Gap; Chief Pharmacist's Mate James T. Cheshire, forty, New Hope; Seaman Second Class Hubert P. Hall, twenty, Floyd County; Fireman First Class Billy J. Johnson, twenty-two, Caney; Fireman Third Class Willard Lawson, twenty-five, Milton; and Machinist's Mate First Class Ulis C. Steely, twenty-five, Corbin. Rosettes have been or will be placed next to all their names in the Gardens of the Missing.[92]

Fireman Second Class Martin Daymond Young of Lewisport is also named in the gardens. His twin sister, Daisy Young Hawkins of Lewisport, grieved for him until her death in 2002 at age eighty-five. "I still miss him," said Hawkins in a newspaper interview published two days before the fiftieth anniversary of the Pearl Harbor attack. "I think about what could have happened—the family he could have had."[93]

About December 17, 1941, Millie and Harvey Young of Cloverport got the telegram that their son, Daymond, was missing in action: "It was a very sad Christmas," according to his twin sister. "The family gathered at mother's house Christmas day. Everybody was unhappy; some were mad. The gifts were under the tree, but we didn't feel like giving them out. The attack took all the spirit out of Christmas." Even so, the family kept hoping that he might have survived "and they would find him": "It wasn't clear for another year that he was dead."[94]

Russell Arnold Combs, twenty-five, spent six years on the *Oklahoma*. But the Louisvillian was out of the navy and back home on Pearl Harbor Day. His kid brother, Coxswain Clarence A. Combs Jr., twenty-two, was still aboard. "I'm going to re-enlist pretty soon," Russell told the *Courier-Journal*. The ex-sailor wished "he had been there for the action."[95]

Georgia Combs wished both her sailor sons were with her. "I'm worried. My head aches," she admitted, asking one of her boys to get her two aspirin. "This is war to me whether there's a declaration or not. They're shooting at my son." The enemy also fired on Machinist's Mate First Class Harry J. Webb, who had lived with the Combs family before he, too, left for the navy and ended up aboard the *Oklahoma*. The *Courier-Journal* story named two other local tars on the battleship: Bugler Second Class Al Shanks and Baker First Class Jerry Windell.[96]

Combs got a letter from Clarence Jr. the week before Pearl Harbor. She said he talked about signing up for another hitch and said nothing about impending war. Combs quit DuPont Manual Training High School in 1938 to join the navy. The youngest Combs son, Charles, eighteen, vowed to volunteer for the navy if his big brother went back in service. Meanwhile, Russell attempted to be upbeat. "Chances of one particular man being hurt are pretty slim," he said. Meanwhile, Clarence Sr., a brakeman on a Monon Railroad passenger train was away and not due home for a week. The whole Combs family ultimately got good news: Combs survived—so did Shanks, Webb, and Windell.[97]

4

Elsewhere on Battleship Row

Other Kentuckians found themselves in harm's way on Battleship Row. While the *Arizona* and the *Oklahoma* suffered the most casualties and sustained the heaviest damage, the other capital ships were hit, some harder than others. The *West Virginia* nearly shared the *Oklahoma*'s fate. The *California* sank. The *Nevada* tried to escape, but, bombed and torpedoed, the battlewagon was run aground to avoid sinking and possibly blocking the channel.

The *West Virginia*

As many as seven torpedoes exploded against the port side of the *West Virginia*, blasting open its midship and forward hull sections and smashing its rudder. As water rushed in, the dreadnought started listing dangerously. Counterflooding saved the ship from the *Oklahoma*'s fate, and the *West Virginia* hit bottom on a relatively even keel. More than a hundred crewmen were lost, including her skipper, Captain Mervyn S. Bennion, who died on the bridge. His heroism merited a posthumous Medal of Honor and a Purple Heart. Also heavily damaged by fire and bombs, the *West Virginia*, nicknamed the *Wee Vee,* was raised and extensively repaired and modernized. But the capital ship was unable to return to active service until mid-1944.[1]

Seaman Second Class John W. Hamlet of Hartford, the Ohio County seat, could not bear to watch as fire crept toward his captain's lifeless body. He said "everyone on the ship loved" Bennion "like a father": "He wouldn't allow any profanity and the officers had to be good to us. Those were his orders."[2]

A splinter from an armor-piercing bomb that hit the *Tennessee* mortally wounded Bennion at his battle station on the bridge. His life ebbing away, the skipper wanted to know how the battle was going and how his ship and men were faring. When it was obvious the *West Virginia* was sinking, he gave the abandon ship order. When flames threatened to engulf the bridge, he ordered the crewmen near him to leave and save themselves.[3]

It seemed that Hamlet was also eligible for a posthumous Purple Heart. On December 16, 1941, the navy cabled his folks that he was dead. They got an unexpected but welcome telegram on Christmas Day; the navy was sorry it had erred and promised that their son was alive. Both wires spared details; Hamlet filled everybody in when he got home on leave nearly eleven months later. His return made news in the *Owensboro Messenger*, which also had listed him as killed. The follow-up story got his name wrong; the reporter identified him as "James Hamlet."[4]

When interviewed later by a reporter for the *Owensboro Messenger*, Hamlet remembered: "I was below deck reading the comic section of a Honolulu newspaper when a heavy detonation rocked my ship and nearly floored me." When the first aerial torpedo struck the battleship, "none of us thought of the Japs or war," he said. "We thought a magazine had exploded somewhere. And even when the command ordering us to battle stations thundered over the ship's communications system, it still didn't occur to me that we had been attacked. Everything had been so peaceful and quiet there we just didn't think of war."[5]

The general quarters alarm sounded seconds after the first torpedo slammed into the ship at about five minutes to eight. "The minute I got on deck," Hamlet said, "I saw what was happening. Torpedo after torpedo was falling around us. The sky was full of planes. There was an inferno of smoke and fire." He ran for his battle station on the bridge. The Kentuckian found the "gray-haired, kindly" fifty-four-year-old Bennion fighting for his life but still in command: "A piece of shrapnel hit him as he was issuing his commands. Blood gushed from his side but he kept on until finally he collapsed and sank to the floor. He ordered some of us to prop him against the wall."[6]

He recalled Bennion repeatedly urging: "Are we getting any [planes]? Just get me some planes. Don't bother about me. Shoot down those planes." Ultimately, it dawned on Bennion that the *West Virginia* was doomed: "The captain ordered us to abandon ship. He told us to leave the bridge and wouldn't let us carry him down. 'Get the wounded off" was one of the last orders I heard him utter, his voice having grown very weak."[7]

Hamlet remembered watching helplessly as flames crawled slowly toward the bridge: "We were horrified. . . . We turned our heads. We couldn't watch any longer." After the first attack wave was over, he joined a fruitless search for Bennion's remains. Survivors watched the second wave from Ford Island, unable to fight back, but cheering "every time one of the enemy planes was hit": "It was something like a football game."[8]

Lieutenant Commander Thomas T. Beattie's report fleshes out Hamlet's account of Bennion's death. From Louisville, Beattie was with the captain when he fell mortally wounded. The *Wee Vee*'s gunnery officer, Beattie was breakfasting in the wardroom when he heard the alarm over a loudspeaker. He rushed for the bridge with Bennion "just ahead" of him "proceeding in the same direction."[9]

Beattie and Bennion took up their battle stations in the armor-plated conning tower as dive-bombers started pounding the ship, scoring several hits. Bomb blasts knocked out telephone communication with the rest of the ship, so Beattie suggested they go to the bridge and dispatch messengers on foot. They reached the bridge as bombs continued to rain down on Battleship Row. Beatty was unscathed, but Bennion "doubled up with a groan" and slumped to the deck "very seriously wounded," likely "by a large piece of shrapnel." Beattie loosened the captain's collar and sent a sailor to bring back a pharmacist's mate.[10]

"[The *Arizona* suddenly] blew up with a tremendous explosion and large sheets of flame shot skyward," Beattie recalled. He suspected a magazine was hit and was worried a *Wee Vee* magazine might similarly let go. The *Wee Vee* was listing from torpedo strikes; there was also the danger it might capsize like the *Oklahoma*. Neither of these catastrophes happened; the *Wee Vee* settled to the harbor bottom relatively upright.[11]

Beattie did all he could to save Bennion, who refused to leave his post. He sent Lieutenant Commander D. C. Johnson to the bridge, hoping he could coax him down. Johnson brought help—African American mess attendant Doris Miller, "a very powerfully built individual." Somebody had put the captain on a cot, which Johnson and Miller turned into a litter. They managed to muscle the captain to a ladder. But, when "the cot sagged and almost broke," they returned him to the bridge. Bennion, in great pain, "requested to be left where he was."[12]

Miller spied an unmanned machine gun, got behind it, and started blazing away at the enemy planes. His bravery earned him a Navy Cross, second only to the Medal of Honor. Mess Attendant Second Class Clark Simmons of the USS *Utah*, who was also African American, said out loud what many thought at the time: "This was a courageous young man, and it was always believed that he should've gotten the Congressional Medal of Honor. And the only reason why he didn't get the Congressional Medal of Honor was because he was black."[13]

Beattie spent the rest of the raid in charge of getting wounded men off the ship. They were loaded onto launches and taken to Ford Island, the hospital ship *Solace*, and the Pearl Harbor Naval Hospital. All the while, bombers and strafing planes kept pounding the *Wee Vee*.[14]

Simultaneously, another deadly peril arose: fuel oil burning on the water and drifting over from the *Arizona*. The crew was powerless to battle the wind-borne blaze. "We had no water on board as the fire mains and machinery were out of commission and we were unable to do any fire fighting at all," Beattie said. He wanted a closer look at the threat. So he climbed into a motor boat and ordered the coxswain to head sternward, toward the fire. "The smoke was so heavy I could not see aft of the bridge," he remembered. "As I got into the boat a sheet of flame swept on top of us and we barely managed to get free of the fire." Finally, the boat made it aft, where "the burning oil . . . swept past the ship." When Beattie got back aboard the *Wee Vee*, he "realized then that the ship was lost."[15]

Seaman Second Class Lee Philip Ebner, who survived on the signal bridge, had a standard reply for anybody who asked him about Pearl Harbor: "You can't believe it going from peacetime to wartime in two seconds." The Louisville sailor would sometimes add: "And I could see at least three years ahead of me, at least, being at war. Yeah, I knew that much."[16]

Ebner, twenty-two, said he was safer on the bridge than sailors were elsewhere on the battlewagon. Most of the 106 crewman who were killed were inside the ship and probably never saw the enemy. Nonetheless, Bennion's death was proof, as if it were needed, that the bridge was anything but a haven.[17]

Ebner was in the signal gang, whose main job was to watch for signals from other ships in the harbor. Shortly before 8:00 A.M., he saw low-flying aircraft headed toward Battleship Row. "Some of the first planes came straight across," he recalled, "and they were, I didn't realize at the time, they were dropping torpedoes." He got a good look at one: "It came right over us, and . . . when I saw that red circle I knew it was [a] Japanese plane. And you could see the pilots; they . . . had the leather helmets, the goggles." He said the *Wee Vee* crew had never had an air-raid drill in the harbor, only at sea.[18]

After the crew was ordered to abandon ship, Ebner and some of his shipmates helped get oil-soaked crewmen into boats that came alongside the *West Virginia*. The boats also transported Ebner and other crewmen—some had to be pulled from the water—to the Pearl Harbor submarine base. "I lost everything I had below decks," Ebner said. "I just came out with the clothes that I had [on]." After mustering with the *Wee Vee* survivors, he volunteered to join the signal gang aboard the USS *Mahan*, a destroyer that earned a quintet of battle stars in the Pacific theater.[19]

Pearl Harbor was the first and last battle that eighteen-year-old Seaman First Class Arnold Jacob Owsley of the *West Virginia* saw. A shortage of cash evidently cost him his life. "He was up for furlough [on December 1] and hoped to return here for a short time," the *Kentucky Post* reported on December 17. "But lack of funds forced him to stay in the islands." The Covington sailor is buried in the Punchbowl.[20]

Owsley had been put in a Cincinnati orphanage by his father after his parents' divorce. He ended up in foster care before returning to his father and ultimately joining the navy. "The last letter his family received from him was in October," according to the *Kentucky Post*.[21]

The attack canceled thirty-four-year-old Boatswain's Mate Second Class J. W. Mourray's holiday homecoming. Back in Covington, his mother, Louise Breitenstein, "said she received a letter from her son dated last Thanksgiving Day saying he expected to be home December 12," the *Post* reported. Mourray "was looking forward to seeing his four-year-old daughter, Jerry," for the first time in two years.[22]

The navy lost no time in telegraphing Able Seaman Isador Owen's family in Bellevue, near Covington, that he did not die on the *Wee Vee* after all. Even so, the former star footballer probably did not expect the good news to rate a front-page banner headline in the *Post*: "Owen, Reported Killed, Is Safe." A subhead on a later article explained: "Navy Message Says Mistake Made in Wire."[23]

The erroneous wire came on December 17, reporting that "Izzy" Owen had been killed in action. Thus his name, according to the paper, "was written . . . among the heroes of northern Kentucky who have given their lives for their country." That name had to be erased three days later. "Boy, what a swell Christmas present!" one of his big brothers exclaimed when the cable correcting the mistake arrived.[24]

Owen cut short a promising grid career when he quit high school midway through his junior year and joined the navy in January 1941. Seventeen when he was sworn in, he had played fullback on the Bellevue team that won the Northern Kentucky Conference championship in 1940. After the navy declared him dead, his teammates and the school's cheerleaders saluted him in a special assembly program. The principal, George Wright, and the coach, Edgar McNabb, praised him in brief remarks. And according to the *Post*: "A minute of complete silence was followed by the blowing of 'taps.'" The second message from the navy promised that Owen "[had] been located" and was safe. The telegram also said to expect a letter from him.[25]

The Louisville native Molder First Class George O'Hara Branham of the *Wee Vee* was the second member of his family to perish in battle on a US battleship. "A tragic sidelight to his death lay in the fact that he died on a ship in the same fleet as the U.S.S. Oklahoma, the battleship on which his father, G. C. Branham of Louisville, a warrant officer, was killed in the First World War," said the December 18 *Ashland Daily Independent*. George, twenty-four, had visited Ashland many times and had several friends in the city. His sailor cousin William Branham of Ashland was fatally injured when he fell from a roller coaster at the San Francisco Exposition in 1940. Petty Officer Branham was the father of a two-month-old baby girl.[26]

The navy left Argie Cobb of Cleaton no room for hope, telegraphing him that his son, Seaman First Class Tyrus Pershing Cobb, was "lost in action at Pearl Harbor." His reported death made for front-page news in the December 17 *Owensboro Messenger*. The paper ran a photograph of the twenty-two-year-old sailor in his dress blues and "Donald Duck" hat. The name of a man's ship was spelled out in gold letters on the front of the flat hat, but, because it was wartime, it was blacked out in the *Messenger* photograph. Three days after the navy told the Muhlenberg Countian that he lost his son, another wire arrived declaring: "[Ty] has been found, and is safe." The *West Virginia* sailor "sustained no injuries and is now on duty."[27]

It is evidently unknown where or how Fireman First Class Milton Knight Jr. of Paducah lost his life on the *West Virginia*. But William Knight never forgot the last time he saw his big brother. It was in 1938. "I had gone to caddy [at the Paducah country club] that day," he remembered. Their father, Milton Sr., was driving the sailor to the railroad station. "They came by and he told me goodbye."[28]

The Knights were farmers, and Milton Jr. "didn't like the farm," William recalled. "There was not much back then for a young man—there wasn't no future. We were still recovering from the depression. It was just a matter of personal choice for him and he wanted to go into the Navy. He just happened to be like all the rest of them who were just caught up in the middle of it." Because the sailor-to-be was seventeen, his father had to sign his enlistment papers.[29]

The Knights did not stray far from the family radio on Pearl Harbor Day. News was spotty. "There was some optimism because we just didn't know the amount of devastation and the particulars," Knight said. "[The government was not] releasing all the information on it. You just had to wait and see . . . knowing that [Milton] was stationed there. We were just wondering and waiting."[30]

The wait ended with the telegram that they hoped and prayed would not come. "We were very brokenhearted," said the sailor's sister, Virginia Knight Davis. "It was a terrible Christmas. We had a choice whether we could bring him back or bury him there. But we decided because it had been so very hard on our mother that we didn't want her to have to go through any more." Knight was buried in the Punchbowl.[31]

The *Tennessee*

Two bombs hit the *Tennessee*—also known as the *Big Ten*, the *Rebel*, and the *Ridge Runner*—knocking out its second and third fourteen-inch gun turrets. In addition, burning debris from the *Arizona* set the dreadnought ablaze in several places. But it stayed afloat. After initial repairs at Pearl Harbor Navy Yard, the battleship steamed to the West Coast for more work later in December and was back in active service in May 1942. Five *Tennessee* crewman perished in the attack.[32]

Seaman Second Class Tom Higdon might have planned to hit the sack early on the night of December 7, 1941. After all, he was slated to play center field against a rival baseball nine from the *Tennessee*. The game, set for 8:30 A.M., December 8, was called on account of war.[33]

An eighteen-year-old Kentuckian from Owensboro, Higdon was "taking it easy" topside on the teakwood-planked main deck when he "saw the planes coming across the bay": "Nobody expected anything that morning."[34] He joined a scramble for battle stations when the general quarters alarm sounded, punctuated with a verbal: "This is no drill." He paused only to close a hatch. He remembered: "A streak of bullets hit behind me on the wooden deck and didn't miss me by more than a foot."[35]

About five minutes into the attack, the battlewagon raised a storm of antiaircraft fire from its three- and five-inch batteries and fifty-caliber machine guns. The captain received orders to sortie the harbor and was ready to go by 9:30, but the order was canceled for battleships. Escape for Higdon's ship would have been almost impossible anyway. It was hemmed in by the torpedoed and sinking *West Virginia* on the port side and Ford Island to starboard. Astern, flaming fuel oil was drifting over from the *Arizona*. "We were like a bunch of sitting ducks," Higdon said.[36]

The *California*

Early in the attack, two torpedoes slammed into the *California*. A subsequent bomb hit and a near miss led to more flooding. Nonetheless, the battlewagon dubbed the *Prune Barge* had steam up and was set to get under way when a large sheet of burning oil drifted down Battleship Row and threatened to engulf it. The abandon ship order was passed but later canceled. When the crew returned, it was impossible to staunch the flooding, and the *California* slowly settled in the water. It touched bottom on December 10 with its main deck and superstructure above water. Salvage crews raised it in March 1942, and extensive repair and modernization work continued until January 1944, when the *California* returned to active service. Almost one hundred of its crew were killed in the Pearl Harbor attack.[37]

At age seventy-seven, Jim Hamlin was philosophical about the navy listing him among the ninety-eight *California* dead. He remembered an old navy saying: "10 percent do not get the message.'" His dad, Green Hamlin of Lisle, got the wrong message in a telegram dated December 16: "THE NAVY DEPARTMENT DEEPLY REGRETS TO INFORM YOU THAT YOUR SON JAMES THOMAS HAMLIN FIREMAN FIRST CLASS U.S. NAVY WAS LOST IN ACTION IN THE PERFORMANCE OF HIS DUTY AND IN THE SERVICE OF HIS COUNTRY XX THE DEPARTMENT EXTENDS TO YOU ITS SINCEREST SYMPATHY IN YOUR GREAT LOSS X." The wire asked Hamlin not to tell anybody where his son died "TO PREVENT POSSIBLE AID TO OUR ENEMIES." The telegram also advised Hamlin that, if the navy found Jim's body, it would "BE INTERRED TEMPORARILY IN THE LOCALITY WHERE DEATH OCCURRED" and that the family would "BE NOTIFIED ACCORDINGLY." On New Year's Eve, Green received another telegram saying that his son was "NOW REPORTED TO BE A SURVIVOR." The message said the navy deeply regretted "THE ANXIETY CAUSED YOU B[Y] THE PREVIOUS MESSAGE." Meanwhile, Petty Officer Hamlin had been remembered in services at Harlan Baptist Church, where he was a member. A *Harlan Daily Enterprise* story quoted the telegram in reporting his death.[38]

Hamlin was a sports editor from 1938 until he joined the navy and was one of Harlan's best-known young men. A 1936 graduate of Harlan High School, he was on the football team and was a lover of all sports. "Of course, Jimmy was no better than anybody else's boy who has died at his post fighting for his country," the paper quoted the sailor's coal miner father. "I have another son, Green Edward, and I want him to take up where Jimmy left off, and I'd go if they would take me." He said Green Edward had already volunteered for military service.[39]

Jimmy and Green Edward's dad lost no time letting the *Enterprise* editor, Kyle Whitehead, know that Jimmy was alive. He cited the December 31 telegram and added that, shortly before the wire arrived, he had "received a post card from Jimmy, dated at Pearl Harbor on December 8, the day after the sneak attack of the Japs": "It merely said 'I am well. A letter will follow.'"[40]

December 7 had looked promising for Hamlin; he had liberty. Dawn broke clear and warm. Reveille blared through the battlewagon's loudspeakers at 6:00 A.M. Hamlin rolled out of his bunk in B Division, three decks below the *California's* big smokestack; he was looking forward to swimming and sunbathing with his buddies at Waikiki Beach. He had spent Saturday at the storied seaside spot. But he had also taken time out to order a Christmas present for his steady girl back in Lone Oak, a Paducah suburb. The friendly clerk at the Montgomery Ward store promised him that the gift, a $9.95 radio, would be shipped promptly from Chicago to Almyra Craig, whom he met in Lone Oak in 1937, the year of the great Ohio River flood.[41]

After donning his tropical uniform—white T-shirt, shorts, and socks and black shoes—he headed for breakfast. A half hour later, he ambled topside to the main deck expecting to shell out a dime for a copy of the *Honolulu Advertiser.* "Sweatshirt" Clark, the *California's* unofficial in-port paperboy, had managed to get some copies before the paper's presses broke down. Only two thousand copies were run off; the fleet got most of them.[42]

Paper in hand, Hamlin sat down to read in the shade under a big canvas awning that had been stretched for church services. The breeze made it hard to turn the pages, so he retreated below to the Emergency Boiler Control Room. The steel-walled compartment offered neither sunshine nor pleasant harbor view, but at least he could peruse his paper. Deep inside the ship, he neither saw nor heard the first Japanese planes that appeared over Pearl Harbor. The general quarters alarm sent the crew racing for their battle stations. "I thought it was a heck of a time to have an air-raid drill," he remembered. "But it didn't take me long to realize it wasn't a drill."[43]

The torpedo and bomb strikes filled the inside of the ship with dust jarred loose from a maze of overhead cables, wires, and pipes. The sailors feared it was poison gas. Hamlin recalled: "Six men and I were ordered forward to the gas mask locker." A chief petty officer met the party and ordered Hamlin back to Number Three Fire Room to help get the ship under way; steam was up, and escape seemed possible. Soon after the rest of the men continued forward, Hamlin heard an explosion from a bomb or a torpedo in the direction they went: "I don't know whether or not those men were killed, but I never saw them again."[44]

Water was gushing in through holes the torpedoes blasted out. The ship was ablaze and threatened with burning oil on the water, oozing over from other stricken battlewagons. It was obvious that the *Prune Barge* was not going anywhere except maybe to the bottom of Pearl Harbor. Anyway, Hamlin said he heard the abandon ship order when "somebody shouted it down a passageway." (A temporary order was issued at 10:02 and canceled at 10:15, "flames from the water having cleared the ship.")[45]

Hamlin started forward toward the log room but found his path blocked by fire and twisted, broken steel. He turned around and headed aft, through officers' country, to the fantail, where the Stars and Stripes were to have been ceremoniously hoisted at 8:00 A.M. The ship's band had been warming up for "The Star-Spangled Banner." Hamlin spotted musical instruments littering the *California*'s teakwood main deck. He said a band member told him they had struck up the National Anthem just when the attack started: "He said they never played faster in their lives and they finished."[46]

Outside the officers' quarters, he saw a sailor slumped against a bulkhead. He knew the man as one of the clerks in the ship's "geedunk stand," where sailors could buy cigarettes, ice cream, candy, and notions. He recalled: "We took the fellow inside and laid him on a couch in the ward room. But we later found out he was dead." When he reached the quarterdeck, Hamlin spotted what he thought was "the biggest submarine [he'd] ever seen." It was the overturned *Oklahoma*'s 583-foot steel hull.[47]

Hamlin leapt off the *California*. After he bobbed to the surface, he saw a lifeboat loaded with men, some wounded, and swam for it. He grabbed a handy rope draped along the boat's gunnel and held on for the short trip to Ford Island. Suddenly, a Japanese plane strafed the helpless sailors. With machine-gun bullets splashing in the oily water, Hamlin let go and started swimming again: "That boat was just too slow for me." He soon reached the island and hightailed it for an airplane hangar that was crowded with refugee sailors, soldiers, airmen, and marines. "It seemed to dawn on everybody at the same time that this was a fine target," Hamlin said. So everybody scattered to find shelter elsewhere.[48]

Hamlin found a handy ditch, where he rode out the second wave of attacking planes. After the enemy had gone, he went back to the *California* to help fight fires and keep the battlewagon afloat. The *Prune*

Barge sank but upright with its main deck above water. Hamlin worked past nightfall, helping carry usable equipment off the ship. He narrowly evaded death again when, bone tired, he slipped and fell off a gangway into the dark water. He was unhurt, but an officer ordered him to find someplace to get some sleep: "He told me that wherever I went, to go whistling or singing because they were shooting at anything that moved." It was widely feared that an invasion would follow the air raid. "I don't remember what I sang, but I remember I said, 'Please don't shoot' at the end of every verse." Hamlin caught forty winks in the balcony of a Ford Island movie theater.[49]

Hamlin's swim through fuel oil had ruined his snow-white uniform. On Ford Island, he pieced together a new one, helping himself from a pile of clothes scrounged from all over. It was hardly regulation: chambray shirt, khaki trousers, a marine shoe on one foot, a navy one on the other.[50]

Good news followed bad for Green Hamlin. But initially at least news traveled in the opposite direction for Florence Davidson, a widow who had moved with her four boys to Indianapolis from Kentucky in 1937. On December 16, she got a postcard from her sailor son, Lewis Reno Nunnelley, assuring her he was safe at Pearl Harbor. The next day, she got a navy telegram saying he was dead. "Thus Nunnelley, a fireman, third class, became the fifth Indianapolis youth to give his life in defense of his country in the battle in the Pacific," the *Indianapolis News* reported. A subsequent wire reduced the total to four. Nunnelley was alive.[51]

It is evidently not known whether the Lexington-born Nunnelley knew Hamlin, a shipmate. But Nunnelley was among fifteen officers and men cited for conducting "themselves in a distinguished manner in effecting the rescue of personnel trapped below decks in the [*California's*] Center Thrust Block Room, Forward Battery locker and Forward Distribution Room."[52]

By the time Nunnelley made it home on leave a year after Pearl Harbor, he was a veteran of seven more naval battles in the Pacific. The nineteen-year-old navy man "could show 'not one scratch,' to attest to the danger he went through," an *Indianapolis Star* reporter wrote. However: "He can show a citation . . . awarded for bravery during one of the battles in which his ship participated. The award was made after Nunnelley was credited with rescuing several men trapped below deck of a damaged ship." The reporter did not name the vessel, but it was obviously the *California*.[53]

The story also said that three of the ships Nunnelley was on were damaged. He left the sunken *California* for the heavy cruiser *Portland*, which was torpedoed in the Guadalcanal naval campaign of November 1942. His visit "provided the first opportunity he has had to see his mother since March, 1941," the story said.[54]

Eddie Klusmeier's mother required the care of two doctors after she read the navy telegram that said he was dead. The wire arrived nine days before Christmas. It did not say how or where Eddie died, but Doris Mossbarger Klusmeier knew her son was a sailor on the *California*. The family tragedy worsened when Doris phoned Eddie's Cincinnati uncle, Richard Coleman. He was only thirty-four, but Coleman died of a heart attack twenty-four hours after he got the terrible news. When he heard his nephew was dead, Coleman had rushed to join the navy, but he was rejected, perhaps because of heart trouble.[55]

Three Louisville Catholic churches had masses in honor of the gunner's mate second class. But, on December 29, a mail carrier delivered the best-ever belated Christmas present to the Klusmeier home. It was a letter from Eddie, dated Christmas Day, and postmarked December 26 from Honolulu. "The cheery thank-you note . . . came as a bombshell," wrote a *Courier-Journal* reporter, who quoted from the missive: "Dear Mom and Dad—I received your money order and was pleased. 'Thanks' and when you write to me, write on one side of the paper because the mail is 'censored' and don't write about anything but about home, like how are you and about how you folks are doing." The young sailor assured the home folks that he was "in good health and doing fine." He asked about Gene, his nineteen-year-old brother, adding: "Has Kenney [apparently another brother] written home lately? I hope you all had a merry Christmas and I wish you a happy New Year and lots of luck." He signed the letter, navy-style, "Love—Klusmeier, E. A."[56]

The story said: "The Klusmeiers presented a heart-rending family scene last night as they sought frantically but knowingly without hope to find a happy answer to the questions that the circumstances of the past thirteen days had posed." Eddie's mother called the letter her "third great shock in two weeks." She was weeping over her son when it arrived. "Now you won't cry any more, will you mother?" shouted Matthew,

Eddie's seven-year-old sibling. Since the family had gotten word from Eddie, "neighbors said the grief-stricken mother has been torn between moments of joy and bursts of sadness brought on by the question before her of 'Is my son really alive!'" Doris Klusmeier lost fifty pounds from illness and mourning. Eddie had gone to du Pont Manual High School and had joined the navy on March 12, 1939. He went through boot camp at the Great Lakes Naval Training Base near Chicago and last visited home on May 22, 1939.[57]

Eddie thought he would get stateside leave in June 1942. "I'm coming home," he promised in a telegram to his family asking for $75.00 traveling money. "The Klusmeiers met all the trains for two days, but Eddie didn't show up," said another *Courier-Journal* story. "Eventually another telegram arrived explaining that the expected furlough hadn't come through after all." He finally got home on February 7, 1943. "But Mrs. Klusmeier kept quiet about it, because, she said, 'seeing is believing.'"[58]

Klusmeier had no idea why the navy reported him dead. But he said he was aboard the *California* during the attack and "couldn't believe [his] ears" when he heard the dull explosion from the first torpedo that hit the ship. He was hanging out his washing to dry but rushed to his battle station and "did a little firing" until the abandon ship order came. He and some other crewmen swam the short distance from the stricken ship to Ford Island but "were ordered to return within a few minutes," the *Courier-Journal* story explained. "The crew again returned to shore and spent most of the day fighting roaring fires."[59]

Klusmeier swore his nonappearance in the summer of 1942 was a bigger disappointment to him than to his loved ones. "But the $75 came in handy," the bluejacket confessed. At the same time, he wondered whether his Kentucky colonelcy was valid. Governor Keen Johnson, a Democrat, had sent a posthumous commission to Eddie's family soon after he was reported killed. "Am I a Kentucky colonel even though I'm alive?" he wanted to know.[60]

The *Maryland*

Two bombs exploded on the *Maryland,* causing relatively minor damage and some forward flooding. Four crewmen lost their lives. Later in

December, the *Old Mary* steamed to the West Coast for additional repairs, and the battleship was back in active service in February 1942.[61]

The *Maryland* mail clerk Jack Roberts of Hart County was topside when the attack began. Racing to his battle station, he thought he saw one of the first Kates that torpedoed the *Oklahoma*. "He was no more than, at the outside, twenty foot up," said the then eighteen-year-old. Roberts added that, if he had had a rock, he could have hit the pilot "right in the mouth with it."[62]

Roberts forsook his family farm for the navy in April 1940. He was in the super-dreadnought's post office when he heard the general quarters alert, which he said was punctuated with "this is no joke, or words to that effect." His battle station was below, helping send powder and shells topside to the eight big guns, mounted two abreast in four massive sixteen-inch-gun turrets, two fore and two aft.[63]

Obviously, the big guns were useless against airplanes, so Roberts and the gun crews were released for other duties: "We went out and did odd things. . . . The *Oklahoma* had been hit and was capsizing. The first thing I did . . . I took a fire axe, as directed by someone, and cut the mooring line to keep it from parting and flying and probably wiping out a number of people." After the attack, he and other crewmen were issued rifles and ordered to patrol the ship and Ford Island, no one knowing "whether the Japs was going to make a landing or not."[64]

That night, Roberts joined a tugboat crew working feverishly to save the *West Virginia* from the *Arizona*'s fate. His job was "to hold a hose to shoot water into [the ship] . . . to keep the magazines from exploding." He confessed he was afraid of "what might happen next": "I spent most of the night holding that hose pumping water into [the *West Virginia*]." He agreed that the situation was somewhere between order and chaos: "It's possible some people knew what they were doing but others didn't—doing what you were told, and I guess hoping it was for the best."[65]

On December 8, Roberts was put aboard a motor launch that plied the harbor pulling sailors and marines—alive and dead—out of the oily water. The launch also transported stranded crewmen where they needed to go. Roberts said sailors from ships that were sunk or heavily damaged were without quarters: "All the *Oklahoma* people had to be taken somewhere else." He noted that it was difficult to describe the carnage, thick blackish-gray smoke rising from bomb- and torpedo-blasted ships that were still ablaze: "You were just doing what [you were] directed to do. . . . [As] a young sailor at that time that's what you'd expect to do. . . . It was no fun and games."[66]

Quartermaster Third Class Stan Van Hoose was asleep on a cot in the *Maryland*'s wheelhouse when "boom, boom, boom" woke him up. He peered out a window and "saw planes flying all around": "And then . . . one plane crashed into the Ford Island buildings." He figured the pilot had blacked out in a practice dive. "Then one plane came across from the liberty area in the navy yard, and he dropped something in the water, and I saw it was a torpedo," said the Paintsville son of a coal miner who farmed on the side. When Van Hoose spotted the red rising-sun insignia, he knew the "damn Japs" were there. He survived the Pearl Harbor attack, spent thirty-two months in the Pacific combat area, and fought in seven more sea battles. He figured all that evened the score with the enemy "for waking [him] up at Pearl Harbor."[67]

Meanwhile, Van Hoose headed for his battle station, where he donned earphones so he could hear the navigator: "I got to watch what was going on, the whole deal. . . . I saw the *Oklahoma* turn over alongside of us. . . . She was tied up to our port side; she saved us from getting torpedoed." Between the first and the second attack waves, he said he saw the *Nevada* start its unsuccessful sortie: "As she passed us, they started giving her torpedoes and bombs." Van Hoose, who joined the navy in 1940, stood by in the *Maryland*'s wheelhouse in case orders came to follow the *Nevada* out of the harbor. He was to take over for the quartermaster should he be killed or wounded. It was apparent that the *Maryland*, sandwiched between the capsized *Oklahoma* and Ford Island, could make no escape attempt. The next morning, Van Hoose, who had wanted to be a sailor since he was a boy in the Appalachian Mountains of landlocked Kentucky, raised the Stars and Stripes over the *Maryland*. The big ship had sustained some damage from bombs and strafing; three men were dead and thirteen wounded.[68]

The *Nevada*

Toward the end of the torpedo plane attack, a single steel fish exploded against the *Nevada*'s port side just below its twin forward turrets and opened a gaping hole in the hull. Though water gushed into the ship, the crew managed to get it under way at 8:40 A.M., about a half hour after it was hit. When the battlewagon started steaming down the channel toward the navy yard, dive-bombers pounced, scoring several hits and near misses that caused more damage and triggered fires. When it looked like the *Nevada* might sink and block the harbor entrance, it was run aground. The dreadnought sank on December 8 but in shallow water. Sailors ashore and on other ships had rooted for the battlewagon as it attempted to escape Pearl Harbor, earning the *Nevada* the nickname the *Cheer Up Ship*. It stayed on the harbor bottom for more than two months and became one of the navy's first arduous salvage projects. Fifty members of the crew perished in the attack. Eventually, the vessel was raised, and, after stopgap repairs, it was able to return to the West Coast for permanent repair and modernization. The *Cheer Up Ship* was put back on active service in October 1942.[69]

"It was about 8 A.M. and I was on my way to this brunch they always had laid on for three or four hours every Sunday," remembered Seaman First Class George Callahan of the *Nevada*. "But on my way they sounded the alarms and blew the whistles on board and around the base. It was the general quarters alert, and that meant that everybody was to return to their ships and man their battle stations."[70]

A Pulaski County native, Callahan joined the navy in 1940 and had been aboard since February 1941. General quarters sounded at 8:01. Callahan recalled: "Just as I looked up and saw planes flying overhead they announced that the planes were Japanese." At 8:02, antiaircraft machine guns opened fire on Kates approaching the *Nevada*'s port side. Callahan was evidently part of a five-inch gun crew: "We were ordered to fire, and I fired the gun. But with my little gun I would have to make a direct hit to do any damage."[71]

Machine-gun fire destroyed a Kate before the pilot could launch its torpedo, and, according to Callahan, the plane "crashed about 100 yards off *Nevada*'s port quarter." A five-inch shell stopped another Kate, the projectile likely detonating the torpedo and blowing the plane to bits. Despite the storm of antiaircraft fire, one Kate managed to drop its deadly load. The torpedo smashed into the *Nevada*'s port bow, gouging "a large hole . . . below her two forward turrets." Callahan said the torpedo strike shorted out the port-side electric system, immobilizing his and other guns.[72]

Bombs started raining down on the battlewagon about 8:30. Ten minutes later, the *Nevada* started its run for the open sea. Captain Francis Scanland and his executive officer were ashore; Lieutenant Commander Francis Thomas, a reservist, was the senior officer aboard. Assuming command of the ship, Thomas ordered what seemed like mission impossible: get the *Nevada* under way and out of Pearl Harbor.[73]

The *Nevada*'s dash had a magical effect on all who witnessed it. "To most she was the finest thing they saw that day," Lord later noted. "It was less of a pageant close up." Naturally, the ship was a tempting target for swarming dive-bombers, whose pilots "obviously hoped to sink the *Nevada* in the entrance channel and bottle up the whole fleet." Consequently: "[Vals] hit and near-missed her repeatedly, opening up her forecastle deck, causing more leaks in her hull, starting gasoline fires forward and other blazes in her superstructure and midships area." Ashore, the navy brass feared the capital ship might indeed sink and trap the fleet. "Stay clear of the channel," warned more signal flags. Thomas got the message and ordered the *Nevada* run aground at Hospital Point.[74]

Meanwhile, Callahan saw a shipmate die instantly: "A seaman was on top of a ladder when a piece of shrapnel took part of his head off and he fell down the ladder and landed at my feet. I didn't suffer even a scratch but I was scared." Callahan added: "At least I was alive. A lot of guys were killed on the *Nevada* like that guy I saw. I'll never forget that boy, never."[75]

The *Nevada*'s crew sought shelter ashore. "A bunch of us gathered at the Aloha Stadium and camped out there for two days," Callahan remembered. "We waited for U.S. ships and planes to come rescue us."[76]

Callahan's shipmate, Storekeeper Third Class Earl Emery Davis, was relaxing in his bunk reading a Honolulu paper when he heard what sounded to him like an explosion. "On Sunday morning you got to goof off," explained Davis, an Indiana-born Kentuckian from Owensboro. "We had been practicing maneuvers for, I would say, close to a year and a half, or at least over a year." He figured the blast was part of another drill.[77]

Davis still took the racket for practice when the command "man your battle stations" came over the loudspeaker "just matter-of-factly." More explosions, seemingly from Ford Island, followed. So did another alert: "They hollered over the PA system, 'Man your battle stations on the double. The Japs are bombing Pearl Harbor.' Then we got on the run."[78]

Davis hurriedly pulled on "a tee shirt, and tropical shorts and . . . shoes," and rushed off to join a five-inch antiaircraft-gun crew on the port-side boat deck just aft of the bridge. The gunners began shooting at "Jap planes all over—bombers, torpedo planes, pursuit planes, everything coming in at us." Davis confessed he was scared at first: "But after you get that first fear, you forget it. All you think about is protecting your ship and your life and you fight with everything you've got and we threw everything we could at 'em."[79]

Davis said the torpedo planes were too low to hit: "We couldn't train down enough to get 'em. . . . The only ones [who] could hit 'em was the marines up in the crow's nest . . . shooting down with the fifty and thirty caliber machine guns. . . . We was shooting at the guys that was where we could train on 'em up in the sky."[80]

Davis said he saw the bomber that nearly killed him: "In fact, our whole gun crew seen him coming in from the stern . . . and we knew it was going to get us. . . . So what did we do? We done the wrong thing." He and eight others in his crew quickly ducked under the bridge overhang. The plane's bomb smashed through the bridge and exploded, wiping out the captain's office and quarters and triggering a massive fire.[81]

"We was standing right in front of the door," Davis noted, "and all the flames come right out at us, and all I remember is someone screamed—I think it was me—it might have saved my life because I didn't suck in any of that flame and all of a sudden a black curtain was pulled down over my face." When he regained consciousness, he saw two sailors: "I wasn't aware if they brought me back to life or what, but . . . when I stood up my whole body was just like you had taken a blowtorch and blowtorched my whole body." His skin "was just hanging and dripping off." The concussion from the blast blew his clothes off: "All I had on was the waistband of my tropical shorts and my shoes; the rest of it was gone."[82]

Davis saw dead men all around: "I knew I couldn't do nothing for 'em, so I went to the officer of the deck and told him, 'You got men with arms and legs and everything else blowed off. I'm bad burnt. I'm not hurting, because I'm in such shock.'" Davis said that, because the *Nevada* was already aground, he asked the officer of the deck if he could swim for the Ford Island hospital. He agreed, and Davis "swam under burning oil and everything else": "But I made it to the beach." He refused offers to take him to the hospital: "I said, 'No, if I sit down, then the leaders in the back of my legs is gonna draw and I won't be able to straighten out my legs." So he walked four blocks to his destination.[83]

Davis said he was sprayed with tannic acid, "a purple, almost black stuff," swaddled in bandages, put to bed, and injected with morphine. He added that, each time they replaced the old bandages with new ones, he would tell the doctor: "I can feel myself dying a little more." He was sent stateside on a hospital ship that arrived in San Francisco on Christmas Day. Weeks of care in the burn unit at the Vallejo Naval Hospital followed. He was treated with a spray of sulfanilamide powder and liquid paraffin. All the while, he remained bedbound twenty-four hours a day "with a glucose needle in one arm and a blood plasma needle in the other arm," his arms tied to boards because he "didn't have the skin to hold the fluid in."[84]

When Davis was finally well enough to walk in June, he said it felt like his entire body had gone "to sleep with all the pins and needles." He was declared fit enough to return to the *Nevada,* which had been repaired and was docked in Bremerton, Washington. He was granted sick leave to visit his mother in Tell City, Indiana, in July 1942. She promised him: "You go back aboard that ship, you will never be touched again." He spent the rest of the war unharmed, fighting the Japanese and the Germans, the latter on D-Day.[85]

5

Cruisers, Tin Cans, Friendly Fire, a Cutter, and Marines

Many, if not most, of the Kentuckians at Pearl Harbor were aboard the nine battleships, most likely because they were the biggest ships in the navy. But other Kentuckians were serving on smaller warships, notably cruisers and destroyers, but also auxiliary vessels. A cruiser chaplain with a Bluegrass State connection inspired one of the most famous tunes of World War II.

The attack naturally canceled Sunday services all over Pearl Harbor. Thus, Chaplain Howell Forgy of the heavy cruiser *New Orleans*—nicknamed *NO Boat*—encouraged the crew to "praise the Lord and pass the ammunition." His book "*. . . And Pass the Ammunition*" contains one of the most detailed accounts of the attack. Forgy began the day daydreaming about Murray, where the New Jersey native had been pastor at the First Presbyterian Church when he joined the navy.

Forgy is still credited with saving the church. Before his advent, the congregation was small, struggling, and lacking a permanent house of worship. The Presbyterians met on Sundays wherever they could find room, including at the Calloway County courthouse and Murray High School. When the minister resigned in 1938, the church seemed finished. In desperation, some members pleaded for help at a 1939 presbytery meeting in nearby Mayfield. Forgy happened to be in town conducting a revival and, on the spot, agreed to pastor the Murray church. "He found nine Presbyterians, one hundred dollars in the bank, a lot, and a desire for a church," wrote Jack S. McDowell in the introduction to "*. . . And Pass the Ammunition.*" A year later, Forgy headed for the navy with a wife, the choir member Louise Morgan, a Murray State student from Princeton. The shepherd "left a congregation of more than one hundred persons in a new church building." He had overseen the work on a permanent church building; construction started in August 1939 across from the campus of Murray State University, then Murray State College.[1]

At first, Forgy did not get credit for saying "praise the Lord and pass the ammunition." The distinction went to Captain William A. Maguire, the chaplain of the whole Pacific Fleet. Maguire too survived Pearl Harbor. A Catholic priest, he appeared on the cover of the November 2, 1942, issue of *Life*. By then, Kay Kyser and his orchestra had popularized the song, whose lyrics were written by Frank Loesser. Sheet music and record sales were soaring, but the song had yet to achieve hit status mainly because the Office of War Information (OWI) "[did] not want so valuable a propaganda song plugged to death," *Life* explained.[2]

In the story, Captain Maguire admitted he did not recall "putting into words the now famous slogan," hedging: "If I said it, nobody could have heard me in the din of battle. But I certainly felt what that statement expresses." At any rate, the magazine story said Maguire braved "a blistering fire" yet managed "to reach his own ship where he took up a battle station in the stern of the vessel."[3]

Doubtless, the *Life* editors were embarrassed when on November 1 the AP double-scooped the magazine. One wire story had Forgy fessing up to coining the phrase; another one had Maguire repeating that he could not recall saying it and vehemently denying he shot any gun. In a joint interview, "the Fighting Priest of Pearl Harbor" and Bishop John F. O'Hara, the American Catholic Church's military ordinate, stressed that "international law and the Geneva Conference" forbade chaplains from fighting. They agreed to meet the press "to affirm the truth." The chaplain said that during the air raid "he was on several battleships, ministering to the wounded and encouraging the men." The interview was conducted in New York, where Maguire was on temporary duty. He said that he arrived in the Big Apple only to learn—to his "dismay, annoyance and chagrin"—that he had supposedly inspired the song title.[4]

The other story named "Naval Lieut. Howell Forgy, 34, strapping ex-football player from Haddonfield, N.J.," as the phrase's source. The "somewhat shy" Presbyterian explained that Lieutenant Edwin Woodhead of Boise, Idaho, was standing near him when, "suddenly," they "saw a Japanese plane fall in flames." Forgy swore "unchaplainlike." Woodhead yelled: "Break out the ammunition." And a shell relay line began. Recalled Forgy: "The boys were getting dog-tired. All I did was slap them on the backs and smilingly say, 'Praise the Lord and pass the ammunition, boys.'" The AP correspondent compressed the story a tad. The chaplain admitted that he got profane when he saw a Japanese plane shot down, but he was on deck then. He was below when he said, "Praise the Lord and pass the ammunition."[5]

Not everybody liked the song. Some Seattle men of the cloth panned it as "a jazz tune of blasphemy against Christ and the church," the British United Press reported. "Clerics of several faiths made public statements which held the song as sacrilegious." Focusing on Forgy, they insisted that "Praise the Lord and pass the ammunition" was an expression "unbecoming to a member of the clergy." Like Maguire, Forgy knew not to handle any ammunition or shoot at an enemy. But the Reverend Robert T. McFarlane, a Presbyterian chaplain for the army, admonished: "The only ammunition of a chaplain is prayer with and for our men in the service. His only weapon is the cross, for spiritual and moral welfare of those men." He chided: "When he starts passing the ammunition he becomes subject to [the] same treatment as regular prisoners of war and is not then classed as a non-combatant."[6]

The Baptist pastor Ralph E. Knudson said the song "seems a bit irreverent and certainly does not help either the war or religion." The Reverend Carl H. Sandren, a Lutheran, added his disapprobation to criticism from a dozen other ministers. He harrumphed that "Praise the Lord" was "too indicative of our modern paganism and is in sharp contrast to songs out of other wars such as our national anthem and 'Battle Hymn of the Republic.'"[7]

The *Virginia Methodist* leaned toward pacifism and wanted radio stations to stop playing the song: "There's no denying that the tune is a catchy one, but the words are no credit to America's chaplains. . . . [W]hether the song is sacrilegious . . . may be debatable. . . . It certainly is no great credit to sing with great gusto about a 'sky pilot' who becomes a killer." But the song earned plaudits from some congregants and clergy. For the rest of the war, the flock at Denver's Liberal Church recited the Lord's Prayer and sang "Praise the Lord" at the end of every service. At a Brooklyn temple, a cantor who usually sang "O Jerusalem" as a standby made "Praise the Lord" part of the service.[8]

Meanwhile, John O'Donnell, the *New York Daily News* Washington correspondent, knew a juicy story when he saw one and jumped on the "Praise the Lord" flap. He claimed, tongue in cheek, that the dispute over who said "Praise the Lord and pass the ammunition" promised "to become as historic as the Bacon-Shakespeare feud." The OWI's blessing on the "ripsnorting battle hymn of the Navy" was "crescendoing back on the ear drums" of the agency "with a dull, if not sickening, thud." Never mind that Maguire and Forgy did not fire a gun, touch a single shell, or compose a single word in "Praise the Lord." Because the song said a "sky pilot" became a combatant in the heat of battle, the OWI found "itself in the dilemma of sanctioning an act by a chaplain in direct violation of Navy regulations, as well as the Geneva Convention."[9]

An OWI spokesperson defended the agency, advising O'Donnell: "We're not interested in the authorship of the chaplain's phrase. . . . It's the song itself that the Office of War Information endorsed. The song has guts. It isn't namby-pamby and doesn't stink like most of the stuff that has been written since we entered the war." He posited: "Although a chaplain might be ethically a non-combatant, he would be allowed to take care of himself in a case 'of self-defense.'" Captain R. D. Workman, the navy's chief of chaplains, said the civilian was dead wrong. "We operate as clergymen and under the Geneva Convention," he lectured. "We wear the Cross of the Church upon our sleeves. We are non-combatants." Workman was most worried that the fighting chaplain in the song would hand the Japanese "the opportunity to say we have thrown over the Geneva Convention and that they can now do anything they want with our prisoners." He cited a chaplain on Guam, which fell to the Japanese on December 11, 1941. "The last we heard of him, he was all right, treated according to the rules of the Geneva Convention," McFarlane said. "What do you think is apt to happen to him now?" Ultimately, the controversy faded, and the tune ended up one of the most popular American songs of World War II. "Praise the Lord" stayed on *Variety* magazine's "10 Best Sellers" list for three months. More than 450,000 copies of sheet music sold in two months.[10]

After surviving seven major sea battles and the near sinking of the *New Orleans,* Forgy was stateside in September 1943. On his return, the navy officially recognized him as the source for "praise the Lord and pass the ammunition," but he might not have cared.[11] The padre said he heard the song everywhere he went and admitted he would "be content never to hear it again." Why did Forgy think he coined the phrase? "Because I've always liked the theology of the Old Testament which is based more or less on the theory the Lord helps those that help themselves." The chaplain explained that he was much more concerned about how battle affected a person's faith: "I learned more basic religion in my first five minutes under fire than I did in my seven years in the seminary and in preaching." Forgy was reunited with his wife in Haddonfield, where Louise and eleven-month-old Michael, whom Forgy had never seen, were staying with the pastor's parents. Louise later said Forgy "admitted repeatedly" that he said "praise the Lord and pass the ammunition" but maintained that he did not "use all the unchaplain-like language tacked on the battle cry."[12] Forgy was back in Murray on October 1 to speak on the college campus, where he was honored at the annual faculty-student reception. "The more I see of the Japanese, the more I know the greedy immoral Japanese Empire must be demolished," he said in his remarks. In addition, he charged the students to "rebuild the world" and "plan the future." He praised the American fighting spirit and called for the destruction of war's causes—"greed, avarice, fear and hatred"—because "they are worse than war itself." "There are no atheists on battleships, either," he continued. "Especially in night battles."[13]

It seems likely Forgy visited the Presbyterian church or met with some of his ex-parishioners. Perhaps he told them that Murray was on his mind when he woke up on December 7, 1941. The *New Orleans* was at Berth 16 in the navy yard and dependent on power from the dock. Still abed, Forgy peered at the early morning sky through the porthole over his bunk and marveled at "a circle of Maxfield Parrish blue." He said that "the bright sunlight splashing into the room" reminded him of spring Sunday mornings in Murray. He figured it was a little past noon there, when Presbyterian worship usually concluded. He envisioned the faithful he left behind a year ago: "high-school teachers, college professors, farmers in their Sunday bests and squeaky shoes, the village merchants and their wives milling about on the lawn of the little red brick church."[14]

Forgy imagined the churchgoers were discussing the upcoming Ladies' Aid Society bazaar and congregational supper: "The men from the country would be exchanging views on the hog market and what the war in Europe would do to the tobacco crop price." He suspected: "The pretty girls of the college would semaphore smiles to the boys, signaling their willingness for a coke date at the Hut [a popular hangout near campus] or an invitation to next week's dance." He wrote that the "ribbon-hatted" farm girls "completed this picture of the typical American town that the magazines often tried to show but in which they never quite succeeded."[15]

A slight jarring of the ship interrupted this daydreaming. Forgy tried to close his eyes and in his mind's eye "look back across four thousand miles of sea and land to that little church." He could envision the Bakers driving home from Sunday services toward "their trim, pretty home" close to the Murray State campus. He figured "old Mr. Rogers" was at the wheel of "his ancient Model T Ford, . . . heading for the farm out east of town." He wished for another Sunday dinner with the elderly gent, breaking bread with him at "his warped old pine table" and hearing "him explain [the] . . . code of life which guided him in his praying and plowing." He also longed to listen to the farmer's "endless volume of proverbial anecdotes into which he dipped to find a story applicable to the newest problem of the Rogers ranch, the First Presbyterian Church, or the grain market in Paducah." He could nearly taste "some of the ham my old friend cured over the hickory smoke in the little shack behind the farm-house." His mouth watered as he mused on "the home-made sausage, the southern fried chicken, and Mrs. Rogers' tomato and red pepper relish that would be on the table this and every Sunday."[16]

His mind back aboard ship, Forgy mulled over his sermon, which he expected to deliver to the crew in two hours. The title was "We Reach Forward." The text would be based on Paul's advice to forget "those things which are behind" while "reaching forth unto those things which are before." Forgy planned to use Paul's words to remind the crew that their "fate lay in the days ahead and not in those that had passed." Instead, he would speak some of the most famous secular words of World War II.[17]

Meanwhile, the ship again moved slightly. Forgy figured a tug was shifting the heavy cruiser to another berth. But he also heard "a muffled rat-tat-tat" as if a kid were "running a stick along one of those white picket fences back home." Then: "The tranquility of the Hawaiian morning . . . suddenly exploded into the deafening clang-clang-clang of the general alarm." He "wondered why the officer of the deck could never get into his head the fact that the general alarm was not to be tested on Sundays." He figured the mistake would have the skipper "on his neck." But the alarm droned on. Over the ship's loudspeakers came the shrill peep of the bosun's pipe, followed by: "All hands to battle stations! All hands to battle stations! This is no drill! This is no drill!"[18]

Forgy was still skeptical. He knew the army had been on alert throughout the Hawaiian islands until the night before: "This must be some admiral's clever idea of how to make an off-hour general quarters drill for the fleet realistic." He exited his quarters, bucking a parade of marines scrambling topside to machine-gun and antiaircraft batteries. The leathernecks were griping and swearing "about GQ—especially at this hour, when their Sunday-morning-after-Saturday-night liberty was interrupted so abruptly."[19]

When Forgy heard "a rhythmic thudding against the side of the hull," he guessed crews on other ships were firing five-inch antiaircraft guns. He heard the rat-tat-tat again, this time suspecting it might be machine-gun fire. His battle station was the ship's sick bay, where he met the senior medical officer. The doc was as puzzled as the padre but told him he saw a plane fall from the sky in flames. The chaplain thought that was "carrying a drill pretty far." Forgy figured "this might be the real thing."[20]

Forgy excused himself to go topside and "take a look." He saw "the mighty *Arizona* . . . sending a mass of black, oily smoke thousands of feet into the air": "The water around her was dotted with debris and a mass of bobbing, oil-covered heads." Men—hundreds of them— were "splashing and trying to swim": "Others were motionless." He witnessed "flashes of orange-red flames" spurting from the antiaircraft guns, bright against grimy black clouds, Battleship Row's funeral pyre: "The cage-like foremast of the *Arizona* poked through the smoke at a crazy, drunken angle." The *West Virginia* "was sagging amidships, and her bow and stern angled upward." Forgy watched the *Oklahoma* "rolling on her side, . . . her big bottom . . . coming up": "Hundreds of her crew [were] jumping into the water. Dozens of others were crawling along her exposed side and bottom, trying to keep up with the giant treadmill."[21]

Forgy heard the drone of aircraft engines and saw a Japanese plane "gliding down toward Battleship Row." The pilot "seemed to be loafing in, deliberately taking his time to pick out just what he wanted to hit." The chaplain saw the enemy aviator drop his bombs, his helmeted head "sticking out of the cockpit." He remembered "something mocking about the big rising-sun balls under the wings of the plane." He "gaped with a sense of fascinated helplessness" and wished he could "reach out to stop those bombs before they hit."[22]

Forgy watched dive-bombers pounce on the *California:* "The bombs hit her admidships, right by the stacks. A flash, fire and smoke jumped into the air all at once." The Val pilot sped away; he escaped even though "the sky all around the plane was laced with streaming trails of tracers." Forgy wondered whether "the devil himself could have immuned those planes against our shells." He pondered "this new, horrible, evil power that turned Pearl Harbor into a bay of terrible explosions, smoking ships, flames, and death."[23]

Forgy felt better when he saw a Japanese plane fall: "We'd got one! They could be hit." He said the crew yelled "like freshmen at the first touchdown of the day": "I guess I shouted and screamed as loudly as any one." He evidently swore, too, because the master-at-arms remarked: "I guess chaplains can cuss like bo'sun's mates when they have to." Forgy confessed that the sailor might have been right.[24]

A lieutenant sidled up to Forgy. He was assigned to the ship's main batteries, which were not firing because they were useless against attacking airplanes. He grinned and confided: "Padre, I figure if the Lord is going to look after any one in this, He's going to look after you. If you don't mind, I'll stick close by." The officer was joshing, but, when Forgy dashed for the sick bay on the double, the lieutenant was "close behind."[25]

After the attack, Captain J. G. Atkins reported that, at some point, electricity from the dock failed or was cut, darkening the *New Orleans* below decks, and leaving the ship with only auxiliary power. Preparations to get under way drained the auxiliary batteries and dimmed emergency lighting to the point that it was almost useless. Worse, the lack of power and lights greatly reduced the ship's defensive firepower because all guns and hoists had to be operated by hand.[26]

In the darkness, Forgy and the lieutenant could see daylight streaming in the wardroom through open portholes, which invited strafing and provided all too convenient entrances for water if the ship started sinking. They joined an African American messman in closing them "against the awful panorama outside." The messman was singing "Swing Low, Sweet Chariot," defying "the enemy's chariots swooping down with their deadly loads." Forgy and the lieutenant "wondered how many seconds or minutes or hours would pass" until they and the *New Orleans* would "become a part of the terrifying funeral pyre that now was Pearl Harbor."[27]

Back in the sick bay, Forgy found the doctor and his instruments ready. Outside, he heard a big gunner's mate yell, "Get those —— —— lines down the hatch to the magazine." In the "dim blue battle lights," he saw ropes tumbling down through the hatches. Suddenly it hit him. The ammunition hoists had no electric power: "The gunners topside were ducking machine-gun bullets and shrapnel, training their guns by sheer guts and sweat." Worse: "They had no ammunition other than the few shells in their ready boxes."[28]

Forgy said every available crewman pitched in to help lug the heavy ordnance to the busy gunners on deck: "The big five-inch shells, weighing close to a hundred pounds, were being pulled up the powerless hoist by ropes attached to their long, tube-like metal cases. A tiny Filipino [messman], who weighed little more than the shell, hoisted it to his shoulder, staggered a few steps, and grunted as he started the long, tortuous trip up two flights of ladders to the quarterdeck, where the guns thirsted for steel and powder." Meanwhile, a dozen men mustered at the idled shell hoist. There was no rest for the ammo bearers. A sweat-soaked Jewish sailor, a Brooklynite, still winded from a trip topside, grabbed a shell and nearly crumpled: "His legs tried to buckle . . ., but he wouldn't let them."[29]

Forgy, an ex-footballer, wanted to boost a shell: "The cool metal of the shell casing against my shoulder and neck would feel good. I would be busy and feel better inside. But a chaplain cannot fire a gun or take material part in a battle." Nonetheless, he admitted to feeling something less than Christian charity toward the enemy fliers: "Those devils—coming out of the sky without warning and sending to their death thousands of men of a nation at peace—were violating every rule of God and man."[30]

He added: "There was little time for more reflection. . . . Minutes turned to hours. Physical exhaustion was coming to every man in the human endless chain of that ammunition line. They struggled on. They could keep going only by keeping faith in their hearts. I slapped their wet, sticky backs and shouted, 'Praise the Lord and pass the ammunition.'"[31]

After the first wave departed for their carriers, Forgy went topside and saw that "the sky had turned into a rolling mass of black with billowing clouds from the flaming ships in the harbor." He met a lieutenant who vowed that the attack was "the end of the Japanese Empire." The remark struck the padre as absurd: "He was talking about the end of the Japanese Empire while the battle line of the United States fleet lay burning and sinking before our eyes." But the junior officer "was saying what few of us had yet had the chance to think," Forgy said, adding that "Japan would pay for her treachery" and that the lieutenant "typified the young American dedicated to the task of exterminating the foe who was striking his comrades to their death in the treachery of this sabbath morning."[32]

Forgy said everybody figured the enemy planes had come from an aircraft carrier and would return refueled and rearmed. Indeed, a second wave of planes was already on the way. So the *New Orleans*'s crew braced themselves and scanned the skies for round 2: "Every man and officer grew tense. There was an odd feeling in our stomachs as though we were hungry but at the same time didn't want anything to eat. Our mouths were dry from the nervous strain, and our tongues were swollen. We wanted to slosh saliva about in our mouths, but there was none." There was no water either; lines had been shut off when the ship was made watertight: "We thought gum would help—but there was no gum."[33]

The second wave struck about 8:55. Forgy spotted the planes, a "thin V of silver specks . . . coming over for high altitude bombing this trip, at about fifteen or sixteen thousand feet": "The din and clatter began once again." He saw a five-inch shell explode just behind the V's point. A trio of the attackers was hit and began spiraling downward, trailing smoke. "It was the only three-for-one shot I have ever seen." But most of the formation got through and dropped bombs. Three landed in the water near the *No-Boat;* two were duds. Another came "uncomfortably close," splashing down between Forgy's ship and the *Ramapo,* which was laden with high-octane aviation gasoline. Forgy and his shipmates around him hit the deck and waited "for the tanker to let go with a blast that would blow everything within a quarter-mile to

Kingdom-Come." Only shrapnel rattled against both ships; Forgy and his flock thanked the good Lord that damage was slight.[34]

Nobody was killed or wounded on *NO Boat*. But Forgy knew hospitals ashore would be crowded with hundreds of wounded men. After the second attack ended, he got permission from the cruiser's executive officer to see what he could do to help at the naval hospital. He smelled ether, "sickening and heavy." He saw doctors, nurses, and staffers "moving on the double . . . setting up beds in hallways, in the aisles of wards, anywhere a bed could fit." He roamed among the cots, comforting men who were still conscious. Cards attached to the beds listed the patient's name, religion, and injuries: "Some of them bore no name; many sailors' dog-tags had been burned off along with their clothes and flesh."[35]

Forgy ran into Lieutenant Harry Walker, the *New Orleans*'s junior medical officer and a former star end on the University of Kentucky football team. He had gone to the hospital on December 3 for an appendectomy: "I was surprised to see him on his feet so soon and asked him what he was doing walking around." Walker, who interned at the Mayo Clinic, replied with a grin: "I got myself all taped up and seem to be holding together. You know, Padre, just like in football. When your ankle got hurt you taped it up, and it didn't hurt so much. Well, I've got my guts all taped up. It's just the same." A nurse stopped Forgy as he left the hospital. She confided that Walker "got out of a hospital bed and has already been on his feet more than six hours": "He has performed several dozen operations and amputations." The chaplain was "proud of Harry, proud to be from the same ship and proud to have entered the navy from the same state." He bragged to the nurse: "He's from Kentucky. Kentucky's famous for its thoroughbreds, you know."[36]

Forgy's shipmate James Gilbert Edwards of Louisville went to war hungry: "It being Sunday morning, why, it was holiday routine. When the Japanese attacked . . . I was standing in the chow line getting ready to go down to eat breakfast."[37] Edwards was an eighteen-year-old gunner's mate third class who had been in service a little less than eleven months. He later recalled: "I always wanted to join the Navy after I saw a sailor who lived up the street from me when he'd come home on leave." When he showed up at the Louisville recruiting station, he did not quite measure up; he was a half inch short of the minimum height requirement, five-foot-four. The helpful recruiters suggested he try to stretch: "So I stretched a quarter of an inch and they waived the other quarter because they said, 'You will probably grow some more after you get into the Navy.'"[38] After boot camp, Edwards ended up on the *New Orleans* at Pearl Harbor. The landlubber had never been on a ship before a troop transport took him to Hawaii. He said life aboard *NO Boat* was "good once you got into the routine of it."[39]

The first job Edwards was given was with the deck division, helping three other shipmates square away the captain's gig, a small boat the skipper used as his water taxi. He found his next assignment more to his liking. He joined the crew that loaded the gunpowder for blasting the ship's float planes off their catapults. Neither the single-engine scout planes nor their mother ship were going anywhere on December 7, 1941; the *New Orleans* was tied up for engine repair in the navy yard.[40]

From the chow line topside, Edwards could make out aircraft swarming over Hickam Airfield. "We were standing there wondering what kind of planes they were. We'd had aircraft recognition classes, but it was all on German planes."[41] When the crew discovered the aircraft were Japanese, he said: "I just thought, 'What were those people thinking about, attacking Pearl Harbor?' I guess I was more mad than anything else."[42]

Edwards said that the first Val dive-bomber must have missed its target because its bomb "evidently . . . didn't hit anything": "But the second dive-bomber hit one of the hangars, and you could see it." The explosion demolished the hangar. Suddenly, Kates, special shallow-water torpedoes strapped to their undersides, roared low over the ships in the navy yard racing for Battleship Row. The bosun's mate of the watch piped the crew to battle stations at 7:57 A.M., punctuating the warning, according to Edwards, by yelling: "The dirty SOBs are bombing us!" Edwards rushed to a five-inch antiaircraft gun. He was a hot shell man, tasked with catching shell casings after the gun fired and tossing them out of the way. Before they could defend their ship, the gunners had to cut away a canvas awning that was shading the guns.[43]

"We had our guns firing within about five minutes. . . . [A]s far as to who shot down what planes it was impossible to tell because everybody was shooting," Edwards said. There was no time to be scared:

"When you are firing a gun, then you are busy and the fear don't bother you too bad. But when you are just settin' there, waiting for something to happen, that is when the worst part of it is."[44]

Edwards said other ships and piers in the navy yard blocked his view of Battleship Row. But, even if they had not, he was too busy to watch the destruction of the battlewagons. He did not see the *Arizona* blow up: "But we heard the explosion and felt the concussion." He said the *New Orleans* escaped with only minor damage but came within a whisker of blowing up. A bomb, apparently aimed at the cruiser, went off in the water close to it, the destroyer tender *Rigel,* and the *Ramapo:* "That bomb, if it would have hit that Ramapo, it would have caused a tremendous explosion." Though bomb splinters poked sixteen holes—from one to six inches square—in *NO Boat,* Captain J. G. Atkins reported no casualties on his ship. Likewise, nobody got hurt on the *Rigel* or the *Ramapo.*[45]

All three ships were sitting ducks, *NO Boat's* predicament made worse by the loss of electricity. Edwards recalled: "So we had to ram these eighty-pound shells by hand and they had to pass the shells from the magazines up to the guns. . . . [T]hey got everybody that wasn't assigned to [a] . . . gun and they formed like a bucket brigade from the magazines up to the guns and they were passing these shells from man to man."[46]

Edwards said that the *New Orleans* crewmen stuck to their battle stations until about 3:30 P.M. Because the eight-inch guns, mounted three abreast in three turrets, were not firing, their crews were detailed to rescue men stranded in the water. They set off with the cruiser's three motor launches, two whaleboats, the captain's gig, and a motorboat. Edwards stayed on board.[47]

Edwards remembered that rumors ran rampant after nightfall. Supposedly, Japanese Hawaiians were engaging in sabotage in Honolulu. "There was no sabotaging Japanese in Honolulu," he said. Stories—also false—spread that the Japanese army was landing, presumably after more air attacks.[48]

The heavy cruiser *San Francisco* was across the dock from the *New Orleans.* Machinist's Mate Second Class John Locker remembered rolling out of his bunk on *NO Boat's* sister ship at 7:00 A.M. He remembered breakfast—scrambled eggs and milk-soaked grits. He remembered listening to his brand-new $14.00 radio on the fantail: "I remember everything else but what happened to that radio. I just don't know."[49]

The Paducah sailor was tuned in to a Honolulu station when the roar of airplane engines drowned out the music: "It was terrifying to get a baptism of war so quickly and abruptly. At first, everybody was just running around like chickens with their heads cut off."[50]

Locker was not scheduled for duty. He planned to stay aboard the *San Francisco* and "just sunbathe and listen to the old radio." War swiftly changed his plans. He got a brief but clear look at the attackers just before the general quarters alarm sounded, sending him dashing to his battle station—the forward engine room deep inside the ship: "The planes came in low. They headed right broadside toward Battleship Row. When somebody near me said, 'Say, those planes have got red balls painted on the undersides of the wings,' we knew they were Japanese and knew we were under attack." He described the warplanes—Kates— as "a kind of olive drab": "You could see the men sitting in the pilot's seats."[51]

Escape from Pearl Harbor was impossible. The heavy cruiser was under overhaul in the navy yard, its oil-fired boilers dismantled. Locker recalled: "We couldn't get under way. We were told to just start putting it back together as fast as we could."[52]

The *San Francisco* was virtually defenseless, too. The cruiser was "without operative armament or major calibre ammunition on board" and thus "restricted to the use of small calibre arms." The ship's "major contribution of an offensive nature consisted in augmenting the gun crews of the New Orleans": "The quick transfer of men and officers permitted that vessel to open fire with 5″ guns in very short time." Locker stayed put, shut behind watertight doors, and surrounded by tons of steel. Hence, he could neither hear nor see the carnage around him.[53]

"At that time," Locker noted, "I wasn't worried about torpedoes. There were too many piers and too many other ships for torpedo planes to make any runs at us. Bombs—that was what we were worried about." When he emerged from the engine room after the first wave was over, he saw the *St. Louis* steaming away, its crew "throwing everything loose topside over the side": "They didn't even bother to take it below."[54]

Locker said that almost everybody was ready for the second wave of attackers: "We were pretty well organized by that time." The Japanese "didn't do as near the damage": "They didn't stick around too long either." After the enemy departed, he got a chance to survey the destruction: "It was hard to believe the *Oklahoma* capsized. I didn't know the water was that deep around the battleships. I thought the superstructure would keep them from going all the way over."[55]

Nobody was killed or wounded on the *San Francisco,* which was unscathed except for a "searchlight . . . damaged by bullet or fragment from unknown source."[56] Locker figured he and his shipmates would soon be facing landing craft and troopships loaded with Japanese soldiers: "The average sailor at Pearl Harbor really did think there would be an invasion and that we would be captured and become prisoners of war." He had heard enemy planes had blasted Hickam and Wheeler Airfields: "We had practically no Army protection and there was practically no air force."[57]

Locker saw more combat in the Pacific, climbed the ranks to lieutenant, and retired from the navy in 1966, thirty years after he enlisted. He noted: "I look back and think to myself of all the places I had been in the world—and I had to be where World War II started for the United States." His memory of Pearl Harbor was vivid for the rest of his life, "except for that radio": "I don't know if I threw it up in the air, over the side or what."[58]

Locker could not have seen Joe Sanders when the light cruiser *St. Louis* steamed past the *San Francisco.* The seaman first class from Mayfield was at his battle station deep inside the number 2 gun turret. Sanders and a shipmate had been looking forward to spending most of the day on liberty, taking photographs in the lush green hills above Pearl Harbor. But duty called first; after reveille, and before breakfast, Sanders donned work clothes and joined the deck force, swabbing a forward section of the main deck. No matter, he said: "You were proud of your uniform and proud of your ship."[59]

After the deck force finished its task, the men broke for chow. At 7:56 A.M., Sanders was below, putting on his whites after a shower. He had no idea that topside a pair of officers had spotted "a swarm of dark, olive green aircraft flying low toward Ford Island from the general direction of Aiea [hills north of Pearl Harbor]."[60] Nor was he aware that, while those aircraft "dropped bombs and made strafing attacks," another "dark olive drab colored plane bearing the aviation insignia of

Japan passed close astern and dropped a torpedo."[61] The *St. Louis* went to general quarters as soon as the raid started. Sanders heard that his shipmates opened fire before they were called to battle stations: "Captain [C. A.] Hood said he thought Commander [C. K] Finch, the exec, gave the order to commence firing. Mr. Finch said he thought the captain had given the order."[62]

No matter, Sanders recalled "thinking what the hell is going on": "Then I took off for my battle station as fast as I could go." He headed for the number 2 turret; the *St. Louis* had five turrets, each one bristling with triple six-inch guns. Before he climbed inside the steel box, he caught a glimpse of a Kate roaring over the concrete pier in the navy yard where the *St. Louis* and the light cruiser *Honolulu* were berthed. He said the torpedo-bomber disappeared behind the cruisers' superstructures on its way toward Ford Island. He managed to make out the red rising-sun insignia on the speeding aircraft's fuselage and wings. "But," he recalled, "it really didn't dawn on me it was Japanese." Anyway, the Kentuckian glimpsed no more of the air raid. Inside the turret, he took up his position at the breeches of the big guns and stood by for orders: "I couldn't see a thing, but I could feel the concussions from bombs going off and ships exploding all over the place."[63]

Sanders said his ship was in poor shape to fight. The *St. Louis* was listed on "limited availability," he explained. "Our radar was being installed and there were scaffolds, reels of cables and all sorts of equipment all over the deck." Electric power had been switched off to six of the ship's eight five-inch antiaircraft guns, mounted two abreast in four turrets. Two of the ship's six boilers were shut down for repair. The *St. Louis* seemed easy prey for the predators.[64]

But gunners gamely shot back with 1.1-inch and fifty-caliber machine guns while other sailors hastily cleared the deck of equipment so the five-inch guns could swing into action. "The problem was, we were on auxiliary power from the dock," Sanders said. While the power cables were spared, a sailor used an acetylene torch to burn off the gangway. Another man hacked away the water hose, leaving a twelve-inch hole in the side of the cruiser. It took a sailor just ten minutes to weld a metal plate over it. Below decks, crewmen prepared to get the ship under way and managed to raise steam in the half dozen working boilers. At 9:31 A.M., the power cables were cast off and the 608-foot warship began backing away from the dock. Antiaircraft guns banging away at the enemy planes, the cruiser made for the harbor mouth and the open sea.[65]

Before the *St. Louis* got away, two torpedoes streaked toward its starboard side, possibly fired by one of the midget submarines. They missed, exploding against a shoal. The cruiser, steaming at twenty-five knots, cleared the harbor and began zigzagging on a southerly course with the object of "locating and attacking the enemy carrier which was reported as being to the south of Pearl Harbor." The carriers and their escorts were north of Oahu and steaming home.[66]

The *St. Louis* sustained only slight damage from strafing and bomb fragments. Nobody was killed or wounded. Anxious to reassure his folks, who of course knew none of that, Sanders wrote home on December 9:

> Dear Daddy and Mother:
> Guess you are kind of worried about me. I am all right so far. It sure was hell Sunday morning. I had just started to put my liberty clothes on when the Japs attacked us. We were tied up to the dock when it happened. We would have been damaged or even maybe sunk if we had not got out of here. We were the first ship out of here. I guess you read in the paper about the result of the air raid so there is no use of me telling you anything about it.
> I had a little Christmas present for you and Daddy but I may not get to send it now but will try.
> I'm so tired and sleepy that I can hardly hold my eyes open. It seems like a year since Sunday when we started out.
> I don't have very much to write and I haven't got very much time to write.
> So I guess I'll finish. Answer soon.
>
> Love, your son, Joe.[67]

From December 7 to the end of the war, the cruiser was known as the *Lucky Lou,* Sanders said: "It seemed like the ships all around us were badly hit or sunk, but we always came through pretty much okay." (During the 1943 Battle of Kolombangara, an enemy torpedo bent the cruiser's bow, but nobody was badly hurt.) Meanwhile, the *St. Louis* returned to Pearl Harbor on December 11. Sanders was shocked at the devastation. But he said the most sobering sight was "all those wooden boxes—coffins—piled up on the docks": "There must have been hundreds of them."[68]

Seaman Second Class Clarence Meece of Somerset was a relative newcomer to the light cruiser *Raleigh*, anchored on the other side of Ford Island from the *New Orleans*, the *San Francisco*, and the *St. Louis*. The air raid caught him with his trousers down; he was in the head. A Kate pilot bore down on the ship; his aim was perfect. The steel fish plowed through the *Raleigh*'s church launch, which was easing up to the cruiser's port side, and exploded. "It raised the ship up about a foot and me about a foot higher than that," Meece said. "I wasn't real salty then, and I didn't have any idea what had happened."[69]

The torpedo hit Fire Room 2, flooding it, Fire Room 1, and the engine room. Fire Room 3 was the steaming fire room, but water and leaking oil put it out of commission. The *Raleigh* started listing to port when a glide bomb hit astern. Though it failed to explode, the bomb "penetrated right through the ship" and detonated in the harbor mud, rupturing an oil tank on its way through the ship.[70] "I've still got an oil-soaked dollar bill I went back later and got out of my locker," Meece said, adding that Fire Room 1 was his battle station. "But I probably wouldn't have been there. We were on auxiliary power from Number Four Fire Room."[71]

The crew struggled to keep the *Raleigh* afloat. Counterflooding was tried, but the ship still threatened to heel over. So the crew was ordered to jettison as much topside weight as possible. "The planes went off on a scouting trip; everything else went over the side—catapults, torpedo tubes, torpedoes, booms, ladders, boat skids, stanchions, anchors, chains, rafts, boats, everything," Walter Lord wrote.[72] More help was on the way; pontoons and a lighter were lashed to the *Raleigh*'s port side as a makeshift outrigger. More lines were run to the quays. Gunners did their bit to lighten the ship by shooting a storm of antiaircraft fire at their tormentors. "We had lost our main power, and they were firing them manually by percussion," said Meece, who helped pass shells up to the busy gunners from below decks. The *Raleigh* stayed afloat with more help from two tugs that showed up in the afternoon to provide welcome power and food.[73]

Seaman Second Class Charles McGehee of the light cruiser *Detroit*, moored ahead of the *Raleigh*, always wondered whether lucky timing saved his life. The Calhoun sailor was on liberty in Honolulu Saturday night when he befriended a crewman from the *Oklahoma*. He invited McGehee to visit him on the battlewagon the next afternoon: "If [the Japanese attack] . . . had happened in the afternoon, I guess I'd have gone down with the Oklahoma." The *Detroit* and McGee survived; his newfound friend evidently did not. "I've never been sure but I think he died. I never saw him again."[74]

McGehee enlisted in the navy in January 1941 and joined the *Detroit* the following September. He was topside reading a newspaper and enjoying an apple when the attack started. "To this day," he recalled, "I don't know if I ate the apple and threw the paper away or ate the paper and threw the apple away, or ate both." McGehee wondered whether he might have seen the first bombs fall on Pearl Harbor. Both landed on Ford Island. When he spotted a low-flying Japanese plane pass his ship, he said: "I knew we'd had it." He was wrong. The *Detroit* escaped damage; nobody was killed, and only two men were slightly wounded. Even so, it was a close call. The target ship *Utah*, astern of the *Raleigh*, was also torpedoed, but it capsized and sank.[75]

Though FDR called December 7, 1941, "a date which will live in infamy," V. C. Kidd remembered it as the date Japanese pilots broke up his card game on the destroyer *Tucker*. "We were sitting on the fantail—four of us—playing hearts," said Kidd, a machinist's mate second class. "We thought they were [US planes] just practicing. . . . But we found out real quick that they weren't our planes and they weren't practicing."[76]

Kidd had liberty; after cards, he planned to go ashore. He could not believe how low the torpedo-bombers were. "They were only 25 or 30 feet in the air," he said. "They were so close you could see the faces of the pilots."[77]

Kidd said that, since the *Tucker* was undergoing an overhaul, it could hardly have been more vulnerable: "We had a reduction gear torn down and it was supposed to take two days to get it back together. We did it in four hours."[78]

Before he scrambled below decks to his battle station in the engine room, Kidd saw the heavily armored *Arizona* explode in an enormous fireball. He worried about the lightly armored *Tucker:* "You could sink a destroyer with an ice pick. But a battleship—I didn't know what to think, everything was happening so fast."[79]

While Kidd and the engine room crew worked desperately to get their ship moving, gunners on the *Tucker* started shooting at enemy planes. It was claimed that one member of the ship's crew, manning a fifty-caliber machine gun, fired the first American shot at the attackers. But as Kidd noted: "Everybody was too busy to be scared. You got scared after it was all over, when you had time to think about it." He said that the *Tucker* steamed out of Pearl Harbor at 2:00 P.M., ready to meet the enemy, but the enemy was long gone. He noted that he had joined the navy despite warnings from his uncle, a sailor himself: "He told me don't do it, that they'd put me on a destroyer."[80]

Kidd survived World War II unscathed. But twenty-year-old Seaman First Class Clarence Gunther Jr. of the destroyer *Farragut* was wounded twice in quick succession. "I just thought to myself," he later recalled, "if this is gonna happen very often, and if [this] war is gonna last very long, I'm in trouble. Here I've done been hit twice is less than three minutes." The Frankfort sailor survived the rest of World War II and the Korean War without a scratch.[81]

The *Farragut* was nested with the destroyers *Dale* and *Monaghan,* the latter tin can famous for helping sink one of the Japanese midget submarines that sneaked into Pearl Harbor. Gunther was in his bunk reading a newspaper when the general quarters alarm went off. He was not happy; like Kidd, he had liberty. He confessed that he was perturbed even at his skipper, Lieutenant Commander G. P. Hunter, for pulling what he figured was a drill. (Hunter was ashore on liberty.) "They had six days a week to do this stuff, and they should have left us alone on Sunday," he griped. Besides, he wanted to read a newspaper he had "just paid ten cents for." Everybody scrambled for his battle station anyway. Gunther remembered crewmen "running over top of each other and trying to get to their gun stations as fast as they could and taking short-cuts and going up ladders that you should be going down." Some sailors took their time, certain the alarm was only practice, and got shut below decks.[82]

Topside, Gunther felt "more or less like a sitting duck." He saw the flashes from the onrushing planes' wing-mounted machine guns.

Helmetless, in a white T-shirt and matching shorts and socks, he rushed astern, where he was a pointer in a five-inch gun crew. When he joined the navy in 1940, he was "an eighteen-year-old that never had nothing in his hands bigger than a sixteen-gauge shot gun." Like thousands of other sailors across Pearl Harbor, he was bewildered by "all these planes flying around with the red circle painted on them." The only planes he knew were American, and he didn't know whose planes he was seeing until the bombs started falling: "We didn't know the Japanese was all that mad at us. And Lord only knows we wasn't mad at nobody up until then."[83]

Gunther added: "You just don't know what, what's going on. What are they doing this for? Who's doing it? What have we done to somebody to make them mad enough to come over here and blow us up? I'm thinking this, yeah, because . . . what have we done to anybody? I mean, we was friends with everybody in the world, we thought."[84]

The *Farragut's* five-inch guns opened fire at 8:12 A.M. The machine gunners joined in when the enemy planes were in range. The *Monaghan* and the *Dale* left the nest and steamed away, the *Farragut* following just as the second wave struck. Besides bombing and torpedoing the battleships, the first wave pilots strafed targets of opportunity. Gunther guessed that the pilots figured that, "if they hit anything, fine, if they didn't, why, they lost nothing but a few bullets." He also surmised that the fliers were "more or less feeling things out to see what was going to happen" in advance of the second wave.[85]

By the advent of the second wave, Gunther was able to think about what was happening with "these people flying over there and dropping bombs on your ships and tearing up your play toys that you ride around on." When the second wave hit, it had dawned on him "that somebody done, done, done you wrong."[86]

Gunther said that trying to shoot down the wrongdoers was a lot harder in battle than it was during practice, when gunners aimed at canvas sleeves pulled by plodding target tugs: "They're not going all that fast. When you take a plane that's coming at you at 350, 400 miles an hour, why, it's a whole different story all together."[87]

Gunther was wounded just after the *Farragut* started its run for the open sea. Though the Kentuckian was hit twice and carried away to sick bay, Captain G. P. Hunter reported: "No casualties." A bullet struck Gunther's left leg just below the knee, soaking his sock and shoe with blood. Even so, he said, he stayed at his battle station until a shipmate admonished him to "get [his] leg looked after." Seeing his relief man standing by, he left the gun. No sooner did he start for sick bay than shrapnel from a nearby bomb blast laid open the knee on his already wounded leg. He crumpled to the deck. "I should be home," he thought to himself. "I was scared."[88]

Gunther hesitated to look at his leg: "I thought maybe I didn't have one. . . . I didn't know if I had one there or whether they left it laying back there on the deck 'cause it was numb." After a tourniquet was tied above his knee, he headed below. A pharmacist's mate bandaged the bullet wound after putting his thumb underneath the wound and dumping the hole "full of Merthiolate." He then stitched up the shrapnel wound and showed Gunther to a chair.[89]

Gunther said that fear crept in after the attack: "You stop and start thinking about what you'd went through and what you had done and . . . you had never seen anything like it before, and hopefully you'll never see anything like it again, then you start, you start getting scared, and that's when you start shaking." He said Hunter put him in for a Purple Heart but added that he never received the medal. He was later told that he was ineligible because the United States did not declare war on Japan until December 8.[90]

While Gunther pumped five-inch shells at the enemy planes, Seaman Second Class J. C. Riley of the destroyer *Case* supposedly flung his baseball bat at the foe. From Benton, the Marshall County seat, Riley said he did not remember the toss but recalled losing the bat: "Somebody said I threw it at a plane, but I don't know. To this day, I don't have any idea what happened to it."[91]

Riley remembered just about everything else about the Pearl Harbor attack: "Some days you can't forget. This was one of 'em." He was a shipfitter on the *Case,* which was in a nest of six destroyers. Like the *Tucker,* Riley's ship was undergoing routine overhaul. As clocks on the *Case* ticked toward 8:00 A.M., he was topside taking practice swings with his brand-new bat. He had bought it the day before at the Honolulu Sears, Roebuck store. "I played first base on the ship's baseball team and was just kind of goofing around—we had a game with the team from the *Reid,* another destroyer [in the nest], over on Aiea after church services," he recalled.[92]

Riley stopped taking his cuts to watch some planes flying in from the north, the direction of Wheeler Airfield: "I figured they were up pretty early on some kind of maneuvers." He saw the formation break apart, dive low and head for ships at anchor. "Pretty realistic," he thought as he saw some of the planes line up on the *Detroit* and the *Raleigh*. "That's when I saw one of 'em let go with a torpedo. It headed straight for the *Raleigh* and when it hit her it seemed like she jumped ten feet straight in the air."[93]

The pilot pulled up and turned back toward the *Case*. "That big red ball was plain as day on the wings," Riley recalled, "and I knew who was bombing us." He yelled for somebody to sound the general quarters alarm. Somebody did, and the *Case* came alive with sailors sprinting for their battle stations. Riley ran forward, losing track of his bat, and running smack into a torpedo tube. He fell flat, grabbing his throbbing right knee, as a dozen or so sailors stumbled over him. He managed to pull himself up and limp to his battle station inside the ship's number 2 gun turret just below the bridge: "When I got there, there was just one other member of the gun crew present and the gun was inoperable anyway." The sights had been disassembled as part of the overhaul. Unsure what to do next, Riley climbed out of the turret. The executive officer shouted down from the bridge, telling him to go forward and haul down the navy Union Jack—forty-eight stars and the blue field from the Stars and Stripes—which was fluttering from the bow staff.[94]

Riley obeyed as planes roared overhead after torpedoing ships and dropping bombs on Ford Island. "When I got there [i.e., the bow staff], I couldn't reach it," he recalled, "so I climbed the stanchion, unsnapped the flag and brought it back while those planes were buzzing around like bees. See, a Navy ship doesn't get under way with the Union Jack flying." The captain aimed for his crew to put the ship back together and escape Pearl Harbor.[95]

While some of his shipmates shot at the enemy planes with fifty-caliber machine guns—and apparently helped down one—Riley and the five-inch gun crews stood by ready to help. Over the din of battle, Riley heard some *Reid* sailors "cheering like they were at a ballgame": "I never saw anything like it." But, he said, when "a plane flew over and almost knocked our mast off," the rooters scattered for cover.[96]

Riley also spied the *Reid*'s two forward five-inch turret guns open-ing fire on high-flying horizontal-bombers and dive-bombers. The con-cussion blew out windows on the *Case*'s bridge and, according to Riley, missed the enemy: "They were the worst shots you ever saw." Even so, the *Reid*'s skipper claimed his gunners downed a plane. Though the tin cans were strafed sporadically, nobody was killed or wounded on the *Case* or the *Reid*. Both ships got under way and steamed out of Pearl Harbor, the Reid at 10:10 A.M., the *Case* at 4:00 P.M.[97]

"I never understood why we weren't attacked," Riley said. "I guess it was because we were where the planes flew over after bombing on Ford Island where the battleships were." The *Case* passed Battleship Row on its way out to sea. "When we got to the *Oklahoma*," Riley remembered, "we paused to let a tug get by with equipment on board to help get the men out who were trapped and banging on the bottom of the hull. That was the saddest moment in my life. It was like the world had come to a standstill." Yet he bore no ill will toward Japan and even suggested a get-together some day between the attackers and defenders at Pearl Harbor: "Yes sir, I'd really like to see that."[98]

Seaman Second Class James Barnes, from Nortonville, about sixty miles east of Benton, was a sailor without a ship when the Japanese showed up. He called the attack "just plain old hell": "There isn't any other way to describe it." He was assigned to the USS *Long*, a destroyer-minesweeper that had departed Friday with the cruiser *Indianapolis* bound for Johnston Atoll, six hundred miles away, for a mock bombard-ment on December 7. He, Fireman Second Class Zell Zellner, and another sailor stayed behind to run the motor launch. Several shipmates were on weekend liberty when the *Long* left. Barnes and the other sailors were detailed as water taxi drivers, ferrying their shipmates to temporary quarters on other vessels. "Liberty was over at 12 o'clock midnight," Barnes told the *Madisonville Messenger*. "When we went back to pick up the guys . . . they were telling us that the Japanese [Hawaiians] were put-ting up plywood over the windows there at the bars and stores along the highway." Of course, the implication was that they knew the attack was coming and were not telling the military. Apparently, several servicemen believed such rumors of duplicity. Another story had Hawaiian Japanese secretly setting up radar in a sugarcane patch to help guide the enemy planes. Other stories purported that a Hawaiian Japanese milkman used his truck to knock the tails off 150 fighter planes rowed up at Hickam Airfield and that Japanese Hawaiians piloted some of the planes that bombed Pearl Harbor. None of it was true, but it was typical of the conspiratorial fantasies and outright dissembling that circulated before and after the attack.[99]

"Almost immediately a whole folklore centering on Hawaii's Japanese sprang up like a crop of toadstools from the fertile soil of suspicion and hysteria," Prange, Goldstein, and Dillon wrote. The most famous and arguably most ludicrous tale of treachery was the one about Hawaiian Japanese plantation workers cutting arrows in sugarcane fields to guide enemy pilots to Pearl Harbor. "Missing Pearl Harbor from the air over Oahu would be like missing a base drum in a telephone booth," Prange, Goldstein, and Dillon added. Yet the most worrisome tale—that Japanese Hawaiians poisoned drinking water—may have come from Ford Island. The pipeline was not working; a clever supply officer solved the problem by turning a trio of swimming pools into emergency reservoirs. Naturally, the water had to be boiled: "All such rumors and reports were checked as expeditiously as possible. None of the cases investigated proved to be authentic." Nonetheless, rumors of sabotage, largely rooted in hysteria and racism, led to the internment of some Japanese Americans in Hawaii and thousands of Japanese Americans stateside.[100]

Barnes and his buddy Zellner bunked on the destroyer *Hull*, then went back to work Sunday morning, transporting sailors to church services. "I'd just taken 20 guys to church over at Pearl City landing," he remembered. "We'd just unloaded them when the first bomb hit Hickam Field, right off to our right, across from us." He did not see but only heard the blast: "I thought some of them idiots over there were playing."[101]

Then Barnes saw the bombs, the torpedoes, the explosions. He saw ships sag, explode, and catch fire. He saw some men, many wounded, swimming for their lives in the oily water and others floating lifeless: "Harbor Patrol just told us to go over there and do anything we could to help anybody. So we just started picking up dead people and injured people. I guess we had over 150 [corpses] stacked up on the hospital dock, which came right out there in the Pearl Harbor base. . . . We picked up hundreds of men dead, legs off, heads off. We'd take them down to the hospital dock and lay them out. Somebody would come along, check them and see if they were still alive. They did find several of them alive." Barnes recalled stopping the launch to rescue a badly burned sailor: "We were trying to get him out of the water, and his arm come off at the shoulder. He didn't live very long, though."[102]

Nor did Ensign Hubert Hugo Menges of Louisville, but the enemy did not end his life. Panicky Americans did. Menges flew Wildcat fighters with the Fighting Six, a squadron assigned to the *Enterprise,* which arrived off Pearl Harbor on December 7. The nearly 20,000-ton, 825-foot, *Yorktown*-class aircraft carrier dubbed, "The Big" was due back at 7:30 A.M. But stormy seas slowed refueling, and at 6:15 it was still about 250 miles west of Oahu. The carrier was "too far away to be a target and too late to tangle with the Japanese fleet," Martinez said. Unaware of the impending attack, the *Enterprise* launched a scouting flight of nine Dauntless dive-bombers toward Pearl Harbor at 6:30 A.M. After sweeping ahead of the carrier, the planes were to land at the Ford Island Naval Air Station. Around 8:30 A.M., the flight blundered into the raid. Friendly fire claimed two planes. Zeros knocked down four, and one ran low on gas and crash-landed on Oahu. The rest managed to land at Ewa Airfield or the Ford Island airstrip.[103]

Spoiling for a fight with the enemy fleet, the carrier's skipper sent bombers and fighters to find the elusive enemy carrier the *St. Louis* was seeking. All six enemy flattops were north of Oahu and steaming home by midmorning, so the search was fruitless, and all the planes returned to the *Enterprise* save a half dozen Wildcat fighters. By the time they got back, it was too dark to land, and they were sent on to Ford Island Naval Air Station. The air traffic controllers in the tower had been warned by radio that the F4Fs were on the way. To make sure they got down safely, the operations officer dispatched "reliable men" in "cars, [on] motorcycles, etc." to tell riflemen and machine gunners not to shoot. Rear Admiral Patrick N. L. Bellinger, the senior naval air commander in Hawaii, issued several warnings to ships in the harbor that the navy planes were coming. He also told army aircraft gunners to hold their fire.[104]

Menges and the other pilots saw the Ford Island airstrip lighted in anticipation of their arrival. The fliers had their running lights on and came in low as ordered. Fearing the planes were Japanese, soldiers and sailors opened fire. "In less than five seconds, the entire Pearl Harbor area was firing," wrote Lieutenant Commander Earl B. Wilkins, who watched in horror from Ford Island. Tracers crisscrossed the dark sky. The gunfire, wild as it was, was bound to hit somebody. The planes were puttering along at 500 feet with their flaps and wheels down.[105]

Lieutenant (junior grade) Fritz Hebel, the flight leader, raised his flaps and wheels, shoved the throttle forward, and fled north toward Wheeler Airfield. Hit by army gunners, he crashed and was fatally injured. Menges died when his Wildcat was shot down and crashed onto the veranda of the Palm Lodge near the waterfront in Pearl City. Four pilots survived; two bailed out, and the others made it to Ford Island, one landing on the runway, the other on the golf course.[106]

When it hit, Menges's Wildcat started a fire that burned down the lodge. Officials were unable to recover his charred remains until December 11. He was unrecognizable; one of the surviving fliers positively identified him only by the wristwatch still attached to his arm.[107]

On December 8, the *Honolulu Star Bulletin* claimed that the planes were enemy aircraft "headed toward Pearl Harbor to begin the sixth air raid on Oahu." It noted: "At 9:04 [P.M.] Pearl Harbor reported heavy fire with tracer bullets and bombs falling on other sections of town." A report from Democratic territorial governor Joseph B. Poindexter's office said that the "raid" ended at 9:10 P.M.[108]

The story also said that Hickam Airfield's acting assistant fire chief claimed that the Palm Lodge "blaze was visible from all parts of Honolulu." He added that the aircraft were "flying very low with running lights on." The paper also told its readers: "Fifteen hundred volunteers were reported still combatting the blaze at 10:10 P.M., an hour after it started."[109]

Navy officials quickly learned that Menges was dead and how he died. But, as the *Louisville Courier-Journal* reported, the official telegram that arrived at his parents' house in Louisville on December 23 said that the ensign, "formerly. . .a carrier boy for The Courier-Journal," was "missing in action." According to the report, Mrs. and Mrs. Charles Menges got the standard admonishment "not to reveal the name of the ship on which their son was serving or the location of the action in which he was lost." They undoubtedly knew he was a pilot on the *Enterprise* and almost certainly suspected the Japanese shot him down or damaged or sank his ship. The report did not say. In June 1943, when the paper announced the naming of the *Leopold* and the *Menges,* the story said the two "Louisville heroes" died at Pearl Harbor. The implication was that the enemy killed them both. (The Leopolds, of course, knew how their son died.) Like Private Dawson, Ensign Menges was interred on Oahu. Dawson's and Menges's remains came home on the same ship in 1947. Menges was buried in Evergreen Cemetery. His funeral notice did not tell how he died, only that he "passed away Pearl Harbor Day, December 7, 1941." It is evidently unknown when Charles Menges and his wife learned their son's true fate.[110]

If the fire that consumed Menges and his fighter plane "was visible from all parts of Honolulu," Giuseppe "Joe" Incontro could have seen the blaze from the coast guard cutter *Taney,* tied up in the city harbor. He was in the galley preparing Swiss steaks Sunday morning when the crew heard a racket outside the ship. When somebody asked him what to do, he did not waste words on a reply: "Just keep cooking."[111]

Incontro, who lived in Owensboro after the war, said that it took everybody about ten minutes to figure out Pearl Harbor was under air attack. They "saw the smoke" and concluded that they were "being bombed," the Nebraska native recalled. The *Taney* was officially part of Navy Destroyer Division 80, though the vessel still had its coast guard crew. After the attack started, the ship went to general quarters, and the captain prepared to get under way. But no orders came to exit the harbor, and the *Taney* stayed put. Shortly after 9:00 A.M., when the second attack wave appeared over Oahu, the *Taney*'s antiaircraft batteries opened fire with three-inch guns and fifty-caliber machine guns. But the planes were too high to hit, and the cease-fire order was given after twenty minutes.[112]

"We didn't have time to think of where anyone was or what they were doing," Incontro said. "Everybody was very scared. If anybody said they wasn't scared, they were crazy." He found time to dash off a letter to his mother "saying I don't know if we're going to make it or not or even if this letter will make it." It did, and he did. "I guess I was one of the lucky ones," he said.[113]

The Marines

Thomas Crump was as tough as marines go. But he admitted he "was absolutely scared to death" when the attack began. "Never in my life had

I ever witnessed or known anything like that," said Crump, a twenty-year-old private who was standing guard duty on the *Pennsylvania's* gangplank. He eluded death and made sergeant major before he retired from the corps.[114]

Crump joined up in 1940 and was ultimately posted to the marine barracks at the Pearl Harbor Navy Yard and assigned to the navy yard police. It had been an uneventful Sunday morning watch until shortly before 8:00 A.M., when, he told the *Louisville Courier-Journal,* "all of a sudden, all hell broke loose": "We could see the planes coming into the harbor, and you could actually see them drop the bombs." He saw one miss the *Pennsylvania,* which was laid up in dry dock behind the destroyers *Cassin* and *Downes.* All three warships were easy targets; bombs destroyed the tin cans. Another bomb struck the *Pennsylvania;* the concussion knocked Crump flat. A man five feet away fell dead.[115]

The Mississippi-born Crump ended the day with shrapnel wounds to his lip and the back of his head. Bombs bowled him over several more times, but he stuck to his post until 5:00 P.M., at that point helping keep back wives and children desperately searching for loved ones on the blasted and burning ships. "You could see the harbor afire," he recalled. "It just was amazing." He witnessed men stranded in the oily water and trying to swim under the flames. When they surfaced for air, "the oil would stick to their skin and just burn the flesh off their face." He said he was "not trained for the action and damage" he saw at Pearl Harbor because "there was such massive destruction and devastation and mutilation of bodies": "I saw so much during the bombing it makes me feel sick inside to talk about it and think about it."[116]

Crump spent the last six years of his marine career as a recruiter in Louisville—he made his home in Jeffersontown, near the city. He also started the first marine junior ROTC program in the county at Louisville's Seneca High School. He went back to Pearl Harbor but steered clear of the navy yard. He was retired when he returned for the fiftieth anniversary of the raid. He saw the gleaming white *Arizona* Memorial spanning the decomposing hulk of the *Pennsylvania's* sister ship: "Oil seeps . . . from the water, up to the top, and it's almost like tear drops coming up there begging for help."[117]

Private Hubert Gregory, another marine, marched smartly off to World War II. He and his marine barracks company were trooping in regulation formation to their assigned guard duty posts when they spotted a gaggle of low-flying airplanes. "All of a sudden you could see the bullets from the planes strafing the ground," he told the *Paducah Sun.* "It was such a surprise. . . . I didn't even know who was attacking us, and I don't think anybody else did, either. Then I saw the Rising Sun on the planes—they were flying so low it was like you could reach out and grab them."[118]

Gregory, twenty, from Glasgow, grabbed his M-1 off his shoulder, snapped in an eight-round clip, and started banging away at the planes. The men had been issued just one clip apiece. So, when they emptied their rifles, they dashed for cover. The twenty-one-year-old Gregory hid behind a big tree. The company had been trained on thirty- and fifty-caliber machine guns, both weapons capable of downing a plane, especially the latter. "But of course we didn't have them with us," he reported. "It took us 30 or 45 minutes to get our hands on them, and we fired those guns until they were red hot." He said that, because Battleship Row was only a few hundred yards distant, "there were planes all over the place": "It seemed like such a long attack, but it really wasn't. You always thought you'd be the next one to get it. . . . [T]hat stayed in your thoughts."[119]

So did the carnage Gregory witnessed after the enemy flew away: "There was so much smoke and fire—you just can't forget it. There was lots of confusion, and everybody was all torn up. . . . Then the focus turned to putting out the fires and looking for the wounded." Gregory was unhurt and counted himself among the fortunate: "I've always felt lucky because I could have been one of the ones who didn't make it. Thousands of good men didn't."[120]

Private John Edwards Wood also counted himself among the lucky marines. When he got back from breakfast, he heard some of his tentmates in the Fourth Marine Defense Battalion gassing about seeing planes and hearing antiaircraft fire. Some were wondering who was having maneuvers that Sunday morning, so Wood, who lived in Glasgow after the war, decided to have a look for himself. As he told the *Franklin Favorite:* "I went out between the tent rows and saw planes that were high and seemed to be following the coast line down from Honolulu toward Pearl Harbor and Hickam Field. You could see one plane right after another."[121]

Wood's battalion had left the navy base at Guantanamo Bay, Cuba, bound for Wake Island. The ship paused at Pearl Harbor on December 1. "We were actually in transit," Wood said, adding that, when the Japanese attacked, the battalion's rifles were still crated up. "I wasn't right down in the harbor area; I was outside it between Pearl Harbor and Honolulu."[122]

Wood, twenty-one, was unsure whether the attack was a drill or real until he saw "one plane burst into a ball of fire": "That was too real to be maneuvers. When we found out it was the real thing, they started breaking open storage crates and giving everybody a rifle and ammunition." The North Carolina–born Wood said they were ordered to shoot at the planes even though they were too high to hit. But nearby antiaircraft batteries opened up with potent firepower: "A plane circled around and you could see that red ball under [the wings]. . . . The plane didn't drop any bombs but flew toward Honolulu."[123]

He said that the antiaircraft gunners were firing over the heads of the marines, who were flat on their bellies, hugging the ground: "It was just too close for comfort. We ran up there to a building that was under construction; it was a marine base later named Camp Catlin." The building had a roof but no sides: "We all jumped over inside of it and . . . laid down against that concrete footing and put our hands over the back of our heads and were just hoping [the antiaircraft shells] . . . wouldn't come any closer to us than they were."[124]

Wood remembered that, when the firing stopped, "everybody that was in there kind of raised up and looked around." He said his head was about a foot from another marine's head: "We both raised up and looked at the same time." Neither spoke, but Wood said the other man's "face was white, just as white as it could be": "I just wondered to myself if my face was as white as his. That was the most uneasy moment I had during the attack that morning."[125]

Before he joined the marines, Wood fought forest fires and built roads in the Depression-era Civilian Conservation Corps. As hard as that work was, Wood said it did not prepare him for battle since he had arrived on Oahu only six days before the attack: "While we were in boot camp some of the boys were talking about where they wanted to go after boot camp and someone said Pearl Harbor. The rest of us didn't even know where Pearl Harbor was; we never had heard of it. As far as

I know I ended up being the only one from my platoon that went to Pearl Harbor."[126]

Marine Private First Class Ellis O'Neal of Carrollton was stationed at Ewa, seven miles west of Pearl Harbor. He hitched a ride to war in a bread truck. "We didn't have a bakery at our base," he said. "They'd send this truck every morning to Pearl Harbor and they'd pick up bread." The truck returned "with all these blocks of ice and bread in the back": "We jumped on the back of the truck, about a half-dozen of us, and pushed all this ice and bread off onto the ground." Having made room for themselves, they told the driver to make a beeline for the flight line.[127]

Ewa was hit early and hard. The enemy damaged or destroyed every plane in the first attack. Like General Short, the marine brass feared sabotage and ordered aircraft rowed up wingtip to wingtip in the open. Parked near the runways, the fighters and bombers were especially vulnerable. Nonetheless, braving a storm of machine-gun and cannon fire, pilots and ground crews tried to get their planes in the air or drag them out of harm's way. It was to no avail; the attackers left the flight lines afire and in shambles.[128]

Other attacks followed. The only bright spot in an otherwise dismal day was the absence of eighteen scout bombers that were aboard the *Lexington* and bound for the US base on Midway Island.[129]

O'Neal was an aircraft mechanic, but he was watering flowers when the air raid began. He saw the planes and figured it was another drill. Other marines who spotted the red rising-sun insignia guessed that the aircraft were from the "red" team. O'Neal knew the raid was real when machine-gun and cannon rounds started kicking up dirt a hundred feet from him: "They made several passes over the field like that. One right after the other. . . . The planes started burning."[130]

O'Neal said: "[The enemy pilots] weren't interested in us at all. They wanted the planes. They made no effort to take any of us out at all. . . . They knew we weren't going to hurt 'em." But the marines tried, scrambling to the barracks for their rifles, which were unloaded. On weekends, he explained, the bullets were locked up across the airstrip. To get at the ammo would require running a gauntlet of strafing fire, wide open with neither cover nor concealment. Hence, they hijacked the bread truck.[131]

The driver raced across the airstrip, stopping and starting randomly, hoping to spoil the enemy pilots' aim. He and his passengers made it;

the marines tumbled out, broke the locks off the ammo crates, loaded their rifles, and started shooting back. O'Neal remembered: "I don't know how many rounds I might have fired, but I don't think we ever hit anything to do any damage. . . . You'd have to be a pretty good shot to hit 'em. You'd just be more or less shooting. And they were more or less laughing at us while they were shooting at us. Even some guys were using pistols."[132]

The marines managed more firepower than O'Neal realized. They salvaged working machine guns from shot-up planes and stuck them on makeshift mounts. Somebody discovered that the rear machine gun of a scout bomber still worked and trained the weapon on the enemy. Ewa machine gunners downed at least one plane and claimed another probable. O'Neal was not hurt, but three marines were killed during the attacks, fourteen others were wounded, one fatally.[133]

6

The Dungaree Navy

Sailors who served on auxiliary vessels or support units ashore dubbed themselves "the Dungaree Navy." Sailors on battlewagons and other large warships often had to turn up for inspection in dress blues or dress whites. Full-dress inspections were less frequent on the likes of tenders, repair ships, tugs, and landing craft, where uniform regulations were more relaxed. Enlisted crews spent most of their time in chambray shirts and bell-bottomed jeans, the latter called *dungarees.*

Anyway, the USS *Curtiss* gunnery officer Eugene B. Hayden of Owensboro must have been proud of his men for helping sink a midget submarine and shooting down some planes. But the lieutenant missed the action. He was among nine officers and fifty-five men ashore, at home or on liberty. The attack was mostly over by the time he was able to catch a boat to his ship, a seaplane tender.[1]

Lieutenant Hayden found the *Curtiss* in bad shape, having been strafed, bombed, and hit hard on the starboard side by a Val his gunners shot down as it pulled out of a dive on Ford Island. The plane caught fire and crashed into the starboard side of the *Curtiss* against the ship's number 1 crane. The impact caused the gas tank to explode, setting the tender on fire, and causing the crew to abandon the number 3 gun temporarily. Seven minutes later, a bomb hit the ship. The blast killed twenty men and wounded fifty-five more. One man was reported missing.[2]

Hayden was still asleep when the attack started. The lieutenant, his wife, Julia, and their three-year-old daughter, Sue Gene, lived in a small court near the army's Fort DeRussy and beside the Hale Koa Hotel. Walter Pack, the *Curtiss* chaplain, was their neighbor. Hayden said: "The sound of gunfire, really just a distant throbbing . . . first woke my wife and then myself. She shook me and said, 'That sounds like gun fire. Why are they doing that on Sunday morning?'"[3]

Hayden listened for a few minutes before he remembered that, a few days before, the fleet was advised that some of the gunnery practice areas had been shifted. Hayden suspected that a breeze was "blowing the sound in" from the new areas. But he conceded that Sunday morning was "kind of a funny time for them to be shooting."[4]

A few minutes later, Julia rolled out of bed and switched on the radio. "Planes are apparently attacking Pearl Harbor," an excited announcer reported. The news propelled her spouse out of the sack. He saw a young army captain across the street. He yelled at him, hoping to find out what was happening. "I guess you [navy] guys are getting the same treatment we had last week," he replied, referring to an army alert. The captain explained that everybody was supposed to act like it was a real attack without warning. They even had to hustle "down to their Army stations and go through a battle exercise and then return home." Hayden guessed it was probably the navy's turn, shrugging: "It looks like we're in for it this week."[5]

By the time Hayden got dressed—in civilian clothes—the radio crackled with more bulletins reporting the planes as Japanese. He remained skeptical even though he could hear more noise and now spied smoke rising from Pearl Harbor. He decided to investigate and headed for his car with the padre and another young officer housed at the court. He said he stopped and thought to himself: "Well, this might keep me aboard ship for a long while. I'm not going to need money and my wife will, so I ran back and handed her my wallet and said, 'You'll need this more than I will.' I think that scared her more than anything else when I did that."[6]

Hayden said that he hopped in his car with his passengers and the trio rode off to their first battle. None of them knew what to expect when they arrived, if they arrived. The carpoolers headed west along their "usual route towards Pearl Harbor." This made them go through Honolulu: "And according to our custom, coming from the Waikiki area, we went along the coastline and the coastal roads and streets. The closer we got to Pearl Harbor, the more we began to realize that there really was something going on. The radio was still blaring out."[7]

They drove along Ala Wai Boulevard, noticing "various small machine guns units being set up along the side of the road." They also spotted air-raid wardens in "old time World War I helmets . . . appearing all over the area, particularly along the roads." As the threesome neared the highway to Pearl Harbor and Hickam Airfield, they saw more wardens forcing civilians off the road to clear the way for military traffic. "Most of us were in civilian clothes," Hayden said. "We normally would keep our uniforms aboard ship and wear civilian clothes home in the evenings." A military ID was stuck on the car, so the wardens waved them through.[8]

Most of the wardens Hayden saw were Asian Americans. He recalled: "I'm sure some were Chinese, some were Japanese, some were Filipino, but they were . . . members of the Civilian Air Raid Group and were doing their job that morning." He discounted rumors of sabotage by and disloyalty among Japanese Hawaiians: "I believe the majority of the Japanese people were really loyal. In fact, I think many of them would consider themselves much more American than Japanese. After all, Hawaii has many Orientals. And they were simply Japanese by birth just like there were nationals of England or Germany or anywhere else. They just simply were of Japanese ancestry and that was all. They were not loyal to Japan."[9]

At Hickam Airfield, army guards took a quick look inside the car and motioned them on. At Pearl Harbor a guard saw they had ID cards in hand, peeked in the car, and sent them on their way. Hayden noted: "In retrospect, he may have been a little bit careless [because] . . . obviously people could have come in and committed a fair amount of sabotage. On the other hand, it was all so very necessary to get the personnel back to the ships. So, I presume they had received orders considering that getting the personnel back was of greater importance than the possible infiltration of some saboteur." After dropping off his riders, Hayden headed to Hospital Point, the customary landing area for boats from the *Curtiss*.[10]

The attack was petering out by the time he reached the dock. Hayden remembered seeing "all these ships smoking in the bay" and sighting "a few Japanese planes coming down." He figured the aircraft were "reconnaissance planes." But he saw evidence of strafing—"a burst of machine gun fire from the planes and occasionally . . . a streak or flashes in the water or near the ships where bullets were entering." It was all surreal, he said: "It felt in a sense that I was watching a newsreel. It did dawn on me as I was standing on this open dock that this was no place for a fellow when there was shooting going on." He retreated from the dock and took refuge, such as it was, behind a coconut palm. "I could at least kinda watch the dock for something coming in and felt that I had a little protection although after a while the coconut tree I was behind seemed pretty small. I went and looked around for a bigger one, but there weren't any."[11]

Finally, two boats arrived. Somebody on one of them said that the *Pennsylvania,* dry-docked nearby, was on fire and that its magazines were expected to blow. (They did not explode.) No matter, boats were ferrying wounded men to the hospital. They were also shuttling crewmen to their ships. Hayden needed a lift to the *Curtiss* and thus hitched a ride. When the boat shoved off, he felt as if he was in a theater watching "the panorama from a newsreel": "I can well understand how people back in the states couldn't believe it. I could not have believed it then and yet I was seeing it."[12]

On the way to his ship, Hayden had a clear view down Battleship Row: "I could see the *Arizona* sitting down. I could see the *Oklahoma* turned over." He did not realize that the *Arizona* had blown up: "She looked lower in the water, but at the same time she was upright. There was a lot of smoke around her." He saw smoke rising from other super-dreadnoughts, too, and witnessed "a lot of activity going around:": "There were ammunition cans, floatable cans, strewn all over the harbor, many bits of debris." He did not remember seeing any bodies in the water or men struggling to swim to safety since they had "swung wide of the battleships on the way to the *Curtiss*." But, as the boat rounded Ford Island and neared his ship, he caught a glimpse of many planes on fire.[13]

Hayden planned to climb aboard on the *Curtiss*'s starboard side. The tender was listing in that direction from the bomb strike. "I got the impression that it was away over on its side," he noted. "Actually, it was only about five or ten degrees, which did give you sort of [a] frightening feeling as you went up the ladder holding on to the sides and seeing the water way down below you and the ship above you."[14]

The tilt might have seemed worse than it was, but a big part of the *Curtiss* was in shambles. He saw the burning Val "above the hangar that [he] had to go under." Part of the hangar was ablaze from the bomb strike.[15]

When he reached the bridge, Hayden found his assistant gunnery officer, Ensign G. K. Nicodemus Jr. Nicodemus told Hayden that he had given up all attempts at directed fire and told the gun crews to fire at will. He said they had a harder time because new equipment that would have helped them fire faster and more accurately had been sent to the *Albemarle,* a twin seaplane tender that was stateside in Norfolk, Virginia.[16] Nonetheless, H. S. Kendall, the skipper, reported: "Not less than three enemy planes were victims of gunfire from the *Curtiss.*" (He also bragged that the midget submarine "was seriously damaged if not totally disabled by the Curtiss.")[17]

After a while, Hayden joined one of the five-inch gun crews and "worked from there for the remainder of the morning, not that there was much work for a gunnery officer to do since all of the stations were really on their own." When each gunner saw a target approaching, he had to "try to get his gun into a position where he could intercept its course, and hope to fire when [he] . . . had a reasonable chance of hitting the plane." Hayden said it was like applying old-fashioned "Kentucky windage."[18]

Hayden heard that his gunners evidently hit "about three planes": "Most of them were coming in at a fairly low level, sometimes almost on a level with our deck." He also learned that some crewmen shot at their tormentors with rifles and pistols. Supposedly, somebody even threw raw potatoes at the enemy. "If you didn't have anything else and you wanted to get into the fight, you used whatever you could lay your hands on," he said.[19]

Ammunition for five-inch guns like the ones on the *Curtiss* came in two parts: a fused, metal exploding projectile and a metal powder case. Gunners rammed in the projectile, then the case, which had a cork plug in the upper end that fit against the projectile's base. Firing the gun blew out the cork and sent the shell on its way. Hayden said that, early in that attack, some gunners received powder before shells. In their haste to get at the enemy planes, they sometimes fired tools and dummy practice shells, the latter "just simply chunks of metal that normally were used in loading exercises, without explosives or anything in it." He explained that crewmen "threw everything into the gun that they could ahead of the powder and let it go": "There must have been a lot of monkey wrenches and so on flying around in the air out there. And it's amazing that perhaps more damage was not done to adjacent ships and to the city of Honolulu and the naval station of Pearl Harbor."[20]

When Hayden got back to his ship, all the guns were shooting, although "many of them not with their regular crews but manned by anyone who happened to be within reach and could be pulled in to the operation": "There was a lot of very rapid gunnery training going on that morning. Many people who had never been on a gun before became proficient gunners in a short order."[21]

After the attackers flew away, Hayden had time to survey the wreckage all around him. The nearby *Tangier*, a cargo ship that had been turned into a seaplane tender, was smoking heavily, though "there wasn't too big of a fire or anything." Yet the *Utah*, moored ahead of the *Tangier*, "was turned over so that her bottom was up in the air": "There was no indication of how many people had been trapped inside." (Fifty-eight crewmen died.) But he saw rescue workers with acetylene torches "cutting their way into the ship": "Of course, they had no possible way of getting out except a hole were cut in the ship."[22]

Hayden said that, around noon or one o'clock, "things topside finally quieted down" enough for him to go to his quarters and put on his uniform. He said that the main wardroom had been converted into an auxiliary hospital because "our usual little sick bay . . . was also overflowing." Doctors were operating in both places. He was shocked at the sight of dead crewmen "lying out on the floor with the sheets over them" in a small side room.[23]

Hayden grabbed a couple of sandwiches in the wardroom and ate them while he changed into his uniform. He returned to the bridge unsure what to do next: "The harbor had quieted down quite a bit and a good deal of work was going on trying to get the ship's debris cleared away." That sped up repair work. He said that the *Curtiss* was not leaking badly and that the ship had been righted to "a pretty even keel."[24]

Hayden and Kendall credited Nicodemus with blasting the small sub. The ensign was commanding the aft five-inch gun crew. They fired and missed because the gun's sights were not set for a target so close. So he sighted the old navy way—along the barrel—and ordered the crew to fire again: "The recoil of the gun kicked Nick across the deck . . . and certainly bruised up his chest quite considerably, although miraculously he escaped without any injuries that we know of." Hayden was convinced that Nicodemus holed the conning tower.[25] In his report, Kendall commended the ensign for effectively directing "fire on the enemy submarine which unquestionably disabled the submarine."[26]

Seaman First Class H. S. Reeves of Paducah had a different take on who holed the little sub. He claimed that the honor belonged to a gun crew on his ship, the *Medusa,* a repair ship. He said that the midget submarine popped up just he was dashing for his battle station, one of four five-inch guns, the ship's main firepower. According to the twenty-one-year-old sailor, the gunners "just couldn't depress their big guns low enough to hit him." Machine-gun bullets "just rattled off" the conning tower.[27]

Reeves was in the starboard broadside gun crew. After he and his mates eluded bullets from a strafing Japanese plane, he figured they might have a crack at the sub if they could depress their gun and swing it astern. But stanchions supporting deck railing were in the way and could not be removed quickly: "They were pretty rusty. It took guys beating on them with sledgehammers to lay them down." Mission accomplished, the crew swung the gun around, and Reeves said he had the conning tower in his gun's sight.[28]

"Then all of a sudden I saw this hole appear right in it," he recalled. "An old three-inch-fifty anti-aircraft gun above me had got him."[29] (The skipper evenhandedly reported: "Many shots could plainly be seen hitting the conning tower from both the Medusa and Curtiss.")[30] In any event, the destroyer *Monaghan* charged up and finished off the target. With *Medusa* and *Curtiss* gunners holding their fire, the tin can rammed the submarine and blew it up with depth charges. All the while, Reeves was getting his baptism of fire bareheaded: "There weren't enough helmets to go around." That particularly worried a shipmate below, Reeves's brother, Machinist's Mate Second Class L. W. Reeves: "Every time he got a chance, he'd pop out on deck and tell me to be careful or to keep my head down."[31]

Paducah is about forty-six miles west of Golden Pond, the hometown of Reeves's shipmate Vance Leneave (who moved to Cadiz after Golden Pond was removed to make room for the Land Between the Lakes national recreation area). Leneave, twenty-one, was off duty. Reeves, a year his junior, was set to join a paint detail. His job never started.[32]

"We were lying around on our cots, taking it easy," Leneave remembered. "Suddenly, a shipmate, clad only in skivvy shorts, poked his head inside the machine shop and shouted, 'Here come the Japanese!' Cleghorn was his name. How he recognized those planes so fast I'll never know." Seconds later came the general alarm, and sailors hustled for their battle stations. Leneave's was in the foundry, a deck below the waterline: "It wasn't long until I got to thinking what would happen to this place if a torpedo hit us and about how much I'd like to be somewhere else."[33]

Leneave's fellow Kentuckian Reeves was coxswain on a fifty-foot motor launch scheduled for a short journey to the navy yard, where the boat was to be spruced up and painted. He said the general quarters alarm forestalled the trip. He recalled that the alert was less than regulation: "The quartermaster of the watch got on the bullhorn and started yelling, 'General Quarters! General Quarters! Man your guns. This is no vulgar-word, vulgar-word drill!'" Reeves had heard what he thought sounded liked a couple of muffled explosions from over toward the Ford Island seaplane ramp, but he could not tell for sure.[34]

Leneave got his chance to go to war topside. Volunteers were needed to help carry thirty-caliber ammunition to feed two machine guns at each end of the signal bridge, and he pitched in.[35] He and the others must have done a good job. After the attack, A. E. Schrader, the skipper, reported: "Both A.A. [antiaircraft] guns and both machine guns kept up a continuous fire." Schrader "definitely saw four . . . planes shot down": "One fell on the boat deck of the *Curtiss* [the *Curtiss*'s captain claimed his gunners had shot it down] and burst into flames; one dropped [a] bomb close to the stern of the *Medusa* and immediately thereafter disintegrated as the result of a shell hit which I believe was made by *Medusa* #6 A.A. Gun. (A welcome sight.)"[36] Even so, Leneave questioned the barrage's effectiveness: "Our guys seemed mostly to be wasting time and ammunition. Some of them were even shooting with old Springfields and Browning automatic rifles but I guess the shooting made everybody feel good."[37]

The *Medusa* got credit for destroying two Japanese planes and helping send the sub to the bottom of Pearl Harbor.[38] "Later, they painted little Japanese flags on the bridge for the two planes and the sub and wherever we went for the rest of the war people would ask, 'Where did an old tub like that get those flags?'" Leneave said.[39]

The *Medusa* sustained minor damage from strafing and shrapnel. "The only casualty we suffered was one sailor who was struck in the arm by a piece of shrapnel," Leneave said. Though none were from Leneave's ship, bodies floated in the oily water for several days: "The boat crews from the *Medusa* and the other auxiliary ships combed the harbor, picking up the dead. They'd attach lines to the bodies and tow them to the dock." But part of the *Medusa's* work was lifesaving. A crew from the ship helped rescue efforts on the capsized *Oklahoma*. As Leneave noted: "They worked from Sunday until Tuesday getting those men out."[40]

Leneave returned to Pearl Harbor twice after the war. His war mementos included a Honolulu newspaper about Pearl Harbor Day and a chunk of shrapnel he dug from the *Medusa's* deck. "You know," he recalled, "that was one of the cleanest harbors you ever saw before the attack, but it seemed like they never could get all that oil cleaned up afterwards. It was sort of like a reminder of what happened."[41]

Over on the repair ship *Argonne,* docked in the navy yard, Shipfitter Second Class James E. Smith said that he "had a ringside seat" for the attack, adding: "Wasn't nothing between them and me but space."[42] The twenty-year-old Louisville native was a fifty-caliber-machine-gun loader but confessed that the gunners he served were less than marksmen. They shot down the ship's antenna and nearly hit the Fourteenth Naval District signal tower on Ford Island. (The errant fire must have chagrined Rear Admiral William L. Calhoun, the Pacific Fleet base force commander because the *Argonne* was his flagship.) At least one marine corporal could shoot straight; the *Argonne's* skipper credited him with downing a Japanese bomber.[43]

Smith, who went to war helmetless and without a life jacket, also admitted that, before the attack, he "didn't know what a Japanese insignia was": "I knew nothing about the rising sun." So, when he peeked out a porthole above his locker "and saw this big red ball" on a passing plane, he told a shipmate: "Looks like they're having maneuvers early in the morning. Aircraft everywhere." The sailor replied: "Maneuvers, hell! It's the real thing." Smith believed him when he saw a Ford Island hangar blow up. The *Argonne* suffered no casualties and sustained minor damage, though Smith heard the *Arizona* explode and saw the *Oklahoma* capsize and the *West Virginia* sink.[44]

Smith had joined the navy for four years in 1938. He was a short timer, counting the days until his hitch was up on December 22, which meant he might be home for Christmas. He planned to start a farm on the $1,200 navy pay he had saved. He was tired of Hawaii anyway. "The newness had wore off," he told the *Louisville Courier-Journal.* "We got American music only 30 minutes a day. That was from 12 to 12:30. It was 'Singin' Sam the Coca-Cola man.'"[45]

From his Ford Island vantage point, Seaman Second Class Perry Calhoun of Eddyville probably could have seen the *Argonne.* He was on the fourth floor of the big navy barracks on Ford Island and expecting trouble finding an empty rack for drying his duds. The Sabbath was his wash day. Shortly before 8:00 A.M., he heard an airplane close by, looked from a fourth-floor window, and saw it swoop down and drop a bomb on a ship. "A big column of smoke rolled up," he remembered, "and I thought to myself, 'Boy, is that pilot in trouble.'"[46]

Calhoun knew about planes and pilots. He was a metalsmith with Utility Squadron 1, which was equipped with unarmed aircraft that did yeoman's chores such as delivering mail, towing targets, and taking aerial photographs. He said that the most potent weapons in his outfit were old World War I–vintage Springfield rifles: "Some of the boys grabbed them up and started shooting at the planes." He saw one crash near the *Utah.*[47]

USS *Utah* Memorial, Pearl Harbor.

Japanese Zero fighter in the Pearl Harbor Aviation Museum.

Specially modified Japanese aerial torpedo and bomb in the Pearl Harbor Aviation Museum.

Admiral Husband E. Kimmel (Naval History and Heritage Command).

Aerial view of Battleship Row (official US Navy photograph).

USS *Shaw* exploding (Library of Congress).

USS *Arizona* (Library of Congress).

USS *Arizona* wreckage (Library of Congress).

James Allard Vessels (Market House Museum, Paducah, Kentucky).

James Allard Vessels (Market House Museum, Paducah, Kentucky).

James Allard Vessels, seated, and Ross Worth Lightfoot (Market House Museum, Paducah, Kentucky).

USS *Oklahoma* capsized (Library of Congress).

USS *Oklahoma* Memorial, Pearl Harbor.

Samuel Crowder column, USS *Oklahoma* Memorial, Pearl Harbor.

Chaplain Howell Forgy (First Presbyterian Church, Murray, Kentucky).

USS *New Orleans* (official US Navy photograph).

Chaplain William A. Maguire on the cover of *Life* magazine (courtesy of Marion Belote O'Rourke).

V. C. Kidd (courtesy of Gary Kidd).

Clarence Gunther Jr. (Kentucky Military Museum, Frankfort).

The grave of Herbert Hugo Menges, Evergreen Cemetery, Louisville.

US Navy Wildcat fighter in the Pearl Harbor Aviation Museum.

Hickam Airfield damage (Library of Congress).

Wheeler Airfield wreckage (Library of Congress).

Luby Saxon (courtesy of Taira McAfee, Mayfield, Kentucky).

7

The Army

Architects of the Pearl Harbor attack knew that, to destroy the fleet, the raiders had to have air superiority. Hence, several fighters and bombers peeled away to destroy army, navy, and marine air bases and planes on the ground. Their prime targets included Hickam and Wheeler Army Airfields, the largest and most important bases on Oahu. (The Japanese also bombed and strafed Ford Island and Kaneohe Naval Air Stations, Ewa Marine Air Station, and Bellows Army Airfield.) Because the Japanese had no intention of invading Hawaii, they did not go after the army's formidable coastal defenses around Pearl and Honolulu Harbors. They also bypassed Fort Shafter in Honolulu, but some enemy planes did strafe Schofield Barracks after they hit adjacent Wheeler.

Hickam Airfield

In 1935, the army established Hickam Airfield next to the Pearl Harbor navy base and close to the harbor entrance. The base, named for Lieutenant Colonel Horace Meek Hickam, a pioneer army aviator who had died in a 1934 airplane crash in Texas, became the army's main airfield and bomber base in Hawaii and also the air force's headquarters. Hickam Airfield became Hickam Air Force Base after World War II. In 2010, the navy base and the air base merged to form Joint Base Pearl Harbor–Hickam.[1]

On December 7, 1941, fifty-one aircraft were on the ground, and a dozen B-17 bombers were expected from California about eight that morning. The bombers blundered into the attack, with Zeros and Vals working over Hickam. Though the B-17s were unarmed and low on fuel, the big bombers managed to land, nine at Hickam, where one was destroyed on landing and another damaged beyond repair. Three B-17s landed elsewhere on Oahu. A second wave hit at 8:40 A.M. and ended

136

about an hour later. The Japanese fliers destroyed or badly damaged about half the aircraft at Hickam. They also bombed and strafed hangars, the Hawaiian Air Depot, and a number of base facilities, including the fire station, the chapel, the guardhouse, and the large barracks. All told, 121 men were killed, 274 wounded, and 37 listed as missing.[2]

Naturally, the B-17 crews were bone-tired after a grueling fourteen-hour flight from the states. Doubtless, their unexpected reception provided adrenaline jolts. When they neared Hickam Airfield, the airmen suddenly faced a double threat—from both enemy and friendly fire. Zeros were shooting at them, and antiaircraft gunners were shooting at the Zeros. "We were flying into Pearl Harbor fat, dumb and happy, with no ammunition and nobody knowing there was a war going on," the copilot Richard J. Eberentz told his hometown *Louisville Courier-Journal.*[3]

Captain Eberentz huddled with the paper while he was home on leave in January 1943. He had been a second lieutenant when the attack took place. "It was about 8 A.M. and the fireworks were really popping. The anti-aircraft fire was popping all around. I don't blame the boys for shooting at us; they were shooting at everything that might be a Jap plane, and you could hardly tell one from another, but the result was—well, we had to land! You could see those tracers popping right through the wings. It was fascinating."[4]

Eberentz's B-17 landed at Hickam safely, though the *Courier-Journal* headline claimed: "U.S. Ack-Ack Downed Eberentz at Pearl Harbor." He did not say what his crew did after they landed. But, as other B-17s rolled to a stop, the men they were carrying tumbled out and ran for their lives.[5]

Two days after Christmas, Eberentz was nearly killed again, but not by the enemy. His B-17 ran out of gas on patrol, and he ditched in the sea about 125 miles west of Oahu. The crew clambered into life rafts and spent four days in the water. Weary and hungry, the airmen weathered two storms before a navy seaplane picked them up about four hundred miles from where they went down. "Things got twisted and it was a combination of everybody's fault—that's how a lot of things were in those days," confessed Eberentz, who was bitten by an albatross as he bobbed on the briny. He killed the offending fowl and saved the beak as a trophy.[6]

Meanwhile, Second Lieutenant Philip Claudius Sprawls did not hit the hay until the wee hours of December 7. The pilot had been partying at the Hickam officers' club and did not hit the sack at his apartment until 4:00 A.M., after dropping off his date—a Hula dancer—at her place. His digs overlooked Pearl Harbor, from whence the boom of a distant explosion woke him just before eight. He rolled over in bed: "Boom came another one." He blamed the slumber-sabotaging racket on the navy "doing practice on Sunday morning."[7]

Sprawls, a South Carolinian who ended up in Louisville after the war, heard more explosions. When he parted the blinds, he spotted "huge billows of black smoke rising from Ford Island": "So then I knew something was wrong." He started pulling on his clothes "when a projectile of some sort came through the window and into the ceiling" of his apartment. Unfazed, he finished dressing and hitched a ride to Hickam.[8]

Sprawls arrived unhurt outside his squadron's hangar and crossed a street that paralleled the hangar line. He heard an enemy plane, fell to the ground, and covered his face. But, when he glanced over and saw "an airman lying there with his body burning," he thought: "'Oh Lordy, this is serious.'" He got up and bolted for the hangar, where he discovered that all the fire extinguishers had been drained and that water pressure was gone. The squadron commanding officer, expecting more bombing and strafing, ordered his men to hunt cover.[9]

Not everybody did. Sprawls spied some men standing against a wall gawking at the planes: "It flashed through my mind, 'That looks like a position for a firing squad, and I don't believe I'll do that. I'm gonna get out here in the open by this lamppost.'"[10]

Sprawls stuck by the pole as the attackers kept bombing and shooting up the airfield: "And here came one, and I could see the dust jumping up from this machine-gun fire coming right at me. I scooted around that lamppost, got on the lee side of it so fast that I ripped my wristwatch off. When he had passed, I decided I'd get away from that." He had sprinted about a hundred yards when he heard the whistle of a falling bomb: "So I threw myself down in the gutter. . . . The bomb went off and it kicked me up, oh, 12 inches or so off the pavement, and I thought, 'Oh, Lord, if I just get out of this one, they'll never catch me.'" They caught many men but not Sprawls, who afterward wrote an old Clemson professor: "I lived a lifetime in a few hours, but I escaped injuries."[11]

Nineteen-year-old Private Donald L. Ralph earned a Purple Heart even though he survived without a scratch. The X-ray technician got the medal for braving Japanese bombs and strafing fire as an ambulance driver. Not until FDR's December 1942 executive order was the decoration awarded to those killed or wounded "in action against an enemy of the United States."[12]

Ralph, from Ohio County, had just finished breakfast at the new hospital when the Japanese struck: "At first, like everyone else, I thought it was our Navy practicing but when the bombs started to fall it didn't take any of us long to make up our minds that this was the real thing. I ran out of the hospital, grabbed an ambulance and drove it for the remainder of the day."[13]

Luckily, nothing blew out the tires. "But," Ralph remembered, "the ambulance was certainly shot up pretty badly." He and his fellow medics "didn't have time to think about anything except getting the wounded men to hospitals": "We put all of the wounded possible into the ambulance on litters, and others, not so badly injured, would sit up."[14]

Ralph could not recall how many trips he made, but he explained that it was six miles from Hickam Airfield to Tripler General Hospital, where he took the more seriously wounded. "I really gave 'er the gun," he said, adding: "It pained many of the wounded men in the ambulance when I skidded around corners, but all they would keep telling me was, 'Give 'er hell, Doc, and go back after the other guys.'" He said he witnessed "bodies [damaged] in more ways that I could ever imagine." He saw men lying on the ground, helpless, with their legs gone: "And all they'd tell us was, 'Don't bother about me, help the other guys who need help.' That takes guts." He said that, after the raid ended, he "just wondered how in hell" he got through it alive.[15]

William David Payne of Hardin in Marshall County was in the big barracks when the attack started. He could hardly believe his eyes when he glanced from a third floor window "and saw a Jap plane with a torpedo heading toward Pearl Harbor": "The plane was at eye level with me."[16]

His first thought was to flee what he figured—correctly—would be a prime target. After the first wave of attackers flew away the eighteen-year-old Payne rushed to the flight line to help disperse the bombers. More enemy aircraft showed up to shoot up the base. Payne pulled his forty-five-caliber automatic pistol and blazed away: "They were within range, but not much chance of getting one." He said that one of the B-17 pilots asked him what was up: "I told him I thought it was the Japs."[17]

Major George T. Ingram was another Hickam hero. But, back home in Kentucky in 1943, he worried that American outrage over Pearl Harbor had faded. "The trouble back here in this country now is that the people aren't mad," he told a *Louisville Courier-Journal* reporter. "They have lost their anger. They should remember what happened . . . and stay mad. The war might be shortened that way."[18]

Ingram, from Williamsburg, was at the Louisville airport about to catch a plane back to the Pacific theater, where a new assignment awaited him. He hesitated before confessing that he thought Americans were complacent. "Lacking a better word, I guess that's it—complacent," he said. He also admitted that he reached his verdict "only after brief observation" while visiting the home front. He added that he could be wrong. Switching subjects, he recalled the "one-sided fight" at Hickam: "We were sorely outnumbered and the odds against us were heavy. Our boys displayed magnificent courage in the face of those odds."[19]

Ingram earned a Silver Star "for heroism in action during the attack," according to the medal's citation. He was officer of the day on the hangar line at the post operations building. "In order to secure essential information from an incoming plane, Captain Ingram, rather than subject another man to the hazards of direct fire from enemy planes, himself successfully performed the mission," the citation also said. "He then immediately organized and led a group of men to disperse aircraft; directed operations for extinguishing fires, and personally transported wounded soldiers to the Station Hospital in his automobile. His alertness and keen judgment were instrumental in saving many lives and much valuable government property. The courage, leadership, and devotion to duty displayed by Captain Ingram on this occasion reflected great credit upon himself and the military service."[20]

The citation did not identify the type of plane or the information Ingram sought, and Ingram did not divulge details to the reporter. But the plane must have been one of the B-17s. At any rate, he told the scribe: "I didn't want to send any of my men, so I went out on the field . . . and got the information myself." He added: "We knew something had happened that shouldn't [when the attack started]." He said most men first reacted with shock, then amazement, then, quickly thereafter, "fierce, blazing rage." He continued: "There wasn't a man on duty who wasn't fighting mad within a minute after the action started."[21]

Ingram's wife, Mildred Robinson Ingram, and their four children were at the family's Hickam Airfield home on December 7, 1941. But his family was evacuated stateside and ended up in Williamsburg, also Mildred's hometown. George told the reporter that he had spent a short leave with his family but had not seen them since they left Hawaii and had not been back to Kentucky for three years. Besides visiting loved ones, Ingram helped in a Third War Loan rally at which more than $100,000 worth of war bonds were sold "during the first few hours."[22]

A few minutes before the Hickam Airfield attack, the air force private Herman McCarty was getting ready for church. Before exiting the big barracks, he looked "right over the top of Pearl Harbor . . . [and] saw some planes." The twenty-one-year-old Kentuckian from Owensboro "wondered what they were doing because planes didn't fly on Sundays."[23]

McCarty realized that the planes meant to do lethal harm when he saw one dive on Pearl Harbor, drop a bomb, and veer toward the barracks. He spied the red rising-sun insignia: "I was on the second floor and took off toward the hangar but couldn't get out for a while. When we did get out, they had pretty much destroyed all the planes."[24]

McCarty said that, after the Japanese bombed a hangar next door to the barracks, he and others rushed over to help the wounded: "We took doors off the wall lockers to use as stretchers. That's the main thing I did. There wasn't anything else I could do." After basic training, he had been given a choice of three overseas assignments. He picked Oahu, figuring "it would be a good time to see Hawaii." Before the attack, he added, Pearl Harbor was "a beautiful place."[25]

Sergeant Bobby Bailey remembered guys standing in the shade of a barracks porch just after breakfast. The men were nonchalantly peering at a swarm of planes and wondering: "What's the Navy doing practicing on Sunday?" One soldier poked fun at "swabbie pilots" who did not know it was the Sabbath.[26]

A Mississippian stationed at Fort Knox, near Louisville, in 1959, Bailey shared his story with Private First Class Si Surowski, a "*Louisville Courier-Journal* Special Writer." In a story published on December 13, he told Surowski that every December 7 is "like a wedding anniversary": "I remember it like it happened yesterday." Bailey was assigned to the Fifth Chemical Warfare Company.[27]

Bailey said that everybody still thought they were watching a drill even when they saw about fifty planes dive on Pearl Harbor: "We heard their bombs hit, saw the black rolling smoke, but couldn't see their targets and thought this was just Navy Air Force maneuvers. After about 15 minutes of this, one plane headed in our direction. It flew right over the top of us and only then, after seeing the red circles on the wing tips, did we realize we were being attacked by the Japanese."[28]

The plane roared away and bombed the big mess hall where Bailey had breakfasted. As many as thirty more planes followed "at tree-top level, bombing and strafing all hangars, control towers, barracks, the main Post Exchange and all places where troops were gathered."[29]

Bailey said that there was no time to be scared and "no place to run": "It was mass confusion. You have to remember this was Sunday morning, and a lot of the officers were away on overnight passes." He claimed that the Japanese knew "we had only two hangars that didn't have planes in them" and that "they bombed all but those two." He said that the enemy pilots evidently did not know that the base petroleum, oil, and lubrication dump had been converted into the guard-house. He said that the jail "had a few men in it," adding: "The planes leveled it."[30]

Bailey said that he "took off running." As he hurried from "one company street to another," he could "hear the bombs hitting the buildings and the machine-gun bullets busting and going through the window panes": "But the thing that had the most eerie effect was the sound of the engines as the planes went into and came out of their dives."[31]

Bailey said that officers and sergeants ordered the men out of the buildings and onto the parade field: "I was about a block from the field, which had about 200 or 300 men on it, when three planes flying low, wing-tip to wing-tip, cut down at least half of the men on a strafing run. Then to complete their destruction circus, they rolled over and over again as they climbed to prepare for their second pass."[32]

Bailey said that he "really got scared and didn't want to watch them come back": "Shaking uncontrollably, I dived under the building we called the Snake Ranch (beer hall). The only thing I could think of as I lay there was what my Dad had said when I left Jackson . . . to come in the Army June 21, 1941." Bailey's father beseeched him to take care of himself because he felt: "We will be at war before you come home."

Bailey mused that his parent was right and wished he were back in the Magnolia State capital.[33]

Meanwhile, Bailey opted for a change of venue and started running for his company area: "Just after I crossed an intersection, three small bombs hit right in the middle of the pavement and the concussion knocked me flat on my face and covered me with dirt." Luckily, bomb splinters missed him: "I don't know why, but I crawled to the flag pole and hung on as if I were going to be shaken off the face of the earth." When he finally made it back to his company area, he saw his commanding officer, helmeted, in battle dress, and armed with a pistol: "As I looked at him, I thought he was one of the bravest men I had ever known."[34]

When that officer shouted "gather round," a pair of Zeros strafed and set ablaze the company orderly room and mess hall and stitched "a line of bullets up the company street." The men ducked for cover while the officer stayed put. "Fall in," he commanded after the planes were gone. "In a few minutes, we looked like a formation," Bailey said.[35]

The officer told his troops to don battle dress, grab their rifles, and load up with all the ammunition they could carry. Bailey said: "Thank God we had just come off maneuvers that Friday and knew just what to do. With my 03 rifle, all the grenades and the other ammo I could carry, I got back in formation and the fear began to leave us." He noted that the last bombers and fighters had flown off about an hour after he spied the first planes: "Just as it had been indescribable when that living hell broke loose, so it was now with that unearthly quiet broken only by the moans and wails of the injured and dying."[36]

Bailey said that his outfit was given no time to think about what they had endured. They were immediately ordered to dig in on a sandy beach at the harbor mouth to protect Hickam against an expected Japanese landing. About a half hour after the shovel work was done, more enemy aircraft appeared. "This time," Bailey recalled, "they were flying high out of range of our machine guns, but we still threw everything we had at them, including small arms fire." Over their targets, the Japanese aircrews dropped their bombs: "But I'll give the Marines and Navy credit for making it no field day for them. Within minutes, they had the sky filled with antiaircraft fire that had many Japanese planes diving with a one-way ticket." Eighteen years after the Pearl Harbor attack, Bailey still believed the kamikaze mission myth: "We didn't know it at the time but their carrier had sailed away when they left for the second attack and all those Zeroes were all on suicide missions when they dropped their loads."[37]

Bailey said that he saw a plane crash onto one of the largest Hickam hangars. It fell "out of the sky from about 4,000 feet or more and [went] . . . into a long, straight dive": "I thought he would never hit, it took him so long." The pilot seemed to regain control of his aircraft about halfway down: "He leveled off a bit . . . and then went back into that dive to hit the hangar broadside. If I had knowledge of the atom bomb, I would have sworn someone set one off in that hangar. It went up in a mushroom of fire and smoke."[38]

Bailey also said a Japanese pilot "lost his nerve," landed on the airstrip, and climbed out of his plane. When the aviator "made a run for it," "someone cut him down with a Thompson submachine gun," making Bailey "feel good inside." There is no evidence any such thing happened, but there was a story that a daring Japanese pilot performed a touch-a-go on a runway before flying away.[39]

Bailey said that tall tales were plentiful after the last Japanese plane departed for its carrier: "One rumor gave us a much-needed laugh, morbid as it was." He explained: "It seems that when the attack first hit us, someone called Bellows Field about 35 miles away and said that we were being attacked by the Japanese. The reply was 'Change your whisky, or go back to sleep.'"[40]

Eighteen-year-old Sergeant P. R. Davis of Worthington in Greenup County and other noncommissioned officers in his quarters awoke to what sounded like gunfire: "But in reality, [it] was bombs dropping." Davis said that, if anybody else had still been asleep, he would have been jarred wide awake by shouts of, "This is real. We're under attack." Davis said: "We grabbed what weapons were available and scrambled to our posts to defend as best we could. We had just finished a drill and had returned all our arms and ammunition to storage and had only short range weapons with which to return fire—so inadequate against what we had trained upon us."[41]

Davis said that his outfit had been on high alert for an attack through Friday, when orders came to stand down: "The atmosphere was peaceful and quiet. We couldn't imagine anything happening so we were totally caught by surprise. About sixty-five percent of the personnel were already on leave or there would have been more casualties. Bombs fell from the sky like hail."[42]

Davis said that he was maybe a hundred feet from the *Arizona:* "From the smoke from the bombs, I knew it could not survive. Hickam Field had the longest runway and was where the bombers were stored and departed and landed. It was also target zero for a lot of the bombs." The Japanese fighters and bombers hammered the air base. Some of the enemy fell to ground fire: "One crash landed and exploded just across the street from me. One plane had a bomb left that hadn't dropped and we wondered why. The plane kept coming lower and lower and exploded about 100 feet from the ground. I figured the pilot had been hit and was already dead which explained why he didn't drop the remaining bomb."[43]

Davis said that the first wave of attackers departed after "about an hour—a very long hour." When the second wave appeared: "Nobody knew what to do. It was devastating. My last image was of two Japanese planes dive-bombing into a hangar on the east end of the runway." When the Vals flew away, Davis and his buddies had no idea whether the enemy would return: "We were left to assess our damage, tend to our casualties, and try to make sense of a senseless situation. It was utter chaos. We had been told to expect an invasion and to be honest, I don't know why they didn't invade. We would have been helpless."[44]

Wheeler Airfield and Schofield Barracks

Wheeler Airfield

Opened in 1922, Wheeler Airfield is about seventeen miles north of Pearl Harbor and adjacent to Schofield Barracks. The base was named in honor of Major Sheldon H. Wheeler, who was fatally injured in a 1921 airplane crash at Luke Airfield on Ford Island, where he was the commander. (The army's Luke Airfield became a naval air station.) Though Hickam supplanted Wheeler as the Hawaii's main army air base, Wheeler was home to several firsts in aviation history. In 1927, the first nonstop flight arrived in Hawaii from Oakland, California. In 1935, the famous flier Amelia Earhart departed Wheeler on the first solo flight between Hawaii and California. By December 1941, Wheeler was headquarters for the Fourteenth Pursuit Wing and the Fifteenth and Eighteenth Pursuit Groups and approximately ninety planes, most of them fighters.[45]

In the first wave of the Japanese attack, twenty-five Vals dive-bombed the hangars. They came back to strafe the flight line, setting many planes on fire. Four fighters managed to take off and intercept the enemy over southeastern Oahu. A second wave strafed the field but added little to the damage from the first wave. All told, the Japanese destroyed fifty-three aircraft, killed thirty-eight men, and wounded fifty-nine more.[46]

Survivors included Private Raymond Turley, a twenty-one-year-old aircraft mechanic who began the day looking forward to a free steak dinner in Honolulu. He planned to wash down the feast with a cold Coca-Cola. He missed that repast—and his breakfast and lunch, too. No matter, the Kentuckian from Winchester was just happy to be alive.[47]

Turley and two buddies were due a Sunday pass. "We had a little deal going," he said. "The one that woke up the other two was gonna get a steak dinner in Honolulu and all the Coca Cola he could drink. We didn't drink any beer." Turley rose first: "Course, I was raised on a farm and I was used to getting up at four o'clock in the morning. That didn't bother me one bit."[48]

The teetotaling trio had barely begun breakfast in their barracks mess hall when they heard what sounded like a diving plane. Turley remembered: "On Sunday morning, real often, the Navy would come up and they would simulate [an] attack on Wheeler Field and we'd hear 'em come in a dive and then here another plane would come into a dive, and this morning we heard this plane come in a dive and then we heard an explosion."[49]

Thinking a navy plane had crashed, the men rushed to windows in time to spot a dive-bomber drop a bomb and then pull up: "We saw the rising sun on the wings, and we yelled, 'The Japanese are bombing us! Japanese bombing us! Let's get out of this mess hall." Immediately, the soldiers ran for the exits. Turley and his buddies split up, figuring that, if they stuck together, one bomb might kill all three of them. Turley ran toward the headquarters building, where another soldier, "a big tall fella," suggested the two of them take cover against a high concrete curb next to the street. After some more planes passed, the soldier counterproposed that they sprint toward "the east of the hangar line because they were bombing from the west to the east." The duo scampered over a small hill to where crews had been building some temporary wooden barracks.[50]

Turley said that two rows of P-40 fighters lined up on the east side of the hangar caught the attention of a pair of low-flying pilots, apparently at the throttles of Kates. After the duo shot up the parked P-40s, the rear gunners finished turning the aircraft into blazing hulks. "They was loaded with ammunition and aviation fuel and they just . . . melted down," Turley said.[51]

Seconds later, Turley and the other soldier heard "zing, splat," the sound of bullets crashing into the barracks. They jumped into a ditch that had been dug for a waterline and rode out the rest of the attack. Turley said: "I felt like this was a guardian angel watching over me because neither one of us got a bullet or a piece of shrapnel or anything."[52]

Before he got through the air raid, Turley survived a heaving night Pacific storm en route to Hawaii. Soaked to the skin, and barely able to stand on the rolling and tossing troopship, he refused to abandon his post as deck guard. The ship departed San Francisco on December 7, 1940.[53]

The air gunner Clarence Langzell, a nineteen-year-old sergeant from Morton's Gap in Hopkins County, was unable to get aloft and shoot back at the enemy. Assigned to twin-engine A-20 light bombers and P-70 night fighters, he was asleep in his barracks bunk when the sound of diving aircraft woke him up. He figured it was the navy springing another mock attack: "It was the roar of the bombs that drove the men from the barracks and drove home the realization of the attack."[54]

Unable to fly, Langzell joined a twenty-millimeter antiaircraft-gun crew. "Our men seemed neither frightened nor confused, but ran to their stations immediately to fight off the attack," he said. "I don't know whether it was due to discipline or not but something made them do the right thing."[55]

It seemed to Langzell that everybody around him who was not wounded or dead was taking cover. He spotted a nearby truck and ducked under it just as more enemy planes arrived. After they flew off, he crawled out, stood up, and got what must have been the shock of his young life. He had been hiding below a fully loaded gasoline truck. Back home in Detroit, where they had moved to find work, his parents received the shock of their married life. They got an army telegram saying Clarence was missing in action. A subsequent telegram assured them that their sergeant-gunner son was alive.[56]

Sergeant Morris Stacy's family was looking forward to marking his twenty-fifth birthday on Christmas Day. Instead, they mourned his death. "[Stacy] was Louisville's first reported casualty in the Japanese surprise attacks on Sunday," according to the December 10 *Courier-Journal*. His widower father, the former Louisville resident James H. Stacy, had moved to West Virginia to work on the railroad. He phoned Falls City relatives with the news that his son had been killed at Wheeler, where he was assigned to the Seventy-Eighth Pursuit Squadron. Stacy was reportedly five-foot-ten with dark brown eyes and hair and was known for his dry "sense of humor."[57]

Stacy's sister, Mrs. Harold Martin, told a reporter that she had received a letter from her brother about a month before: "He said then he hoped to be made a sergeant soon." She knew nothing of the promotion until she saw her brother listed as "Sergt. Morris Stacy" on the official casualty list. He had been at Wheeler for two of the five years he had been in the army.[58]

"[Morris] must have been proud about the promotion," Mrs. Martin said, remembering "how proud he acted" when he was home admiring himself and his new khaki uniform in a mirror. Stacy had recently written his sister telling her that he was looking forward to Christmas leave, "when he could combine a celebration and his birthday and Christmas with 'one of those good old dinners.'" But the next letter, his last, said that a Yuletide furlough was doubtful. "Perhaps later," he penned.[59]

When the bombs began falling, Stacy, a radioman, pitched in to help roll fighter planes out of hangars. He and a pilot were getting "a plane into the open" when an enemy aircraft "dived and strafed the field, killing both men with machine gun fire." Although Stacy had been due for discharge in July 1941, he stayed in uniform when he and others "were frozen in their jobs, in the fateful 1941 months." About three months before the attack, he wrote home to his big brother, Morgan Stacy, a Louisville firefighter, warning: "We're sitting on a hot spot here. I realize now, more than ever, what a wonderful country America is. It's worth fighting for. If necessary, I am willing to die for it."[60]

Family members told the *Courier-Journal* that Stacy's remains were to be brought home for burial "in about three weeks." The story also cited another Kentucky soldier listed as killed, Private William C. Creech, the son of Mrs. Martha H. Creech of Cumberland County.[61]

Schofield Barracks

Because the Japanese did not intend to invade Hawaii, Schofield Barracks, which opened in 1908, was not a prime target. The base was home to thousands of soldiers, mostly in the Twenty-Fourth and Twenty-Fifth Infantry Divisions. Their mission was to defend Oahu against invaders from the sea. After bombing and strafing Wheeler Airfield, some Japanese planes strafed Schofield Barracks, but seemingly as an afterthought. Damage was slight, and casualties were few compared to the situation at Wheeler Airfield. Together, the Twenty-Fourth and the Twenty-Fifth Division losses were three killed and twenty-six wounded. In hindsight, the fact that Schofield was only lightly hit (and Fort Shafter left untouched) suggested that an invasion was not in the cards, at least not right away.[62]

Cook Luby "Dick" Saxon, twenty-five, got up early—about 3:00 A.M.—to start preparing breakfast at a Schofield Barracks mess hall. Shortly before 8:00, he heard the wail of air-raid sirens. When he discovered the attack was real and not a drill, Saxon, a small, wiry man, took cover inside a large oven that had not been switched on. He emerged unscathed to see thick smoke in the direction of Wheeler Airfield and a steady stream of ambulances bringing the wounded to the nearby base hospital. The next day, he gathered with other soldiers to hear FDR's war declaration.[63]

Calvin Leisure of Ohio County had just come off night guard duty between Schofield Barracks, where he was stationed, and Wheeler Airfield. He was in a tent, standing in the chow line and looking forward to breakfast, when he felt the ground tremble beneath his boots. Hawaii was earthquake prone, but the tremor was unearthly. "We felt the engines before we saw the dive bombers," he said.[64]

Leisure soldiered in the Twenty-Fifth Infantry. "All I had was my rifle and eight rounds of ammunition," he remembered. "I was standing in shock as the earth began to shake. I could see the Rising Sun insignia on the side of the plane that was just treetop high. I heard the sergeant yelling, 'Get rifles and fire at the first plane that comes by.'" Leisure and several of his buddies dove into a golf course sand trap and blazed away at the enemy.[65]

Private Tommy Lewis of Mayfield, also based at Schofield, helped bury the Wheeler dead. He said: "The ordnance people were supposed to do it. But it was a job everybody had to help with." Lewis also recalled: "They hit an ammo dump and blew up a lot of planes. . . . It was unbelievable. . . . It's like if Mayfield was to be bombed today. All the people not expecting it. Not knowing what to do. Not knowing where to go. Just standing around and seeing things happen they didn't think could happen, would happen or were happening."[66]

Lewis, a combat engineer, was from South Carolina, but he settled in Mayfield after the war and reared a family there. He had joined the army in 1939 and had just three days left on his hitch when the Japanese attacked Pearl Harbor. December 7, 1941, was a day of numbing confusion for him: "We had just come off maneuvers [on December]. When it all started we thought 'Here we go again.'"[67]

Lewis rolled out of his bunk thinking about breakfast; the meal was not to be. When he heard the roar of low-flying airplanes, he ran to the barracks porch with other soldiers. He first took shelter in a barracks basement before climbing out to view the air raid from a baseball diamond: "They didn't bother us much. They were mostly after Wheeler."[68]

Staff Sergeant Frank Weise of Owensboro saw what Lewis saw and figured it was all movie make-believe. "The planes were so close that we saw the rising sun insignia on the wings and the fire flash from their machineguns," he said. "But I thought it was merely part of some special maneuvers for the benefit of M-G-M." Hollywood filmmakers, he added, "were always out there."[69]

Weise, a dental technician, was at breakfast when he heard staccato gunfire over the roar of aircraft engines. When the soldiers ran outside and glimpsed the low-flying planes, they "still didn't think anything about it": "They were always putting on special stunts for the movie people." So he and the others watched the planes fly away, then "went back to finish [their] breakfast."[70]

Before they were through, the earthquake-proof barracks "shook so violently that a window broke," Weise remembered. "Then we really jumped. We knew that wasn't for the movie people. We ran out and saw tracer bullets and knew, then, it was war—the real thing." The air-raid alarm sounded, sending Weise and his messmates running for their field packs and first-aid kits. His helmet fell off: "I stopped to pick it up. The man just in front of me fell dead, his back riddled with bullets. If I hadn't stopped to pick up my helmet, I would have been that man, for he was in the spot I would have been [in] had I kept on running." He hoisted the soldier in his arms and hurried him to the dispensary: "He was dead when I picked him up."[71]

Weise and other medical personnel climbed aboard trucks and ambulances and sped off for Wheeler, the destination of the planes that interrupted his morning meal. "The attack continued for 10 or 15 minutes," he recalled. "We saw the Japs drop bombs on Wheeler Field. . . . We saw the Jap planes power-dive and level off at 200 feet." He said he watched anti-aircraft gunners shoot down nine planes, an exaggeration in the fog of war, adding: "When one fell there was plenty of cheering."[72]

Weise said that he helped tend to a steady stream of wounded and even cut a three-inch piece of shrapnel from a man's leg: "We're not supposed to remove things, that's for the surgeons. But this man was bleeding so badly, that I couldn't stop it with a tourniquet, so I pulled out the shrapnel, filled the hole with gauze, then applied a tourniquet, and sent him to the hospital."[73]

After the raid, Weise evidently suffered from posttraumatic stress syndrome, called *shell shock* in World War I and *battle fatigue* in World War II. "My officer wanted me to go to the hospital to see what was wrong, but I wouldn't go," he said. "I wanted to stay in the Army and help with the job on hand." Weeks after the attack, he fainted and was hospitalized. When he failed to respond to treatment, doctors told him he should leave the army. "I just couldn't think of that so they sent me to a hospital in the states," he recalled. "One day they brought around an honorable discharge for me to sign." When he refused, an officer threatened him with a Section Eight discharge on the grounds of mental unfitness for service. He relented and signed. He was discharged for "physical disability" on July 21, 1942. He went home and landed a job at local hospital. "But I'd sure much rather be back over there," he told a local reporter with whom he shared his story of the attack.[74]

Private Charles Hocker of Beaver Dam, not far from Owensboro, was still in his quarters when he heard what sounded to him like explosions. He had been in uniform for just six months, so he guessed army or navy planes were dropping smoke bombs for practice. He realized his error when aircraft painted with round, bright red rising-sun insignia on their wings and fuselages began bombing and strafing. "Bullets were going everywhere in the barracks," he said. "I saw blood on my right leg."

His wound was minor. But he said that the raiders "killed a lot of my buddies."[75]

Hocker and a friend had tried to join the navy earlier in 1941 because "there was nothing going on in Beaver Dam." He was sixteen, his buddy evidently the same age. A recruiter sent them away, admonishing: "Come back when you grow up." They headed for the army recruiting office, lied about their ages, and got in. "My father signed the papers," he said. "They didn't question anything." After basic training, the army asked him whether he wanted to go to the Philippines or Hawaii. He opted for the latter: "I pictured Hula girls."[76]

In Hawaii, Hocker turned seventeen, the legal age to enlist with parental permission. After the attack, he had to forsake the relative comfort of his barracks for service in the field, bedding down in irrigation ditches, and digging in on banana plantations and elsewhere. He suspected that Japanese ground forces would have conquered Hawaii: "They could have walked right through us. Thankfully they didn't."[77]

Doubtless, Dr. Leonard D. Heaton, the Schofield Barracks hospital chief of surgical services, was also grateful that there was no invasion. He and his staff were swamped with casualties. "The best and happiest days of our lives went up in the smoke of Pearl Harbor, Wheeler Field, and Hickam Field today," the University of Louisville medical school graduate wrote in his diary. 'I wonder if, when and how they will ever return." The attack canceled his plans to attend a lecture at Queen's Hospital in Honolulu.[78]

Heaton was looking forward to hearing Dr. Jonathan Moorhead of New York City, an authority on traumatic surgery. The topic's importance increased exponentially for military physicians on the day Heaton recorded in detail. He was home on the base and about to climb in a car with two other doctors for the drive to the city. They were supposed to pick up another doctor on the way to the lecture: "We hesitated before entering the car because our attention was called to the great number of planes in the air and some very loud distant noises."[79]

A plane "came quite close," and, when the pilot banked to come down Heaton's street, the surgeon "distinctly saw the rising sun insignia on his wings": "Soon he was coming . . . with machine guns blazing away at us." The trio rushed inside the Heaton home. "As long as I live I shall never forget my feelings and emotions when I saw and realized that these were Jap planes and that we were in for the real thing. Something we never thought could ever happen to us here due to primarily our great naval force and implicit faith in such."[80]

Back inside, Heaton told his wife, Sara Hill Heaton, that they were under attack. Their daughter, Sara Dudley Heaton, had nasal bronchitis and was in bed. The couple and the two doctors went outside to see whether the planes were gone. They "distinctly saw dive bombers and bombs over Wheeler Field and much black smoke in the direction of Pearl Harbor": "There were many planes by now all over and around us. I remarked as must have many others before us in situations like this, 'Where are our planes?'" At that instant, another Japanese warplane lined up with the street, "spraying everything and everybody with machine guns": "We rushed back into the house again and at this time I got an urgent call to come immediately to the hospital." He comforted his wife and daughter and left.[81]

The first wounded from Wheeler were already at the hospital. "We immediately set our operating teams in action," Heaton wrote. "We worked all that day up until early evening. I had already set up 4 of these teams on paper and they started to function . . . We were not caught short on personnel or equipment. Such wounds!!—eviscerations of brains, neck, thorax, abdomen—traumatic amputations, etc. No burns of any consequence. No cardiac or neurological operated cases." The army surgical teams treated 117 patients, working tirelessly, calmly, and speedily to save lives and limbs. "Thirty-eight patients died, most of them [having arrived] with fatal wounds." There were no reported cases of deadly gas gangrene. Heaton had already devised a new procedure to prevent the infection that was later used throughout the army.[82]

Back at their house, the Heatons found a spent 7.7-millimeter machine-gun cartridge, "a family keepsake and reminder for the generations."[83] In 1943, Heaton was awarded the Legion of Merit for "his unusual devotion to duty and his excellent judgment . . . which did much to enhance the efficiency and state of readiness and effectiveness of the surgical teams handling that emergency and by so doing rendered service of great value." He had graduated from medical school in Louisville in 1926 and the Army Medical School and field service school in 1929.[84]

Private Albert Patrick of Salyersville was not among Heaton's patients, though he might not have felt well. He did not get back to his barracks until around 2:00 A.M. Nonetheless, he managed to ambulate to breakfast and down eggs and pancakes. "There was just about 12 down in the mess hall," he remembered.[85]

Patrick was awake enough to notice the roar of aircraft engines. "I just pushed the hallway door open . . . and there was that plane right up there. I could even see the numbers on it, I seen his helmet; he had the old-fashioned helmet. It was in a dive, and it released something." The plane was an Imperial Japanese Navy Aichi D3A Val.[86]

Patrick added: "There was a radio on the porch. And it was a-going. And it was a-talking about, 'We are under attack, this is the real thing, report back, report back to your station.'" He and other soldiers climbed on rooftops and shot at the planes with a trio of machine guns: "No officers had arrived, wasn't a non-com, just us ten guys, privates." He said that somebody asked if they downed any enemy planes: "I never saw one go down, but one was smoking as it flew out of sight." Like many military men and women and civilians, Patrick heard rumors of a Japanese invasion. Supposedly, enemy paratroopers were dropping on a golf course: "So we rushed out there. We passed the Arizona sinking . . . little blazes of fire on the water and fellows were trying to get to shore. There wasn't no one on the golf course, though." Before the attack, Patrick had enjoyed his Hawaii posting: "Whoa, that's a good place. We liked it. It was great. It really was paradise."[87]

Sunup caught Private Earl Little of Louisville and some of his buddies feeling a tad unwell, too. They were hung over from a Saturday night on the town in Honolulu. The soldiers had made it to the Black Cat Café for a Sunday morning breakfast when they heard what sounded like distant explosions. They knew neither the location nor the cause of the racket but figured it was a signal to return to base. So they hustled across the street and hopped on a bus.[88]

"We jumped on . . . and the driver refused to take us to Schofield," Little remembered. "I don't know why, but he said he wouldn't take us." Maybe it was because he had fifty-five passengers and only thirty seats. Anyway, he changed his mind after some less-than-gentle persuasion: "So a staff sergeant from Tennessee—I don't remember his name—put a knife to that guy's throat and said, 'You're either going to take us, or you're gonna lose your head.'"[89]

Fifteen minutes later, military police and shore patrolmen halted the bus on a road next to Pearl Harbor. At first, some of the soldiers mistook the swarming planes for "maneuvers or something," Little said. "But we couldn't figure out why all those ships were blowing up." They knew they were witnessing a real battle when they saw "bodies and arms and legs flying through the air" when a ship blew up.[90]

The bus passengers did not have time to be scared, Little said. "We didn't know for sure what was happening. I think we were more in shock than anything else." The soldiers got another jolt when the bus halted at Wheeler Airfield, the stop before Schofield Barracks: "Once we drove in the gate, we could see where they'd bombed the field; there were P-40s burning and bombed-out buildings and everything." Back at the barracks, the soldiers drew their rifles and ammunition and were assigned guard duty. Little, who was in the Twenty-Fifth Division's Eleventh Quartermaster Regiment, was posted to a railroad line near Schofield Barracks. After dark, he confessed to sharing the fear of almost everybody who survived the attack, invasion: "That's when I was nervous, really."[91]

Private Richard Don Lay of Loyall in Harlan County was one of the nervier men on base. He helped shoot down a Japanese dive-bomber over Schofield Barracks—but, instead of giving him a medal, the army kicked him out and sent him home. He had lied about his age when he enlisted in February 1941, swearing that he was seventeen, the minimum age for joining up.[92]

Lay later told a reporter that bomb explosions had jarred him from a sound sleep in his bunk. He ran outside and saw Japanese aircraft "dropping bombs and machine-gunning men in their tents and on Wheeler Field." He hurried "to an ammunition center and took a Browning automatic [rifle] and three clips of ammunition" before ducking for cover under a parked car.[93]

After a bomb hit and blew up about twenty-five yards from him, Lay decided to seek more substantial shelter, so he scampered for "the lower end of the motor pool where there was a .50-caliber machine gun in a dugout." He jumped in with a major who was shooting at planes "so low over us [he] could have hit them with rocks." The duo opened up on a Val as it pulled out of its dive. Lay said he got the pilot with his BAR: "The major hit the plane, which crashed 50 yards away."[94]

After there were no more planes to shoot at, Lay said a soldier came to the motor pool and suggested they hop on a motorcycle and head for Pearl Harbor. "He drove and I rode in the sidecar," Lay said. "We raced to Pearl Harbor at 70 miles an hour. When we got there, about 75 Jap planes were still overhead, some of them dropping bombs."[95]

The duo dismounted. Lay hit the dirt. But the driver—Lay "knew him only as Cruise"—opted to stand "to get a better view." No sooner did Lay tug at the man's trouser leg and urge him to take cover than "he fell, [presumably] shot through the chest, by bullets from a Jap plane." Lay said that he carried Cruise "about 400 yards to an ambulance": "But he was dead when I got him there."[96]

Meanwhile, D. W. Lay had written the Pentagon explaining that his son was too young to serve. He was fourteen when he joined the army. On Christmas Day, the army put Private Lay on a California-bound ship. He was discharged at Fort McDowell on Angel Island in San Francisco Bay. He went home to Kentucky in February and stayed until June 1942, when he and his father went to work at the Norfolk Navy Yard. D. W. hired in as an electrician, Richard Don as a messenger. The teenage vet was unhappy with his position. "I know I could do more important work," he complained at the time.[97]

Richard Don was partial to his dad's trade. "I'd like to be an electrician," he said, "but I'll stay on as a messenger until I can become an apprentice in some trade." He told the reporter that he was unsure about legally enlisting after his seventeenth birthday: "I can't answer that—the time is too far away." He reenlisted on June 9, 1944, at age eighteen.[98]

Lay might not have had a merry Christmas in 1941. But G. A. and Mary Taylor of Louisville did, albeit a day late. Their holiday joy sprang from a letter they received on December 26 from Goebel A. Taylor, their nineteen-year-old prodigal son at Schofield Barracks. He was safe and unhurt. "Pop, if you think it's hell to be married, you ought to be in a war," the missive advised. Private Taylor also admonished his dad: "Don't you sit up by the radio all night listening to short wave to find out if I get killed."[99]

The elder Taylor had been worried about his offspring since he had run away from home in 1939. Goebel fils returned, landed a job as a draftsman, quit in July 1941, volunteered for the army, and shipped out to Schofield Barracks, where he joined the Sixty-Fifth Engineers. "A shell landed in our barracks but nobody was hurt," he assured his parents. "It landed about fifteen feet from where I sleep." Evidently an errant antiaircraft round, the missile failed to explode.[100]

The private promised his folks: "The government will send you a telegram if I get killed. And don't worry about me being killed, I got a horseshoe in each pocket and a string of rabbits' foots around my neck." Mary Goebel forbade her boy to box when he lived at home, fearing his nose would bleed like it did when he was a lad. Her offspring also wrote that he had been boxing and that his nose had not bled even a little bit.[101]

The Army Elsewhere

On December 17, the *Georgetown Times* informed its readers that Robert H. Brooks and William Hostetter, two local youths, were reported killed at Pearl Harbor. Brooks, a soldier, did die but in the Philippines on December 8. Hostetter, a marine, survived the sinking of his ship, the *West Virginia*.[102]

Like Pearl Harbor, the Philippines figured heavily in Tokyo's war strategy. Without declaring war on the United States, Japan planned to surprise and destroy the American fleet in Hawaii on December 7. The next day, Japanese forces would attack the British on the Malay Peninsula and the Americans on Luzon, which included Manila, the Philippine capital. Afterward, the Japanese counted on a rapid conquest of the rest of the Philippines, plus Guam, Wake, Hong Kong, Borneo, British Malaya (including its capital, Singapore), and Sumatra. Ranging on, Japan would seize Java and the rest of Dutch East Indies. Thus, it would have a free hand to develop and exploit the natural resources of Malaya and Indonesia, notably rubber and oil. To protect their far-flung conquests, the Japanese would erect a defense perimeter stretching from the Kuril Islands through Wake and the Marshall Islands and on around the southern and western rims of the Malay Barrier to the border between Burma and India. All that accomplished, Japan's navy and air force could sever communications between Australia and New Zealand and force Britain and the United States to sue for peace. Meanwhile, Japan would finish off, thus placing half the world's population under the economic, political, and military dominance of Tokyo. "This scheme of conquest was the most enticing, ambitious and far-reaching in modern history, not excepting Hitler's," wrote the admiral and historian Samuel Eliot Morrison. "It almost worked, and might well have succeeded but for the United States Navy."[103]

Brooks, twenty-five, of Sadieville, was the "first Armored Force soldier killed in action in the war," the *Louisville Courier-Journal* said.[104] Major General Jacob L. Devers, the Fort Knox commander, quickly moved to name the post parade ground in Brooks's honor. Evidently, neither the reporter nor Devers knew that Brooks was black and passing as white in an all-white outfit. When the general found out, he proceeded with the official naming ceremony.[105]

Brooks was also among the first African Americans to die in the war. The *Georgetown Times* identified Brooks as "Negro." In its story about the rain-soaked ceremony, the *Louisville Courier-Journal* did not.[106]

A half dozen generals plus two score of the highest officers of the US armored force paid tribute "to a brother-in-arms," the *Courier-Journal* story advised. Colonel F. A. Macon read the official order explaining that "Private First Class Robert H. Brooks, Company D. 192d Tank Battalion . . . , was killed in action December 8, 1941, near Fort Stotsenburg, Philippine Islands." Devers signed the order.[107]

The brass stood at attention before the parade ground flagpole, the Stars and Stripes at half-staff. "Facing them," the *Courier-Journal* reported, "a platoon of infantry was drawn up, while further back forty other officers stood in lines." Devers spoke briefly, announcing that Brooks had "died on the battlefield" on "the first day that America entered the war": "For him, the first soldier of the Armored Force to be killed in action, this parade ground . . . will be named 'Brooks Field.'" Chaplain Cleary followed with a prayer asking that "the immortal soul of Robert H. Brooks" be granted "refreshment, light and peace in Thy Heavenly Kingdom through the infinite merits of our Lord and Savior Jesus Christ."[108]

The ceremony ended with three volleys of rifle fire and taps. "The force had honored its dead and returned to the work in hand—avenging him," the reporter wrote. "The flag went back to the top of the pole. The infantry and the band marched away." Meanwhile: "Somewhere north of Manila the men of the 192d—from Kentucky, Wisconsin, Ohio and Illinois—were fighting from light tanks to hurl back the Japanese invaders." They lost the fight. Most of the men were killed in battle, and many of those who were captured died of mistreatment, including torture, on the notorious Bataan Death March or in Japanese prison camps.[109]

The 192nd was a federalized national guard outfit consisting of four companies. The Kentuckians made up Company D. Most of them were eating lunch when the first enemy bombs started falling. Brooks was with two mechanics from the maintenance section. Apparently, he was instantly killed by a bomb trying to reach his half-track to shoot back with its fifty-caliber machine gun.[110]

Before the ceremony, one of Devers's aides tried to find out about Brooks's parents, Adline and Ray Brooks. The Farmer's Deposit Bank had the only phone in Sadieville. When the bank president, W. T. Warring, came on the line, the junior officer asked whether somebody from Sadieville could attend the dedication ceremony. He also asked the banker whether he knew Brooks's mother and father. "His parents are tenant farmers, ordinary black people; maybe you could contact them and see if they could come," Warring suggested.[111]

The surprised aide hung up. The 192nd was all white, so, figuring he must have mistaken what Warring had said, he called right back. "Did you say they were black?" The banker replied: "Yes, his mother and father are very dark." Given that the army was segregated, the aide was unsure about the parade ground naming and ceremony. When he reported his conversation with Warring to Devers, the general responded: "It did not matter whether or not Robert was black, what mattered was that he had given his life for his country."[112]

Because Brooks was light-skinned, he often was taken for white. His fellow tankers knew he was African American and "never questioned it as he was considered 'just one of the guys,'" wrote John Trowbridge, a Kentucky National Guard historian. Brooks was posthumously promoted to private first class. Following the war, his remains were reinterred in the American Military Cemetery near Manila. A memorial stone stands on the parade ground at Fort Knox, and a state historical marker in Sadieville commemorates his life and death.[113]

Kaneohe Naval Air Station

More than sailors and marines were at Kaneohe Naval Air Station, a base for PB2Y Catalina patrol seaplanes. A contingent of army engineers had been sent over to help build some new barracks. All told, the raiders killed eighteen sailors and destroyed or damaged all thirty-three Catalinas at the base. But gunners shot down the first of twenty-nine Japanese planes destroyed in the attack, and Chief Petty Officer

John William Finn earned a Medal of Honor. Severely wounded, and refusing to take cover, he kept firing a machine gun at the attackers from an open position. About thirty miles east of Pearl Harbor by road, Kaneohe is a marine air station today.[114]

Hundreds, maybe thousands, of soldiers, sailors, airmen, and marines on Oahu were eating breakfast or were bound for bacon and eggs. Army private Vaughn Drake of Lexington was in the latter category. "We were getting ready to go to breakfast," he later told the *Lexington Herald-Leader*, "and we heard all these planes flying over and making a lot of noise. We just figured it was the Army Air Corps carrying out maneuvers for practice, like they did a lot. We didn't pay much attention to it."[115]

Drake, twenty-three, was one of the engineer soldiers helping run a temporary electric plant set up for carpenters working on the barracks. When he and other soldiers ambled to the chow line, they "noticed these planes flying over the naval air station, diving and everything": "And we thought, 'Boy, they're really putting on a good show.' Even though we saw the red spots on the wing—which was the Japanese symbol—we still couldn't believe it. . . . About that time, one of the officers had been in contact with headquarters at Schofield Barracks, and they said, 'This is an attack! The Japanese are attacking the whole island!'" Drake saw an enemy plane crash: "Later that day, some of us went over there and tore some pieces out of it." He got what he figured was the control stick: "It's got some Japanese writing on it, which I never did get translated."[116]

After the planes flew away, many on Oahu—military and civilian—worried that a Japanese invasion would follow. The edginess worsened after dark. "So that night, everybody was pretty much on guard," Drake remembered. "A funny thing that happened: We had two stacks of lumber down at the end of the camp that we used to build the barracks with. Well, it came [*sic*] a pretty stiff wind and started flipping that lumber up and down and made a noise."[117]

The popping sound unnerved the engineers, who shot up the wood pile, figuring it was Japanese troops storming ashore. "Next morning," Drake reported, "we looked at it and that lumber was splintered all over the place. I bet 100 shots had been fired into that lumber pile. People were trigger-happy."[118]

David Neal, who was in Drake's outfit, hoped the tall grass of a fallow pasture would hide him from a strafing Japanese pilot. "I fell down a-facing him and when I fell down I rolled about four or five times," remembered the McCreary Countian. "Them bullets was popping like firecrackers hittin' the ground by me there. And I could see that grass just laying over, . . . just like you took an invisible scissors and cut it off."[119]

Private Neal, a twenty-six-year-old draftee, mustered into the army in July 1941. He was eating breakfast when he heard a commotion outside and got up to investigate. He spied "four or five" men standing on a big lumber pile—evidently the soon-to-be friendly fire–riddled wood—and watching planes buzzing over the base. No sooner did one of the men speculate, "They're on maneuvers," than Neal "seen this plane a-coming down": "I seen the smoke from his guns and the tracers. I said 'maneuvers, hell!' He turned that wing up when he pulled out of that strafing dive and there was that red ball on it. I said, 'That's the rising sun.' Some damn fool said, 'That's just a sticker on the [US insignia] star.'"[120]

Neal rushed to his barracks. "About time I hit the barracks," he recalled, "the bugler jumped out there and blowed the call to arms." No sooner did the troops form up than the company commander ordered his men to disperse and seek shelter. Neal said that the brunt of the attack was aimed at the airfield; his outfit suffered only one casualty. Just as a sailor rolled into a waterline ditch, a bullet slashed his belt in two and slightly burned his hip. After the attack, a soldier volunteered to run a bulldozer to help fill in bomb craters and clear away debris. Neal agreed to go along to guard him—with an empty rifle: "I never got no ammunition until about eleven o'clock."[121]

Fort Barrette

Completed in 1935, Fort Barrett was designed to help protect the western flank of Pearl Harbor. Near Ewa Marine Air Station, the open-top concrete strongpoint bristled with two sixteen-inch guns plus antiaircraft batteries. The Japanese strafed the fort, killing a corporal.[122]

When Private Herman Horn of Frankfort awoke, he had no notion he was soon to be Fort Barrette bound. He said his unit had been camped out near the harbor mouth, where they were guarding antisubmarine nets. When the attack started, they were herded into trucks that sped off to crew Barrette's antiaircraft guns. Before they left, the men could see tall columns of thick black smoke rolling up from ships blasted by bombs and torpedoes. Prior to departure, Horn's outfit was issued thirty-five rifle rounds and ordered not to shoot. "They wanted us to save our ammunition," he said, "because the Japanese might invade the island. We could have shot their eyeballs out, but we were told not to fire."[123]

M-1s would have been next to useless against the Japanese airplanes. Anyway, the twelve-mile trip to Barrette was anything but a Sunday drive for Horn and his comrades in arms. Enemy pilots were strafing "everything they saw": "And when they saw our trucks, here they come. When they did, we'd jump off the trucks and hit the cane fields beside the road and take cover." He remembered: "Those of us in the back of the truck would watch for planes. When we'd see one, we'd beat on the top for the driver to stop. Then into the cane fields we'd go." He added: "We didn't fire one shot during the whole attack. It was pathetic. But we were very, very lucky." The next day, his parents learned of his luck when he sent them a short cable, promising to write again as soon as he could.[124]

Camp Malakole

Pearl Harbor's defenses included Camp Malakole near Barber's Point. Since January 1941, the outpost had been home to the 251st Coast Artillery Regiment, a California National Guard outfit that had been ordered to active duty. Organized in 1924 to defend Los Angeles and San Diego Harbors, the regiment was reorganized for antiaircraft defense six years later. The men built the camp themselves, clearing away kiawe trees to make room for barracks and other necessary buildings. The regiment arrived on Oahu in November 1940 and included at least two Kentuckians, John D. Barker and his buddy, John H. Riddle.

Barker, a sergeant from Gimlet in Elliott County, was looking forward to a fancier-than-usual breakfast on December 7, 1941. Mondays through Saturdays, everybody got the same chow plopped onto aluminum trays. On the Sabbath, the men could order what they wanted and dine off china plates. Clean cloths covered mess hall tables, to boot.[125]

Barker arrived about 7:30. He called for fried eggs, sunny-side up, fried potatoes, ham, biscuits, and black coffee. Just as he tucked in, he heard the drone of low-flying aircraft. He kept eating, figuring they were Hickam Field flyboys. He realized his mistake when machine-gun bullets bore through the mess hall's thin wooden walls, shattering his plate, and spattering his eggs. "Those bullets were hitting about six inches apart across the table in front of me," he remembered.[126]

The men were ordered to muster outside even as Japanese planes shot up the barracks, motor pool, mess hall, and antiaircraft-gun emplacements. "With the men lined up outside, they were an easy target for the attacking planes," Barker said, adding that everybody rushed for cover. He crawled under the barracks. He said that one of the men shot down a Zero with a Browning automatic rifle.[127]

8

Civvy Street, Hawaii

Uncle Sam's civilian employees do not rate much space in books about Pearl Harbor. Nor do the wives and children of servicemen. Several men not in uniform were on the payroll at the shipyard, where a number of civilian women were clerks. Others from civvy street worked for the army, including the Kentuckian Ben Fritz, an aircraft engine electrician at Hickam Airfield.

Fritz was used to noisy airplanes, even the ones he heard early on December 7, 1941, a Sunday. "I was not alarmed as the dawn patrol had been doing this every morning," the Harrison Countian wrote home. But he was soon rudely awakened by "a series of explosions [that] rocked the earth, the shack and my bunk; dirt fell into my face."[1]

The thirty-three-year-old Fritz was serving with the Hawaiian Air Depot Volunteer Corps, a civilian paramilitary outfit. Fritz and thirteen other volunteers had arrived at Hickam from Patterson Airfield in Dayton, Ohio, on November 2, 1941. He and some others bedded down in a little cottage, which they christened "our shack." They were close to the hangars, which, along with the flight lines, were choice targets for the enemy aviators. The blasts rousted all the shack dwellers out of their slumber. Fritz was probably sleepier than usual. The night before he met up in Honolulu with some buddies from back home. They parted company at 4 A.M.; Fritz headed for Hickam, the navy guys for their ship, the USS *Arizona*. They never saw each other again.[2]

Wide awake, Fritz peered out the back door and spied "a pursuit plane banking around in the air about a hundred yards away" with "the pilot . . . looking about." He caught a glimpse of "big red spots on the sides and wings of the ship." He said that he was "looking at 'The Rising Sun' of Japan but . . . didn't realize it": "Couldn't think it was a raid and war until I saw a plane with a red spot going down in a sheet of flame over Pearl Harbor."[3]

Fritz and his bunkmates dressed hurriedly, looked out the front door, and spotted "smoke pouring from a great hole in the roof of the repair dock [at Pearl Harbor] less than 100 yards away." They saw "a rising fury of explosions and [heard] the roar of bombs, anti-aircraft guns, various machine guns." Fritz admitted that the din "was little short of terrifying." In the clear, azure sky he gazed at "a great pattern of black anti-aircraft bursts [following] . . . high-flying hardly visible bombers": "The sight was more thrilling than any movie because it was the real thing. Even though surprised, our Army and Navy took only a few minutes to go into action."[4]

After the first wave of attackers flew away, "men began moving about in confusion," Fritz wrote. "A lieutenant wanted men to help keep fire from spreading and we grabbed extinguishers here and there and carried them into a new building adjoining one that was burning." When the second wave arrived, he fled "the building in nothing flat, running for the shack." Bombs rained down anew: "A piece of shrapnel smacked into the ground by the side of one of my friends as he left the building just behind me." His pal later swore that "he made three steps into the air before he landed, making full speed."[5]

Fritz said the second group of attackers were mainly Vals: "A cyclone of bomb explosions and gun-fire shook the earth; the air was thick with dust, smoke and conglomerated smells of destruction drifting with the trade winds. We had no way to combat either." So he stood, he said, weak-kneed near the shack, smoking his pipe, and "ignoring small objects as they whistled by": "I realized I should crawl into a small hole but could not resist watching what I think one of the greatest shows of all time. When you expect to be wiped out instantly, you are more resigned than terrified; I know I was."[6]

"I learned to distinguish the growing whistle of the bombs and to be very close to the floor or ground as they exploded," Fritz said. He witnessed a procession of Vals "streak down from various directions over Pearl Harbor, the morning sun glinting on bombs as they were released." Afterward, the dive-bombers "zoomed twisting upward and away." Fritz's thoughts were on a friend aboard the *Arizona* when he sighted a rainbow "beyond those planes, and above Pearl Harbor outlined against rugged volcanic mountains." He added: "Words I had previously written came to my mind, 'Hawaii is a beautiful place.'"[7]

During a lull, Fritz saw "truck loads of men with full equipment" speeding by. Ambulances were also on the move, and "trucks with mounted guns patrolled here and there." He hopped on a shop tractor and joined other men helping move "certain materials out of storage." But more enemy bombers appeared. "We again abandoned tractors," he remembered, "and again rushed for shelter; again shell bursts spread across the sky as bombers at high altitude held perfect unwavering formation." He spotted "bombs like grains of rice, spreading from under them": "Thus the climax came in a great roar of smoke and flame."[8]

After the attack was finally over, Fritz and others "walked about the yard and picked up fragments of bombs and shell, like you walk about the yard and pick up big hailstones after a storm." He scavenged some of the deadly debris "not 20 feet from where I had been standing part of the time." He and others visited the cratered airstrip and the smashed hangars: "There were planes on the ground burned apart by tracer bullets and in various degrees of destruction; I walked through fire-blackened steel buildings; saw craters in cement floors, doors and windows shattered or blown off; steel framework twisted." He also found "pools of blood here and there where men had died at their machines."[9]

Fritz saw barracks blasted apart and "clothing and bedding scattered." Automobiles were afire; the horn from one vehicle was stuck and blaring. Medics were laboring "over forms covered with blankets": "Men's faces were grey; eyes trying to understand the inhuman savagery; a young lieutenant said he was all that was left of his antiaircraft gun crew and the jacket of [the crew's] machine gun was full of bullet holes." He told Fritz that "four men were shot to pieces before his eyes": "A lad was standing in the harness of the gun; he was grinning and watching upward; if that young man is representative of America, I am damn proud to be one."[10]

Fritz said that a bomb destroyed the post exchange: "Two pools of blood were near its crater; I do not look for these; I just saw them." He also spied the Stars and Stripes atop a nearby flagpole: "I could see jagged holes and a long slit but it was still waving." He ended his letter by assuring the home folks: "We are now going steadily about our work; we are alert and ready for anything." He urged: "Remember Pearl Harbor and remember Hickam Field. I am very confident that I will." Fritz stayed in Hawaii for a while, long enough for him to pen a poem titled "To Ma'am." The verses appeared in the *Honolulu Star-Bulletin* on May 21, 1942.[11]

Fritz, who died in 1996, spoke little of December 7, 1941, according his son, Drew Fritz, who recalled that his dad "kept items related to his experience in his footlocker." He once showed his offspring "a roughly three-by-three-inch piece of red painted metal, perforated with three holes." Drew Fritz said that his father "snipped it off one of the Rising Sun markings on a downed Japanese aircraft."[12]

"Lots of noise from planes" failed to faze Toni Stahl: "This was not unusual as they often had 'dog fights' on Sunday mornings." The Butler County centenarian meant army and navy pilots dueling in mock air combat. "But then we saw an alarming amount of smoke rising in the air and we realized something was wrong."[13]

Stahl, who turned 101 in 2020, was alone with her toddler daughter, Sandra. Her then husband, the sailor Carl Woodrow Clinton, had rented a two-bedroom apartment for his family about fifteen miles from Pearl Harbor. He was at sea aboard the cruiser *Chester*. "We immediately turned on the radio and they were announcing torpedoes had hit 'Battleship Row' and all military personnel were to report for duty, that this was not a drill!" she recalled. "Everyone else was told to remain in house." She also remembered another radio bulletin: "We were told to turn off lights and block all windows so no light could be seen." That night: "Hawaiian guards were all around houses to make sure no lights could be seen."[14]

Toni was born and reared in a navy family in Pensacola, Florida, where in the early 1940s her mother and other relatives still lived. According to a family story, Toni's photograph fell off a shelf in her family home at the moment the Japanese planes appeared over Pearl Harbor. At first, her mother feared it was a bad omen. But neither the picture frame nor the glass broke. So she concluded that, whatever danger her daughter was in, she was unharmed.[15]

While many others on Oahu—military and civilian—expected a Japanese invasion, Stahl said she "didn't even realize that could happen": "I was so young." The navy sent many of its wives and children stateside in March 1942. Stahl and her daughter ended up in Long

Beach, California, and she and Carl divorced. She landed a job packing parachutes for army air force pilots, including the Kentuckian Charles Stahl of Butler County.[16]

After she packed Stahl's chute, Toni realized she left out the ripcord. Afraid her mistake could prove fatal for the aviator, she lost no time finding him: "I still remember what he said: 'Well, you saved my life so I think I better take you to dinner.'" Toni, who had dated the legendary drummer Gene Krupa, agreed to go out with the young flier. They were married two years later.[17]

After the war, Charles got a job as an airline pilot, and the family lived all over the country, having grown with the birth of a son, Andrew Stahl, in 1952. In 1961, Charles retired and moved the family to Butler County, where he died in 1988. His widow worked until age ninety-seven, when she resigned as a volunteer receptionist at the Bowling Green Medical Center. "I remember thinking the Lord was with me," she said of the day of the attack. "He saw me through it very well. But I don't want to go through anything like that again, believe me."[18]

Married to First Sergeant John H. Martin of Schofield Barracks, Frances Martin was looking forward to her first regular run as a base bus driver. She was waiting for schedules to be posted, her bus parked last in line, when a pair of Japanese planes "swooped low over the vehicle," one dropping a bomb about thirty yards away. She guessed the pilot was aiming for a water supply plant. "I was too busy trying to keep my head to be scared," Martin said later. But she added that her "worst scare" came when she couldn't find her son, Leon: "So many families became separated temporarily during the confusion that Sunday. Anxiety caused by these separations really was worse than any fear of the Japs." Evidently, mother and son were reunited.[19]

Seven-year-old Frank M. Reinecke Jr., the son of the marine major Frank M. Reinecke Sr., knew not to tell anything that might be a military secret. So, when a *Courier-Journal* photographer asked him about a ship in his toy fleet, he looked at his mother and asked, "Do I have to?" The little vessels were the only souvenirs he and his mom brought home to Louisville from Hawaii. "I can remember it without souvenirs," Estelle White Reinecke told a reporter for her hometown *Courier-Journal.*[20]

The attack jarred awake the Reineckes; the major was off duty. "We were asleep, but it didn't take long for us to understand what was happening," remembered Estelle, who went to Louisville Girls High School and the University of Louisville. The Reineckes lived in a wood frame house on a beach near Pearl Harbor. "Jap planes came in so low we could see the insignia painted on the wings," she added. No bombs hit close to the house, but she said that "plenty of shrapnel fell all about."[21]

While she revealed little about the attack, Estelle "had much to say" about morale on Oahu and "the quick, grim fashion in which the U.S. armed forces got to work." Still, she confessed: "It would be useless to say we weren't scared. But I don't know of a single instance of panic. Everybody was angry, and knew there was a job to do, and it had to be done."[22]

Estelle said that nearly instantaneously every soldier, sailor, airman, and marine rushed to his post. "And after that first day," the *Courier-Journal* reporter wrote, "there was nothing but the relentless job of readying for war, and the sending home of the wounded and the women and the children. That's why Frankie's Christmas presents were nearly forgone."[23]

The Louisville-born author Naunearle Brinton (Nancy) Shea, the spouse of the army air force colonel A. F. Shea, was sitting at her dressing table, combing her hair. When she heard one explosion followed by so many more, she knew that Hickam Airfield, where her husband was based, was under attack.[24]

Shea spotted Japanese planes flying low past her house before she and her Filipino employee sought shelter in a doorway between two rooms. Next, they ducked under the house. Shea was wearing her Sunday best, a gray-green dress she put on for church. She worried she might ruin it: "The gardener had left the hose running, so there was several feet of mud under the house." Nonetheless, Shea said, she and her employee crawled in, pushing and pulling "one another through a tiny window." When she wriggled inside, she felt "'a small, mischievous run' in her last pair of nylon hose." She mused afterward: "I didn't know if I ever would get out alive," adding that her main concern was for the sorry state of her stockings.[25]

After twenty minutes, the two crawled out, ran for the garage, and hastily built a "fort"—trunks topped with mattresses. Shea peered through cracks and saw a bomb smash into a neighbor's garage, setting it alight. "You develop a certain fatalism," she recalled, "and I think that's what enabled the people of London to take bombing so long." Hence, she decided to abandon their bastion and take her chances inside in comfort. She sank into the softest living room chair and "waited for one of the fragments hailing on [the] roof" to find her. She sat, as the reporter noted, "with the whole island shaking like an earthquake, pictures crashing to the floor, plaster crumbling, and Jap planes roaring over the house, methodically strafing everything in sight until her husband picked his way through the wreckage to take her to the comparative safety of Honolulu." But by the end of the attack she confessed: "I was so furiously fighting mad, I could have manned a machine gun myself."[26]

Shea figured she could have been a sentry, too. Driving into Honolulu with her husband after the attack, she saw male guards checking cars. She decided that women could do the job just as well, thus leaving men "for the real fighting." She also defended Kimmel and Short. "No one could have been more smug, more complacent, more self-satisfied, than America before Pearl Harbor," she said. "It seems cruel to me to make two men the scapegoats for the attitude that was all over the country."[27]

She said she knew the admiral and the general: "It may have been some dereliction in duty in that these men couldn't get together, but the reason they couldn't get together was that they were trying to fight a new war on 1918 lines. They refused to believe that airpower was the striking force in modern warfare."[28]

The military brat Maud McKay said her life would forever be split in two parts: "'Before Pearl Harbor' and 'After Pearl Harbor.'" She, her teenage brother, Jack, and their mother restarted their lives in Louisville, though they had no connection to the Falls City. "Before Pearl Harbor they lived leisurely in Aloha land where her father, Col. J. T. McKay, is stationed," a *Louisville Courier-Journal* reporter wrote in the January 10, 1942, issue of the paper.[29]

The McKays flew stateside aboard a Pan American Airways clipper seaplane. The colonel decided to send his wife and children to safety. They had no idea where to go except somewhere far removed from either coast. "It was almost a case of getting a large map of the U.S., closing our eyes and punching a pin through the Midwest somewhere," Maud explained. They chose Lexington. "Fortunately for Louisville, however, Miss McKay happened to think of an old friend who lived in Louisville," the paper said. So they moved in with Lucille Shay.[30]

McKay had been a sophomore at the University of Hawaii. "The only bright spot in the Pearl Harbor incident was that it interrupted final exams," she said. "All of us were delighted." She claimed that she was not afraid during the air raid: "Neither was anyone else, or if they were, they certainly kept it to themselves."[31]

McKay said that, from their house on a hill, the family "could see the smoke billowing up from the harbor." She remembered listening to a radio announcer telling everybody to stay indoors and stay calm: "His voice sounded pretty shaky . . . but his message kept coming." She added: "The most incredible thing that could ever happen—so we thought—happened when the Japanese bombed Pearl Harbor. We thought it was absolutely impossible, and naturally everyone was stunned."[32]

McKay, who planned to continue her studies at the University of Louisville, said that everybody pitched in to help after the raid: "Just as an example to show you how quick our recovery was, though, the girls whom I thought were wasting their time belonging to a motor corps got right into action the minute things began happening. . . . [T]hey rendered invaluable service in first aid, ambulance driving and the like. They were magnificent!"[33]

Modesty forbade Cecile Cords from telling a *Courier-Journal* reporter what her army air force husband said when "a loud crash" and the roar of airplane engines woke them up in their home three blocks from Wheeler Airfield. Lieutenant Howard H. Cords, a fighter pilot, "was grabbing his flying things and was racing toward the field" before the two "could do much talking."[34]

The lieutenant's spouse huddled with a newspaper scribe at the Louisville home of her parents, Lieutenant Colonel (army) and Mrs. August C. Jensen. "We'll get them yet!" she vowed to the reporter. He wrote that she spoke "without any trace of vengefulness": "She seemed to feel she was stating a very matter-of-fact and indeed an inevitable prospect."[35]

Cords said the attackers focused on hangars, aircraft, and barracks: "The Japs tried to knock out the planes and to keep the crews from getting them ready to fly." She added: "We didn't get hit much at the place where we were. Some machine gun bullets hit the quarters and some bomb fragments ruined some cars, but nobody there was killed." Five of her husband's ground crew lost their lives to bombs or strafing.[36]

Cords said that the attackers "came in so low it was impossible for them to miss." She said that, as the Vals dove, the pilots raked the field with machine-gun fire and dropped their bombs and that, as the planes pulled up, the rear gunners started shooting: "They mowed down every man they could hit. For twenty minutes or more this kept up with the Jap planes flying so low you could see the rising sun emblems on the wings plainly." She repeated a rumor that was making the rounds, that the attack was a suicide mission: "They say they never got back to their carriers and never intended to. . . . The Japs used old planes and they wanted to save their carrier, so they flew in from such a distance that they couldn't have made a trip back." Of course, the Vals, Kates, and Zeros were among the world's most modern carrier-based planes. They flew from six carriers, all close to Oahu, and had ample fuel for the round-trip.[37]

The reporter wrote that Cords spoke about the attack "with extreme reluctance," explaining: "She guards her speech with the care of one versed in things military, and says she does not like the loquacity with which some others who went through similar experiences have given accounts to the press." He gathered that "the Wheeler Field bombing was bad enough without adjectives": "Not once did Mrs. Cords resort to 'terrible' or 'horrible' and any comparable descriptive."[38]

Cords said: "We at the field had a completely different picture from what the accounts would seem to indicate. We saw the bombing and the machine-gunning and then the flames, but everybody was running to his station trying to get planes into the air. I guess it was so unbelievable we didn't have time to think of anything but that. The newspapers seem to want to know what time of day it was, how many planes bombed the field, how many were brought down, and all that. I didn't think about collecting any statistics at all."[39]

Cords did gather grisly mementoes, according to the reporter: "several machine gun bullets that had spattered the buildings, several bomb fragments and parts of a couple of bomb sights from Japanese planes." The reporter surmised: "This indicated Jap planes were brought down close by."[40]

Cords said that she expected to be moved to safety: "When the announcement came giving us only a short time to pack and be ready to leave, it was no surprise. We were evacuated from Honolulu. We passed

Pearl Harbor, of course, but you couldn't get within sight of what happened there." She and her family left on one of three passenger ships that zigzagged across the Pacific and arrived at San Francisco on New Year's Eve. The voyage was anything but festive. Cords said that her vessel "was loaded to capacity" and that "the food and service were of the worst": "But nobody minded." She had not been stateside since she left for Hawaii with her family in December 1940.[41]

The Kentuckian Kenneth Huff was still in Honolulu teaching at the Territorial School for the Deaf and Blind. When the air raid began, students were enjoying a day out of class, "unconscious of what was going on at Pearl Harbor, which is about 10 miles from here," the teacher Alden C. Ravn wrote in a story reprinted in the *Kentucky Standard*, the Kentucky School for the Deaf newspaper. The story said Huff graduated from the Danville school in 1940, as did his fellow teacher, Dr. Kenneth Braly, and their boss, Superintendent Sam Palmer.[42]

The children had just finished breakfast and were playing in the yard around 9:30 when Palmer "quoted the radio, saying that we were at war with Japan," Ravn wrote. None of them were "ready to believe him" until a short time later, when "a shell whistled over [the] yard and landed in a small shed some two blocks away": "That loud explosion and the smoke which entered our nostrils were enough to convince us. Quickly the children were grouped and herded on the porches, awaiting the next burst which never came. At noon we answered the dinner bell as usual, but some of us were too upset to eat at all. That afternoon was not quite the same."[43]

Ravn recounted that the day had dawned "bright, sunny, calm—and peaceful until a few minutes before eight when the hordes of enemy planes appeared over Oahu": "A surprise, it was, indeed!" The next day, the children were sure "the war was over since nothing had happened to convince them that the Japs were not through with us yet": "However, after repeated and careful explaining, they seemed to understand. Their response—no fear." Even so, for the first few nights after the attack, some of the students "dared not undress before going to bed; several even kept their shoes on all night": "But no hostile planes appeared and none have visited us since."[44]

The article said that the school, located about five blocks from Waikiki Beach, had ninety boys and girls, approximately 75 percent of them of Japanese descent: "Each dormitory has a blacked-out room.

The older boys made their own by covering the windows with cardboard or newspapers and blankets. The room becomes stuffy in a short time—due to lack of ventilation and we have to open the door every now and then in order to let in some fresh air. On the whole, both the children and the adults have quickly become adjusted to this kind of life."[45]

Ravn said all but fifteen boys and girls had gone home. Still: "Only the older pupils show that they know there is a war going on and at times they ask, 'When are the Japs coming?' Some of them are anxious to help our Uncle Sam although they are Japanese. One Japanese boy sleeps with an iron bar beside him every night. He says he wants to help our army in case the enemy parachutists attempt to make a landing."[46]

Ravn wrote that the school's new air-raid warning system was particularly effective. An air-raid warden reported that the "newly-installed sirens are loud enough to pull hard-of-hearing people out of bed": "At the first warning blasts each housemother or teacher is to round up her children and remain indoors or wherever they happen to be. When our four bomb shelters are completed, they will proceed to them." Meanwhile, each dormitory had a pair of "crude shelters consisting of tables with mattresses protecting all sides."[47]

Since the attack, Honolulu had had only two warnings, but no Japanese planes were spotted, according to Ravn. He insisted that the school was ready: "Each building now has fire fighting equipment such as extinguisher, fire hose, garden hose, coupler, sand in buckets, shovel, ax and gloves. Also, a ladder can be seen leaning onto a side of each house. 'Be prepared' is now our watchword."[48]

Ravn expected his school to reopen soon but with a new curriculum tailored to fit the war emergency: "Classes will be short, with more stress on vocations, particularly gardening." Some of the older pupils had found jobs and might not come back, he said: "Those left will be seen strolling around with gas masks hanging by their sides. Later steel helmets will be added. These things with our nightly blackouts are our constant reminders of war. Likewise, the words seen everywhere: 'REMEMBER PEARL HARBOR.'"[49]

Julia Hayden lived close to Huff's school. She stayed glued to the radio after her spouse, the navy lieutenant Eugene B. Hayden, departed for Pearl Harbor, the USS *Curtiss,* and the war. She also kept Sue Gene, the couple's three-year-old daughter, close by.[50]

At first, Hayden and other military wives believed that the radio bulletins were part of a drill and even took their kids to play at nearby Waikiki Beach. "But a short time afterwards," she recalled, "we saw something hitting the water over towards Pearl Harbor and we were told that was part of the bombs." When they were warned that the attack was real, the mothers shooed their youngsters back inside.[51]

The women were told not to turn on lights after the sun went down unless they blacked out the windows. "We had nothing to black them out," Hayden said, "so they brought us . . . black roofing paper, which we then tacked over all of the windows, which cut out all air, making it very hot and uncomfortable in the house."[52]

The next morning, word came through that something was up at nearby Fort DeRussy. The concrete bastion on Waikiki Beach near the Hayden home bristled with fourteen-inch, long-range guns. Potent as those guns were, the coast artillery was useless against the Japanese planes, and the guns remained unfired during the attack. The women found a big hole in the middle of a street near the fort, evidence, they were told, of a Japanese bomb blast. Later, they found out that the explosion of an errant US antiaircraft shell gouged the crater.[53]

After inspecting the hole, the navy wives collected their children, met in an apartment, and prepared to set out for the hills above Honolulu. Julia's and Eugene's recollections vary in that she remembered that "someone else stopped to pick him up" and that he gave her the car keys and his wallet. In any event, Julia said, she, Sue Gene, and the other navy spouses and kids piled into the Haydens' car and went to an apartment. They got ready to flee to the hills if need be.[54]

About two days later, Chaplain Pack, whose wife was in Hayden's group, and a sailor from the *Curtiss* unexpectedly showed up. They were so exhausted that they collapsed on the floor and went to sleep. The women pressed the padre about their husbands. He divulged only who had survived and who had not. The women could coax no more information out of him. "He had received orders to only give those two statements," Hayden said. "They were either alive or they were dead, and that was all he would tell us. So that's all I knew, that Gene was alive."[55]

Still, Julia had no idea whether he were wounded and, if so, how badly. She returned to their home but did not discover that he was unhurt until December 14, when he showed up unannounced. "He had not been wounded, that is, physically," she said. "But mentally, definitely. He had two hours' leave and in that two hours he walked constantly, up and down the living room and talked. He had time for a cup of tea and that was it. And he went back to the ship."[56]

Julia said that military dependents were sent a form and ordered to write down whether they wished to remain in Hawaii or be sent stateside. She said: "I put my name on the list to stay because I thought my husband was going to stay." On Christmas Day, wives and children were permitted to see their loved ones at Pearl Harbor. The Haydens sat down to a reunion "on the banks of a cut-out trench" with their three-year-old daughter, who had the doll that "Santa Claus had brought her," and visited.[57]

Eugene knew his wife and child had to return to the States. Back at the family cottage, Julia got a middle-of-the-night phone call telling her that she and Sue Gene were to report to Honolulu harbor the next morning for evacuation. They could bring just one suitcase apiece. "Why, you're mistaken," she said to the caller. "I have my name on the deferred list." He replied: "I beg your pardon, madame. This isn't a request. It's an order. You be there." Chaplain Pack's wife was among the navy spouses subject to the same order.[58]

Before Julia left, Eugene called her, and the couple phoned the Red Cross, inviting volunteers to come and get "all the food and extra things" that they had in the house. Julia added: "Then I got our car, we had no furniture, we were in a furnished place, [and] got the car and things together for [Eugene] . . . to pick up later." The SS *Lurline,* one of the storied Matson liners that had taken thousands of holidaymakers to and from Hawaii, was waiting at the dock. The navy had commandeered the vessel. Julia said that the ship "was a mad crowd of crying, hysterical women and children." Neither she nor Sue Gene got to kiss or hug Eugene good-bye. "My husband came to see us off, but we just waved at him," she said. "He didn't get aboard ship."[59]

The voyage home was anything but a holiday cruise. Sue Gene and her mother ended up with four others in a cabin for two: "We had been assigned one cot for the two of us." A girl in her early teens gave Julia and Sue Gene her bunk and took the cot.[60]

"We were allowed one pitcher of fresh water a day to wash in and to drink at the dining room, nothing else. Which wasn't too bad for me because my daughter was three-years-old," Hayden said. She said the rationing was harder on women with babies.[61]

Because the *Lurline* was so overcrowded, there were not enough life jackets to go around. "I was fortunate enough to get one [and] . . . was taught how to strap my daughter to myself because there was not a life jacket for her," Julia said, adding: "The doctor had given me something to give her in case she fought, and we had to abandon ship. That caused nightmares."[62]

Hayden felt better when she discovered that her husband's assistant gunnery officer, Ensign Henry Nicodemus, was aboard and bound for reassignment stateside. (She explained that the navy put some sailors aboard to augment the civilian crew but said that there were insufficient bluejackets to give any significant help.) Nicodemus had taken charge of a five-inch gun on the *Curtiss* and had been credited with helping sink a Japanese midget submarine at Pearl Harbor. "Naturally, every officer had found out that he was going to be on [the ship] . . . and had given him instructions to take care of their wives," Julia said. "Well, he tried to do what he could to help us out and made it possible for us to use his stateroom when he was on duty."[63]

Nicodemus let Hayden in on a secret after she spotted two escorting destroyers dropping depth charges. He told her that a midget submarine might be tracking the *Lurline* but admonished her: "Don't pass the word on." She never knew whether the destroyers sank the submarine or even whether there had even been one: "But the destroyers disappeared, and there wasn't any more of that."[64]

Hayden said that seasickness plagued neither her nor her daughter. But many others succumbed, including the chaplain's wife. When she fell ill, she left her cabin and asked Hayden to check on her baby son. Hayden collected Sue Gene, went to the cabin, and saw Nicodemus trying to fill in as a diaper changer. The infant was "crying at the top of his lungs": "The young ensign [was] very much perturbed." Nicodemus could not find a diaper and "was really confused [about] what to do with the baby." After Hayden located towels, which she evidently fashioned into a diaper, and a bottle, she returned the infant to his mother. A relieved Nicodemus announced that "he could handle submarines and guns but not babies."[65]

The ship docked at San Francisco on New Year's Eve, and Red Cross volunteers whisked the refugees off to hotels. It was cold, and many of the women and children lacked warm coats and sweaters. The next day, Red Cross representatives assured the women that one or two stores would be open for anyone needing to buy winter clothing. Julia left Sue Gene with another refugee and went shopping with three women whose husbands had died in the attack: "They had small children to buy clothes for."[66]

One of the widows complained about the high prices: "The little clerk, who was quite perturbed about working on New Year's Day, put her hands on her hips and said, 'Madam, do you know there's a war on?' That made quite an impression on me." Ultimately, Julia and Sue Gene moved into a house in Santa Anna. When the *Curtiss* arrived in San Diego, they rejoined Gene.[67]

The army wife Mabel Ackerson and her sixteen-year-old son, Fred, also traveled stateside on a liner. She did not name the ship but confided that it was one the family had thought about booking for a vacation cruise. Back stateside, she was dividing her life into "B.B." and "A.B."— "before blitz" and "after blitz." Ackerson meant Pearl Harbor, not London. Anyway, she and her spouse, Lieutenant Colonel Martin Ackerson, were sound asleep in their Schofield Barracks bungalow when the roar of airplane engines and gunfire woke them up. "Why should they start maneuvers at this early hour?" she griped to the colonel. "Those aren't maneuvers," he replied.[68]

She ran to a window and spotted a low-flying plane with bright red balls painted on its wings and fuselage. She retreated when bomb fragments or bullets shattered the window. Within an hour, she and Fred were whisked away to the presumed safety of a concrete barracks. Later, they were evacuated to a school in Honolulu.[69]

While the colonel went to war, Mabel and Fred stayed in the overcrowded schoolhouse, where about seventy people were jammed into each classroom. They slept on the floor, sweltered, swatted mosquitoes and missed more than a few meals. But the general feeling, Mabel said, was a resigned, "Well, here we are." After five days, Mabel and Fred began their long trek to Louisville, where the colonel had been stationed for six years before the war.[70]

After arriving in California, Mabel and Fred went to Des Moines, Iowa, then on to Kentucky's biggest city, where they visited with another army family. Mabel was accustomed to refugee status. The great Ohio

River flood of 1937 chased the Ackersons from their Falls City home; a Wisconsin forest fire also left Mabel homeless. She and Fred planned to return to her sister in Des Moines. "After being in the army thirty years, I feel I haven't any real home," she lamented. "After the war is over, maybe we'll come back to Louisville for good."[71]

Anna Flaig was still in Hawaii two months after the attack. In a letter to a Danville friend, she said she first mistook the air raid for "an extra special war game!" After all, she added, "we've had so many alerts and blackouts and maneuvers that we just thought it was more of the same until the planes swooped so low that you could see the 'Rising Sun' on them and the bullets flew all around us."[72]

Anna's husband, Captain J. Vincent Flaig, was a physician like his father, the late Julian Flaig. While Dr. Flaig practiced in Danville, the captain was on the staff at the Schofield Barracks hospital. He watched the planes from outside the front door until "bullets from the machine guns struck the car next door and peppered the ground" close by. Anna said that they lived just below the tall towers of the RCA radio station and next to the telephone exchange. Naturally: "[Those structures] made perfect targets so we came in for our share of excitement."[73]

Captain Flaig rushed to the hospital. "They evacuated the women from the Post, but somehow or other they missed me in the roundup as I stayed over here alone the first night," Anna said. She went to the hospital on Monday morning: "But, Tuesday, some of the officers' wives who live in Wahiawa Heights returned and I joined them. Eight of us, plus a two months old and a 6 day old baby, have been staying together at St. Thomas [Hospital]." The women expected to return home soon and hoped to be reunited with their husbands. Meanwhile, Anna added: "Everything is quieting down rapidly and we're cooking and washing and cleaning and ironing as usual, except that we have to crowd everything into a mighty short day because of the blackouts from dusk to dawn."[74]

Anna urged her friend not to worry about her and her husband as "the Island is well defended": "If we hadn't been caught off guard the Japs wouldn't have gotten anywhere with the forces they had. And now that we know 'It Can Happen Here,' and [are] on the alert, they'll have a mighty difficult time repeating such an attack."[75]

9

Keeping the Home Fires Ablaze

Unlike later undeclared conflicts in Korea, Vietnam, and the Middle East, World War II was total war. The global conflict affected virtually every American to one degree or another. The government deeply injected itself into the economy and, thus, into society. But FDR's New Deal—generally popular in Kentucky—had gotten John and Jane Q Citizen accustomed to more government in their lives. Roosevelt carried Kentucky and the country in landslides in 1932, 1936, and 1940 (and would again in 1944). The rationing of sugar, coffee, butter, meat, gasoline, tires, fuel oil, and shoes required sacrifice. But Americans stateside were spared bombing, invasion, and occupation. (There were practice blackouts and air-raid drills even in Kentucky, two thousand miles from the Pacific and a little more than five hundred miles from the Atlantic.) Nonetheless, the lives of most Kentuckians not in service remained relatively stable, given the war emergency. Several colleges suspended sports, but the Derby continued. Listening to the radio and going to the movies became even more popular. Milk and mail were delivered regularly.[1]

The day before Pearl Harbor, *Dive Bomber* went off at the Gayety Theater in Burlington, in northern Kentucky. On the day of the attack, *Keep 'Em Flying* opened at the Malco in Owensboro, in western Kentucky.[2]

Dive Bomber was a drama—in color (still rare at the time)—that starred Errol Flynn and Fred MacMurray as navy pilots. It was partly filmed aboard the USS *Enterprise,* one of the three carriers that the Japanese hoped to sink at Pearl Harbor. The famous comics Bud Abbott and Lou Costello were the stars of *Keep 'Em Flying,* an army air force spoof billed as "a picture too funny for words" and "a bombload of belly-laughs." The movie was supposed to run three days. It did, despite "bombloads" of death and destruction at Pearl Harbor.[3]

When Adolf Hitler invaded Poland on September 1, 1939, starting World War II, most Kentuckians, like most Americans, were not ready to join Britain and France on the battlefield against the Nazis. But isolationism began to wane after Hitler conquered most of western Europe, including France, in 1940. Most Kentucky lawmakers in Washington and most voters back home agreed with the president's plan to supply the Allies with military aid short of American troops. They liked the idea of America as the world's "arsenal of democracy." Except for the hard-core isolationists, they mostly endorsed FDR's Cash and Carry and Lend-Lease programs. The latter, which Congress approved in March 1941, was designed to boost Britain militarily after France fell. At that point, the British stood alone against the Nazis; Germany and the Soviet Union had signed a nonaggression pact in August 1939. On June 22, 1941, Hitler invaded the Soviet Union. Afterward, Washington extended Lend-Lease aid to Moscow.[4]

Pearl Harbor swept away any illusions Kentuckians had about being able to stay out of the war. From Paducah to Pikeville, people demanded revenge. "Victory took precedence over everything else at this point, not least of all because Kentuckians knew that ours 'is a just cause,'" wrote the historian Richard E. Holl.[5]

"Yet for all the changes, daily life remained remarkably stable [in Kentucky]. . . . Even segregation continued, but it seemed ironic that in a war against fascism and for democracy, German POWs could eat in some Kentucky restaurants while their black guards could not," wrote the historians James C. Klotter and Lowell H. Harrison. Indeed. Though America was fighting German, Italian and Japanese tyranny abroad, Jim Crow segregation and race discrimination continued unabated in the South and in border states like Kentucky. Nonetheless, African Americans embraced the war as their struggle, too; thousands of blacks fought—and many died—for their country in Europe and the Pacific theater.[6]

Like nothing else before or since, Pearl Harbor unified Kentucky's often fiercely partisan press. Republican or Democratic, liberal or conservative, Bluegrass State papers were all in for licking the Japanese—and the Germans and the Italians, to boot. Some editorials were reasonably measured given what FDR called Japan's "unprovoked and dastardly" attack. Others shamelessly pandered to racism and xenophobia.

Before the editorials came the extras. On December 7, the Sunday morning papers had been out since before breakfast. The extras hit the streets late that evening or early the next day. Papers had to scramble to line up the requisite staff. The *Paducah Sun-Democrat* was typical.

The paper's managing editor, Joe LaGore, a World War I veteran, was enjoying a leisurely Sunday when he got the news about Pearl Harbor. He recalled: "Somebody called me on the phone or I heard it on the radio, I can't remember." But he clearly recalled what happened next: the boss wanted to put out an extra. So LaGore and Edwin J. Paxton Jr., the publisher's son and the paper's associate editor, got busy rounding up reporters, editors, composing room personnel, printers, and circulation department employees. LaGore tracked down the reporter Joe Mitchell at a local airstrip where he was enjoying a flying lesson. "He was having such a good time he wasn't coming down," LaGore said. "I didn't have any way of radioing him so I had to wait."[7]

When Mitchell finally landed and heard the news from LaGore, his first thought was of his brother, Private E. C. Mitchell Jr., who was at Hickam Airfield. "The whole Mitchell family was concerned," LaGore said, "and he was Mr. Paxton's nephew." News came later that Private Mitchell was unscathed.[8]

LaGore and Paxton managed to round up enough help to put out two extras, one after midnight and another later on Monday. But LaGore said that editors and reporters battling deadlines had to answer phones that would not stop ringing: "People would call and say, 'I've got a boy at such-and-such place in Hawaii, have you heard about him?'" Nobody had, not yet anyway.[9]

Paxton had happened to be at the *Sun-Democrat* office around 12:30 P.M. on December 7 when the phone rang. "I was in the second-floor editorial office," he remembered. "There was no one there but myself; I'd returned to get something I'd forgotten to bring home the previous night after we'd put the Sunday morning edition to bed."[10]

Bill Fellers, a veteran *Sun-Democrat* printer and the publisher's friend, was on the line. "Ed," he said, "the radio station is saying the Japs are bombing Hawaii." Paxton hung up and switched on the office radio; it was always tuned to WPAD. Owned by the Paxtons, WPAD was the town's only station. Expecting news, Paxton heard a commercial.[11]

The associate editor proceeded to flip the main switch to start the twin teleprinters that were wired to the AP office in Louisville. "I could tell from the hum that the wire was now active," he said. "After a pause, both machines chattered briefly." What printed out was: "FLASH—rept FLASH—JAPANESE NAVAL PLANES ATTACKING PEARL HARBOR—Rpt—JAP." Paxton added: "By that moment WPAD was apparently repeating a somewhat more detailed bulletin from CBS, and I moved to the set to listen. There was almost no detail. But it was enough to confirm the AP's flash."[12]

The news confirmed by the old two-source rule, Paxton called LaGore and the city editor, Henry Ward. The trio agreed to summon the staff and get out an extra. (Paxton remembered that the last time the *Sun-Democrat* had put out an extra was in the wee hours of July 23, 1934, when federal agents gunned down the famous bandit John Dillinger outside a Chicago movie theater.) "Neither the radio nor AP had much detail, but bits and pieces of news came over the wires from time to time," Paxton said, adding: "At 3 P.M. Paducah time the Japanese government officially announced its Declaration of War against the U.S. and Great Britain."[13]

The teleprinters rattled with more news: Japan had also gone after the Philippine Islands, Guam, Singapore, and other targets. Paxton said: "Radio WPAD allowed us numerous announcements stating we would have an extra, with latest available details on the story, by 9:30 that night. It would be sold only at the Sun-Democrat office. Business office people who dropped by volunteered to handle sales."[14]

The *Sun-Democrat* was at 408 Kentucky Avenue. (The *Sun*, its successor, is in a modernized version of the same building.) Paxton said that, by 9:00, the street "was jammed with waiting cars, parked double on both sides for blocks both east and west and around all corners on 2nd, 3rd, 4th, 5th and others, including Washington and Broadway. Beginning at 9:30 the sales were brisk and continuous."[15]

Paxton said that more than three thousand extras were sold and that "calls for them continued for days afterwards by people who wanted them for souvenirs." Meanwhile, on December 8, the paper lost its long-time sports editor, Sam Livingston. He joined the navy that morning and fought in the Pacific until the war was over.[16]

Thirteen-year-old Jim Edwards of Wickliffe was a rural paper carrier for the *Sun-Democrat*. He was home, fast asleep, when a blaring car horn jolted him awake about 2:00 A.M. on December 8. Next came "a loud knocking at the front door" by a man calling his name and shouting: "Wake up, wake up!" The noisemaker was his route boss, a Mr. Hughes.[17]

The early morning visitor exclaimed to Edwards "that Pearl Harbor had been attacked and we had a special edition to deliver as quickly as possible." Edwards said his mother lost no time fetching the family Model A Ford from the barn, and off he and Hughes sped on a Paul Revere–like ride. "My route started at the Adam Temple store in Maxon and covered some 15 miles throughout the Maxon and West Paducah communities," Edwards said. "Needless to say, we caused considerable excitement as we went from house to house honking that old Model A horn and me hollering to the top of my voice—'Extra! Extra!—Pearl Harbor bombed!!" He confessed that it was hard for him to fathom the attack: "But after war was declared I sure felt I was helping the war effort by carrying the daily news of it to the people in my community."[18]

Robert Coleman, eighty-seven, remembers the extra: "But I first heard about Pearl Harbor on the radio. It was a cold December day in Paducah." Coleman was a student at the city's segregated Lincoln Junior High School. "We had been studying about the war current events," he said. "I was too young to go to war, but I was surprised, baffled."[19]

"War has chosen us!" the *Louisville Courier-Journal* thundered on December 8. "There is no more excuse for doubting that barbarism has come back into our world." The editorial presaged America's "Germany-first" strategy: "We shall fight to the end. And we must face the terrible truth that the end will not be found in Japan, or on the wide wastes of the Pacific. The end will be found in Berlin." It continued: "Japan's attack on the U.S. is part of the world treachery, the world revolution, which the Nazis have created. Japan's attack on the United States is the final effort of Berlin to distract us from the meaning of modern history, from the simple fact that the men who honor no promises are tearing to bits the civilization of our Twentieth Century." The editorial predicted that the United States "will now unite to beat Japan," but it warned: "America must now unite to finish the job by beating Germany, the source of all our woe."[20]

The *Courier-Journal* was among dozens of American papers to hint broadly or say flat out that Hitler was behind the Pearl Harbor attack. "This concept was absolutely false," wrote Prange, Goldstein, and Dillon. "The Japanese were not German stooges. They planned and carried out the attack entirely on their own, and conducted their own intelligence-gathering to prepare for the strike." Nonetheless, they conceded: "This idea—that the Germans masterminded Japanese foreign policy, strategy, and tactics, and even contributed pilots to the Pearl Harbor striking force—arose almost immediately after the event and persisted for years."[21]

Prange, Goldstein, and Dillon also wrote: "Many responsible newsmen assumed that Japan could never have pulled off such an astounding feat on its own; the Germans must have been back of it. . . . Not only did the press credit Hitler with presenting to Japan a readymade foreign policy, but it also saw his guiding hand in the strategy of the attack itself." They suggested: "One receives the impression that to the gentlemen of the fourth estate, a thorough shellacking at the hands of the demon genius of Berlin would be less humiliating than one administered unaided buy the hitherto-underrated Japanese." Evidence of such an impression is plentiful in the editorial pages of scores of papers.[22]

The *Cincinnati Enquirer*'s Kentucky edition also advanced the Japanese-had-to-have-Hitler's-help theme: "Behind Japan's ruthless and lawless action we can discern the evil hand of Adolf Hitler, who has been trying for more than a year to shove the Japanese into conflict with America, and thus to protect Nazi Germany from the full impact of American naval and industrial power." Japan had "given immense help to [Germany and Italy, its allies], and now is attacking us to help them the more." Thus: "[America] must deal with Japan as our unsought share of the task of shattering the Rome-Berlin-Tokyo threat to civilization." The editorial writer agreed that FDR and the military had no choice "but to begin hostilities instantly in self-defense": "We went to war Sunday just as Poland and Russia went to war, when they found an enemy attacking without the slightest warning."[23]

The *Lexington Herald* editorialized that the Japanese attacks on Hawaii and the Philippines were just what Hitler wanted. It also charged that Japanese diplomacy supposedly aimed at preventing war with America was a "stage show" and "an exquisite exhibition of bowing and scraping as a cover up for a stab in the back." It was abundantly clear to anybody "who goes back to Juno for a parallel" that Tokyo "sent her ambassadors 'with lips dripping honey with and war in the heart,' not as a spontaneous act of the island empire but in carrying out a pattern that has been followed almost to the letter by Adolf Hitler every time he has double-crossed a friendly nation and has undertaken to commit a murderous act of treachery against an unsuspecting friend." The editorial argued that Japanese aggression against Hawaii and the Philippines was calculated to draw America into war with Japan so that Hitler could "turn with the fullness of his fury against England if he can close the back doors in Russia." Hence, Japan acted as a loyal Axis member, "turning the storm of a World War against the country which tried so hard to keep out but which now must defend itself on every side with eternal vigilance and total preparedness."[24]

A *Frankfort State Journal* editorial also claimed that Berlin had egged on Tokyo. The capital city paper dismissed Japan as Hitler's "Nipponese satellite." It also scorned isolationists: "The false security that the pacifists, the America First group and the isolationists have engendered in the minds and hearts of many Americans, the sense of well-being that paid propagandists have created through words of their own or the phrases of their unwitting followers, has suddenly and definitely been shattered and America finds herself facing a menace greater than any in her more than 160 years of independence." The United States would remain "a free country." But: "No real American will further tolerate obstructionist and seditious methods and speech. No real American will fail to give wholehearted backing to the wartime emergency policies as laid down by the President, commander-in-chief of our army, navy and air forces." The paper demanded: "National unity must and shall be the theme of life for every American citizen henceforth until the menace of the totalitarians are [*sic*] wiped completely from the earth."[25]

The *Lexington Leader* and the *Somerset Journal* also praised national unity, but the former also trotted out xenophobia, and the latter panned isolationism. The *Leader* reminded readers that it had said "long ago" that war would unify the country: "Factionalism has been natural, and wholesome. The opposition has exercised a restraining influence. Government has been much more responsible than otherwise it would have been." Henceforth: "Americans will show the world what real unity means, and how they can meet a crisis as one people, intent only on victory and the establishment of right and justice in the world."[26]

The editorialist wrapped up by recalling that, when Japan invaded Manchuria, the *Leader* had warned that Tokyo "had gone Asiatic," that Japan "had returned to its barbarous past, to its dark ages and its ancient policies of force and cunning." Thus, the Japanese "could no longer be trusted or dealt with as a civilized people."[27]

The *Journal*'s editorial writer was unsure whether to lead with "Wake Up, America'" or "We Told You So." He opted for the former and unloaded on isolationists, crowing: "How bitter must be their lot now! They may have been sincere, but theirs was a sincerity of ignorance. . . . We hope that they now see the error of their way, and that they no longer consider those among us to be alarmists and war-mongers, who heretofore tried to wake up America to the danger that now must be real to all of us." He was confident that America would defeat Japan. Still: "[Victory] may take longer than would have been required if some people in our country had used a little more horse sense, and a lot less of the jackass variety!"[28]

The *Paducah Sun-Democrat* predicted: "Sunday [i.e., the day of the Pearl Harbor attack] can be set down as the beginning of the end for Hitler's dream of world conquest. Even though we are at war with Japan we'll be fighting Hitler the more." It continued: "With Japan eliminated as an Axis power and definitely removed as a threat to the peace in the Pacific, we can then turn our entire strength to the main business of crushing Hitler. When this will be no one can venture a reasonable prediction. Enough for us now that we have begun the first step to bring it about, namely, the elimination of Japan from the Axis orbit."[29]

The *Kentucky Post* was gratified to see "the forces of civilian defense" so speedily "mustered to full strength for the emergency that has become a crisis." It singled out the Red Cross, declaring: "In war time no agency in this country does a more important service to mankind, both at home and on the line of battle." Nonetheless, it was disappointed that membership was lagging after "the Red Cross spent such large sums of money and did such a fine job of disaster relief during the flood of 1937." It ended by outlining the organization's dual task in America's brand-new war: "service to aid the morale of the armed forces and services to safeguard the life and health of the civilian population."[30]

Other papers, including the *Mayfield Messenger,* the *Franklin Favorite,* the *Madisonville Messenger,* and the *Middlesboro Daily News* played the race card. "In American slang a coward and a sneak is called 'yellow,'" the Mayfield paper editorialized on December 8. "The Japanese Government yesterday morning when America was preparing to attend Sunday school, lived up to their color and showed it in every respect in their cowardly, behind-the-back attack." The editorial claimed that somebody said Japan's aggression amounted to "biting the hand that fed them." The *Messenger* begged to differ: "No, it reminded more of a snake or a rat that someone had taken pity on and fed and warmed back to life, a dog just would not have been that treacherous." It snarled: "Well, brother, that grinning ape bit the wrong hand this time!" When Germany and Italy declared war on the United States on December 11, the *Messenger* broke the news to its readers with a banner front-page headline: "HUNS, WOPS JOIN YELLOW ALLIES."[31]

Like the *Messenger,* the *Favorite* dished a double helping of bigotry and invective: "If anybody expected other than what America received Sunday from the mongrel, half-breed Japanese, who are as treacherous as a rattlesnake, and likewise as venomous, he or she had most certainly received their misinformation from those of the [famous aviator and isolationist Charles A.] Lindbergh stripe rather than from the great humanitarian, Franklin D. Roosevelt." In his war message, FDR was content to characterize Japan's attack as *infamous* and *dastardly.* The *Favorite* claimed: "Never in all the annals of recorded time was a truer example of hate, cowardice and deceit perpetrated upon an unoffending people than was the outlaw bombing of cities, ships and civilians by the soldiers of the God-forgotten and God-forsaken country, which for the past four years has carried forward a war of aggression against the peaceful, and in some respects helpless, nation of China." It charged that the behavior of the Japanese diplomats in Washington "has no parallel since Judas Iscariot conspired with the plutocracy to betray the Savior": "And even Judas had decency enough left to hang himself in expiation of his infamy."[32]

The Madisonville paper editorialized that the Pearl Harbor attack was the "climactic episode of all the treachery, the covert duplicity of which the contemptible little brown men who seek to enslave free men in the eastern Pacific are capable." Japan was a "face-saving nation of slinkers . . . masters of two-face diplomacy, who smile and cry 'peace' while plunging a dirk between a friend's ribs." But, by making war on the United States, the Japanese had "committed hara-kari among the nations of upright character." The editorial claimed that the Pearl Harbor "attack was typically Japanese, remodeled under a few refinements of treachery as patterned by Hitler." The *Messenger* rejoiced: "At last the ape-men stand revealed. And the revelation will mean their end." Pearl Harbor, too, would silence the "traitorous mouthings by the Lindberghs, Wheelers and Nyes." (Senators Burton K. Wheeler, a Montana Democrat, and Gerald Nye, a North Dakota Republican, were also leading isolationists.) The *Messenger* demanded an end to further "nauseating heavings from alleged peace minorities": "We are at war. The FBI says it is ready now to crack down where cracking down is long overdue."[33]

The *Middlesboro Daily News* insisted that Pearl Harbor was "a perfect example of treachery worthy of Hitler himself." Its editorial agreed that Tokyo sent its diplomats to Washington "to mask the preparation of the Japanese naval and air forces": "While special envoy Saburō Kurusu [who, for the rest of his life, vowed he knew nothing of the impending Pearl Harbor strike] talked of peace . . . Japanese naval forces were even then steaming across the Pacific to the appointed place at sea from which to launch their bombing planes." The editorial writer concluded: "The slant-eyed partners of the Nazis have now proved they had no real peaceful intentions but were only waiting for the opportune time to wage war against the United States."[34]

The *Ashland Daily Independent* skipped the xenophobia and race-baiting. It editorialized: "The first shattering explosions of bombs in Hawaii did one good thing for the American people, even while they took a terrible toll. They woke us up. They dispelled the mist of confusion in which we have been wandering." No longer could Americans rightly ask each other, "Do you think we ought to have a war?" Pearl Harbor answered the question: "We have a war, and it is not of our own making." Japan caught Americans "unawares": "We had not yet brought ourselves to understand the complete duplicity, the shameless double-dealing, and the venomous deceit that lay behind all Japan's dealings. We were innocent. Like Hamlet, we could scarcely believe that 'one could smile and smile, and be a villain.'"[35]

The *Independent* also warned that America's sword—which Japan "has forced from our reluctant scabbard"—"must not be sheathed until Japan as a power in the Pacific and world affairs does not exist." But Japan's defeat "does not mean a war of extermination against the Japanese people": "It means destruction of her navy and air force, together with the means of building another. To this task Japan has herself assigned us." Fighting the Japanese "will be no basket picnic," the editorial conceded, adding: "News from the Pacific will be worse before it is better." Thus: "We must be prepared for bad news, for losses of ships and men." Nonetheless: "We cannot fail to win in the long run, though the run may be longer than we see at this moment."[36]

Likewise, the *Owensboro Messenger* warned: "The world is about to witness an awesome, terrifying sight—this country, prepared as it has never been prepared, powerful as no people in all history has known power and invincibility, and united as it never had enjoyed unity in a crisis of this kind, at war." It admitted: "When reverberations of exploding Jap bombs reached the ears of the American people Sunday, the first reaction was stunned amazement." But: "As the terrible significance of the bombing . . . stole over our people, the rocks and rills and templed hills of this great nation echoed to their indignant cries."[37]

Pearl Harbor, the *Messenger* continued, had turned isolationists into "warmongers," while "interventionists, who have maintained all along that we could not escape the world conflict," now "found their theories unchallenged." America was "not at war of its own choice." Rather, it was "the victim of deliberate, unprovoked attack, executed in the best totalitarian fashion": "Hitler's Far Eastern satellite is the aggressor."[38]

Nonetheless, Japan's goal in attacking Hawaii was unclear to the *Messenger:* "But of one thing the Japs can be sure. This country will reply in kind—ten, yea, a hundred-fold." Pearl Harbor, "the misguided action of the little clique of Tokio war lords and their masters in the Wilhelmstrasse" (the Nazi foreign ministry), had forged national unity that America had "earnestly and unsuccessfully sought since the outbreak of World War II." Thus, Japan and Germany "unwittingly have rendered a great service to the very institutions they seek to destroy."[39]

Danville Advocate-Messenger's city editor, Ben L. Williams, promised that the paper's war coverage would be "entirely one-sided." In a December 8 editorial, he explained: "During times of peace, or near peace, this newspaper, together with all worthwhile newspapers, tried to see and to print all sides of all questions. But now our country is at war."[40]

Williams predicted: "On the surface, life in Danville will proceed much the same as before. But underneath will be a new sense of unity, of striving for a common cause, and the Advocate-Messenger will endeavor to do its best to maintain the high standards required for the good of all and the success of our government at this time of greatest national crisis." He pledged that his paper would keep reporting "the news with the greatest clarity and promptness possible": "But we will also miss no opportunity to boost the welfare of this great nation or condemn in the strongest terms those who stand in the way of our collective security."[41]

The *Pike County News* detected "a mild attack of hysteria since news of the Japanese attack on the United States was flashed last Sunday." So the Pikeville paper's front-page "Here and There" column was headlined: "Let's Keep Our Shirts On." The paper conceded that "news has been scarce and all sorts of wild rumors have been floating about" and that "everybody wants to help 'lick the Japs' and nobody knows quite what to do." So it shared FDR's post–Pearl Harbor advice: "Everyone go about routine duties in the routine fashion until called upon for active service." It warned: "The news we receive during the next few weeks or months is bound to be bad. The aggressor always draws first blood. So there is no reason for us to become disheartened if we hear of severe setbacks in the near future." But it was glad that Pearl Harbor had unified the country: "Never before in its history has America been so strong in patriotism. In the end, national unity and patriotism will bear the fruits of victory." Meanwhile, the *News* pledged that Pike Countians "at home" would serve the country best "by following orders, working and giving."[42]

The Morehead State College (now university) student paper also called for calm. "Now, more than ever, sound, cool, level-headed judgment is needed," the *Trail Blazer* pleaded on December 13. "Panic spreads quickly . . . as quickly as its forerunner[,] rumor. Anger and hate have no place in good thinking. Don't be rash, don't jump to conclusions."[43]

The campus weekly, which billed itself as "Kentucky's Most Modern Collegiate Newspaper," urged students: "Consider carefully where you fit in this war and try to fill your place to the utmost. If the army wants you they will not hesitate to call on you. If you are in school wait until they do call. You can do service for your community in school as well as in the army. . . . Don't act as if tomorrow might not come. There will be a future, there MUST be a future. Trained people will be sorely needed in that future. Prepare now." Hence, when Uncle Sam calls: "Go proudly knowing that the cause is worth the struggle."[44]

The *Kentucky Kernel* staff no doubt disagreed about who had the state's most up-to-date college paper. But the student editorialist at the University of Kentucky's campus paper echoed the *Trail Blazer*'s patriotism: "The Kernel eagerly calls on every student . . . to stand prepared for anything he may be called upon to do. The life of the United States is threatened and University of Kentucky students must stand ready."[45]

The *Kernel* had hoped that America might remain at peace, "aloof" and "planning for the future, solid and strong," as "the great doctor of the world's sickness." But war had been forced on the country: "Instead of the American people climbing over the isolationist-intervention fence, the fence itself has been lifted by the Japanese and moved to such a position that there can be but one side for Americans to take. And that is to throw every bit of strength and spirit the nation can muster into the whole-hearted defense of the country."[46]

In the days following Pearl Harbor, no Kentuckians were more desperate for news from the new Pacific war zone than the families of servicemen and civilians out there. Papers rushed to print what they knew, which usually was not much. "Several Hopkins county boys are with some branch of the armed forces in the Pacific possessions, the hot spots of the Japanese attacks upon the United States," the *Madisonville Messenger* reported on December 9. But the paper had to admit that "no word has been received from any of the servicemen." Likewise, the fate of a civilian woman who had lived in Honolulu for fifteen years was unknown to her kin in town.[47]

The *Owensboro Messenger* knew of "three Calhoun boys" and several others from McLean County "in the war zone." (Calhoun is the county seat.) It did not say whether the "boys" were dead or alive. The *Danville Advocate-Messenger* reprinted a story from the *Interior Journal* of

Stanford that said: "[Five] Lincoln county boys . . . saw action with the Japs." The county seat paper suspected that there were others but explained: "These young men are known to be there as the Interior Journal is being sent to them."[48]

At least sixteen Pulaski County servicemen, "some of them with their families," were believed to be in Hawaii and the Philippines, according to the *Somerset Journal.* Back home, worried relatives were "anxiously awaiting word of their safety." Apparently, no city or county civilians were in the Philippines, though William Tuttle managed a big pineapple plantation on the Hawaiian island of Maui, which Japanese planes did not attack. While his wife was with him, their daughter, Polly, was in Honolulu. Another daughter was in school in Oakland, California.[49]

Arthur and Sara Pressler of Newport feared that they were due an official telegram bearing bad news from Hawaii. The *Kentucky Post* was glad to report that good news arrived by telephone on December 19. When Sara picked up the receiver, she heard a familiar voice urge her: "Keep your chin up; that's what we are doing over here and everything is o.k." It was her daughter, Dorothy. She and her husband, the army master sergeant Howard Biggerstaff, were safe. So was Billy, the couple's four-year-old son.[50]

Personal calls to loved ones stateside had been impossible on December 7. Sara asked the telephone company to put through a call whenever possible. Finally on the line with her daughter, she wanted to know whether the family needed money. They were flush, Dorothy replied. The paper said that Dorothy "could give no details regarding her husband, who has been stationed in Hawaii for seven months." Nor could she say when she could return stateside. Dorothy graduated in 1936 from Newport High School, where she had been prom queen.[51]

Gradually, papers were able to provide more information about loved ones in harm's way. On December 18, the *Somerset Journal* reported the Tuttles safe on Maui. Mr. and Mrs. Walter Kuzee of Camp Ground, in Pulaski County, got a navy telegram saying that their nineteen-year-old sailor son, Seaman First Class Ernest George Kuzee, was wounded, presumably at Pearl Harbor. "The message did not state details of his injury," the paper said. "No Pulaski countian has yet been reported killed in the war." Kuzee, who quit high school to join up, had been in the navy almost a year. The teen was turned down several times because he was underweight. He was accepted after he put on the requisite pounds. Ultimately, the *Journal* learned that Kuzee had succumbed and that Seaman First Class Norman Lee Garland, twenty-eight, was missing. They were the county's first two war deaths. Garland was alive. Sometime later, Bob Day, a buddy from Somerset, spotted him in Australia hefting supplies aboard the *Black Hawk,* a destroyer tender. "Hey Garland!" Day yelled, waving a copy of the *Journal.* "You can't do that. You're dead!"[52]

Papers sometimes had to correct erroneous military cables. Four days after the attack, James Ira Wells Sr. of Browder in Muhlenberg County got a navy wire saying that his sailor son, James Jr., had been killed. But, on December 21, the *Owensboro Messenger* published a paragraph explaining that James Jr. had telegraphed his folks in Muhlenberg County that he was "all right." On December 24, the paper ran a two-paragraph AP story describing the wire as "a five-letter Christmas present that spelled the happiest of all possible yule tidings for them." It was a telegram saying "I am OK" and signed "James Jr." The *Paducah Sun-Democrat* revealed that the former city residents Grace and Hilton Roberts, both civilians, were safe. So were the servicemen Gerry Coyle, Bill Danaher, John Clifton Locker, Leonard Rickman, and Rex Yarbro, all from Paducah. But Fred Ray, formerly of nearby Bardwell, was "killed in action." Lieutenant Commander J. H. Brady of Louisville and his family were alive and well, according to the *Louisville Courier-Journal.* The *Franklin Favorite* reported that the army corporal Billie R. Tucker of Petroleum in Allen County "was killed in action at his post at Pearl Harbor, where his work was to inspect airplanes just before they took off at the airport, there." At the same time, Private First Class George Harold Harris, another Allen Countian "serving in Uncle Sam's Army at Honolulu when Pearl Harbor was bombed," had sent a letter to his folks letting them know that he was "all right."[53]

As they were able to gather additional information about local men in uniform, some papers started running the news in column form. The *Paducah Sun-Democrat*'s "Service Notes" was typical. Jack B. Gish, an army air force private, topped the column on February 8, 1942. Based at Hickam Field, the Paducah man had "received a citation for bravery under fire during the recent Pearl Harbor attack, according to a letter received from him by his mother, Mrs. Ruby Gish of 536½ Harrison street." Gish included the citation, which praised his "coolness of behavior and bravery . . . under fire and in the emergency which followed the attack." Next came news supplied by Mrs. Hazel Wallace, who told the paper that she got a letter from her son, Francis Wallace, who was part of "a weather observation squadron at an undisclosed base in the Pacific." She said the welcome letter "was the first direct mail she had received from him since the attack on Pearl Harbor." On the same day, she got a letter from Francis's commanding officer saying that Francis had been promoted.[54]

To balance the usually grim war news, reporters were always on the lookout for odd and funny stories like ones about Clifford Earl Eakle and Alfred Angel. Eakle had been AWOL and on the lam from Randolph Army Airfield in Texas for more than a month. After he found out about Pearl Harbor, he strode into the Paducah police station on the morning of December 8 and surrendered to Chief W. E. Bryant. "I just heard that Japan had declared war on America, Chief, and I'm a d—— good airplane mechanic," the twenty-two-year-old soldier from Clarksburg, Virginia, told the city's top cop. "I am more than ready to do my part, now." Bryant reported that authorities were coming for Eakle.[55]

The prisoner said that, when he got drafted, he was making $45.00 a week as an attorney, considerably more than army pay. He also told Bryant that he took off because he "became 'despaired and discouraged' in the army." He explained: "Now it's a different story; my country really needs me!"[56]

Alfred Angel's unusual sacrifice grabbed headlines, too. After Pearl Harbor, the twenty-three-old disabled ex-coal miner from Hazard tried to rejoin the army. When Uncle Sam declined to take him back, Angel canceled his military disability claim. Hugh Lewis, the field secretary of the Kentucky Disabled Ex-Servicemen's Board, had never heard of anybody dropping a claim on account of war.[57]

Angel wrote Lewis on December 10, explaining: "I sent you some more papers on my disability two days ago. Please return them to me for I don't think it would be right for a man to ask the government for help with a war going on." He said he would "get a job somewhere or something." Meanwhile, he vowed to keep trying to get back in uniform.[58]

Lewis said Angel seemed to have a valid claim. He had an affidavit signed by his doctor swearing that he was unable to dig coal. Army records showed that Angel was hurt at Fort Bragg, North Carolina, "when he fell over a trash can in the company street while he was running to get into a formation."[59]

Governor Keen Johnson surely would have appreciated Angel's patriotic spirit. On December 9, he issued a proclamation entreating all Kentuckians to rally to the cause. The Democrat ordered that "all activities of the commonwealth be immediately placed on a wartime basis," "specifically urg[ing] capital and labor to put aside any differences and unite to increase production of materials and farmers to produce more food." Johnson had telegraphed FDR pledging that Bluegrass State citizens were "a united people . . . ready to follow" the president's leadership. "We must approach the problem with complete victory as our objective and to achieve that victory will require considerable sacrifice on the part of all of us," Johnson said.[60]

As absurd as it seems today, Johnson and other Kentucky leaders seemed genuinely worried about spies and saboteurs flying in and out of dozens of small, often remote airports across the state. Johnson said that the assistant secretary of commerce in charge of aviation personally asked him to start guarding small airports, though Washington said that more security was not needed "at well-policed" airports in Louisville and Lexington. As a result, the governor proposed legislation that would authorize the hiring of more state patrol officers to serve as airfield guards. His proposal hiked the patrol's annual budget from $300,000 to $1 million to pay for the extra officers. In addition, the legislation authorized state officials to call on mayors to "assign guards to small airports and casual landing fields near their towns." Also, the measure created a version of the World War I–era State Council of Civil Defense. It took the Legislative Council less than two minutes to approve the plan.[61]

The governor was particularly anxious to patrol emergency landing strips in Warsaw, Glendale, and Smith's Grove. Warsaw was on the Louisville-to-Cincinnati air route; Glendale straddled the air corridor between Louisville and Nashville. Johnson evidently figured that enemy agents could somehow use the remote landing fields to spy on air traffic among the three cities—as if Berlin, Rome, and Tokyo did not have more pressing military concerns closer to home.[62]

Most likely because Pearl Harbor was attacked from the air, state and local officials also seemed obsessed with air defense. No German, Japanese, or Italian bomber had anywhere near the range to reach America from Europe or Asia. Neither Germany nor Italy had operational carriers in World War II. But, because Japan had carriers and had proved their prowess, it seemed reasonable that the US military on the West Coast would be on the lookout for them and other Japanese warships.

But Kentucky was deep in the country's interior. Frankfort is 2,360 miles from San Francisco and nearly 730 miles from New York. Tokyo is 6,600 miles west of the Bluegrass State's capital, Berlin 4,450 miles east. Nonetheless, Frankfort officials had an air-raid drill on December 15. Maybe they genuinely feared enemy bombers, or perhaps they just wanted to get their town in the war spirit.[63]

The whole drill was supposed to last fifteen minutes; locals gave it five. Nonetheless, officials praised the public for "a wonderful response." From 3:30 to 3:35 P.M., pedestrians and motorists stopped, "cast a wary eye at the perils of aerial warfare," and heeded the local air-raid signal: a shrieking steamboat whistle atop a downtown building. L. Boone Hamilton, a Democratic county judge, boasted that the drill was perhaps the first one held in an inland American city. Never mind that "the city's streets were filled quickly again" as soon as the warning signal stopped. Forget that "the 'all clear' toots 10 minutes later meant virtually nothing." Hamilton, who was also the Frankfort defense coordinator, and Captain Julius Effron, the local state militia commander, "expressed complete satisfaction with the results."[64]

Hamilton said: "The intelligent reaction to air raid precaution efforts was more than we hoped for. The public will come to find out later the importance of observing the full period of the alarm, whether the whistle is sounded or not." The drill was mainly supposed to test pedestrian reaction, but car and truck drivers did their part, finding parking places or halting just outside the business district. Effron's troops were empowered only to *ask* pedestrians to seek shelter. Even so, "none reported any difficulty persuading persons to enter buildings" where they were supposed go in a real air raid.[65]

The practice produced its lighter moments. A minister heard the whistle and ducked into a liquor store. "A bell-ringing solicitor for a charitable organization"—evidently a Salvation Army volunteer—stood his ground on a street corner and kept ringing his bell. A pair of elderly women ignored the state troops "until they finally grasped the word, 'air raid,'" uttered by one of the uniformed men and scurried into a store. Hamilton and Effron were surprised at how kids went along with the drill: "They, along with the elders, took refuge in stores and, with scores who sat in windows of downtown buildings, peered out at the deserted streets during the alarm." (Citizens of London and other European cities knew to steer clear of windows in bombing attacks. Bombs blew out windows, turning glass shards into additional lethal shrapnel.)[66]

In any event, the County Civilian Council had been planning the exercise for months. The group had "mapped plans for a wide variety of defense measures." Those plans "included [the] location of superior possible air-raid shelter sites, fire and police service, communications, anti-incendiary bomb squads, and civilian rescue and relief." The body had recently announced that it would call on the city council to pass an ordinance mandating obedience "to all air-raid and blackout drills."[67]

The council's post–Pearl Harbor defense program also called for a coed home guard. Frankfort civil defense officials believed that Ashland and Louisville were doing likewise, according to an AP story. The Frankfort women—and presumably those in Ashland and Louisville—were to be "trained and disciplined as thoroughly as soldiers in shooting and other work essential to the defense of the capital."[68]

Volunteers would formally enroll after Christmas. Meanwhile, women could sign up with Judge Hamilton. Ellen Clark, a women's corps organizer, suggested an initial "combat corps" of 125 who would drill at an American Legion post. Plans called for outfitting the women in state militia–style uniforms.[69]

Air raids and blackouts were, of course, real to Frankfort sons and daughters on Oahu and in the Philippines, which finally fell to Japanese invaders on May 8, 1942. On December 9, capital city store owners received lists with names and addresses of local men in the military: "The idea . . . is to have every boy from this city and [Franklin County] remembered with a Christmas present . . . to show them how much their services to their country are appreciated by the folks at home."[70]

Shoppers were to review the lists and put a check mark next to the name of a serviceman for whom they wanted to buy something. A "clearance committee," chaired by Evans Cannon, would purchase presents for servicemen whose names had not been checked off and pay for the gifts from a $30.00 city council appropriation. Cannon, who was also the YMCA secretary, listed more than four hundred men in the armed forces. He wanted the gifts mailed promptly so that they would arrive by Christmas. Apparently, not many names were being marked. Anyway, Cannon warned: "Either a large majority of these boys will not be otherwise remembered, or else friends and relatives are waiting until the last minute to mail their Christmas packages." He begged city and county residents to lose no time in choosing a name and buying a gift.[71]

Cannon said the committee was shooting for "a 100 percent job," but explained that the panel must "have better cooperation to make this achievement possible." He complained that the money from the city was inadequate "because of the large number who must be remembered." Hence, he proposed that groups and individuals chip in to the fund. Donors could phone or write the YMCA or the *Frankfort State Journal*.[72]

Meanwhile, millions of men nationwide were falling over themselves to join up. The *Louisville Courier-Journal* had seen nothing like it in the Falls City since World War I. On the day after Pearl Harbor, minors came with their fathers and mothers in tow. Similarly: "Oldsters who saw service in the last war and men who had been deferred in the draft rushed to the various offices."[73]

The *Journal* said that Falls City volunteers made no bones about why they wanted to join up: "They were fighting mad." James Hochadel, nineteen, of Jeffersonville said: "The more I thought about the dirty, sneaking deal those Japs gave us, the madder I got and when I told my folks I wanted to enlist, they said 'Go to it.'" (Men under twenty-one had to get their parents' blessing to volunteer.)[74]

The navy, headquartered in the Federal Building, inked the most enlistees—more than one hundred by late afternoon, with more still pouring in. Recruiters pledged to keep the office open past midnight or for twenty-four hours a day if necessary. The Louisville native Louis William Magnifico showed up to sign up on December 12. Both his parents were born in Italy, but he said that that was no reason for thinking he "can't be as patriotic as the next fellow." He added that Pearl Harbor made "people remember we're all Americans."[75]

Army recruiters expected to land no more than thirty recruits because regulations prohibited them from taking men older than twenty-eight. George Wesley Hunter, an African American World War I veteran, was eighteen years over the age cap for the army. So he headed for the firehouse at 104 West Liberty and joined the Louisville auxiliary fire service. He said he "wanted to help." He admitted that he knew little about firefighting but said: "I can do what I'm told."[76]

The Covington firefighter and ex-pro boxer Joe Anderson was ten years Hunter's junior. "Colonel Joe" spared neither ethnic slurs nor alliterations in telling a *Kentucky Post* reporter that he was still fit enough to "hit a Heine, kayo a Dago and jab a Jap." He volunteered his services to Congressman Brent Spence, a Newport Democrat, explaining: "The Army needs commissioned officers to serve as physical directors, boxing instructors, etc., and that's where I can fill the bill best." In his heyday, Anderson reportedly had given "all the world's leading middle weight fighters all they could handle (and more on many occasions)."[77]

Meanwhile, back at Louisville's Heyburn Building, forty-six men had volunteered for the Marines toward sunset on December 8, but the office was still jammed with applicants. Sergeant Dale Kier said that a man was waiting to enlist when the door opened at 7:00 A.M. He heard that thirty men had joined as a group in Ashland and that the postmaster in "Madison"—apparently Madisonville—had twenty almost set for their physicals. At Somerset, volunteers and draftees kept the army's mobile Examining Board 8 busy. On December 8 and 9, doctors saw 326 men at the Hotel Beecher Armory.[78]

On December 10, more than one hundred men applied for the army at Fort Thomas. Twenty-seven, including a half dozen aviation cadets, swore the enlistment oath, reported the *Cincinnati Enquirer*'s Kentucky Edition. A number of World War I vets tried to volunteer but were turned away because they were too old. The age limit for reenlisting veterans was thirty-five. On the same day at nearby Covington, eight men volunteered for the navy. The oldest, a navy veteran, was forty-six; the youngest seventeen.[79]

More than a few volunteers packed union cards or came from union families. The Kentucky State American Federation of Labor (AFL) president, Alexander Jeffrey, and the secretary-treasurer, Edward H. Weyler—both World War I veterans—issued a joint statement condemning the "malicious attack by those who despise our form of government" and urging rank and filers "as true trade unionists" to be ready to make any "personal and collective sacrifices necessary" to win the war. They called on union members not to strike "until every avenue of adjustification has been thoroughly exhausted" and urged them to contact the AFL before considering "drastic steps." They encouraged workers to buy war bonds and ended their statement with a ringing appeal: "We toiled and sweated to build the nation. Some will die defending it. Let us all defend the nation as freely as we have used it."[80]

Peter Campbell, the president of the Kentucky Congress of Industrial Organizations (CIO), said his group was making plans to create committees in CIO plants to maximize war production and report to management "anything which appears to be interfering with or threatening capacity production." A member of the US Secret Service in World War I, Campbell cited a CIO resolution pledging his labor group to "a determined and whole hearted support of the great national effort, including 100 percent production, and the rooting out of every form of sabotage and subversive influence."[81]

In addition, the AFL and the CIO moved swiftly to help boost war production in Louisville and its environs. John Grigsby, the secretary of the CIO's Kentucky Industrial Union Council, announced that a drive had begun to get defense plant workers to donate eighty thousand man-hours of Sunday work. Workers were to give up any Sabbath double-time pay they were due and put the lost wages toward buying war bonds and contributing to the USO. "We're not going to win this war with snowballs," Campbell said. "It'll take hard work and lots of it. Proprietors have already indicated they're with us." The five-hundred-strong National Maritime Union at Jeffersonville Boat and Machine Company voted to join the program in cooperation with the company president. Weyler said that the state AFL "will insist on full cooperation of union members in the expansion of defense industries."[82]

Louisville Mayor Wilson Wyatt praised the union groups for approving a joint resolution promising "unlimited support to national, state and local governments." The unions approved the measure on December 15. Pat Ansboury, the business agent for truck drivers' and dairy employees' union locals in the city, presented the resolution to the mayor. "I know those are your convictions and I know they will be translated into action when you are called upon," said Wyatt, a Democrat. "All of us are going to have to sacrifice time, effort and money, some of us our lives, and when the crisis of war is over we face an economic and political crisis that's going to require the united efforts of all of us to solve democratically."[83]

On December 12, workers at the Allen Garment Company in Franklin claimed that they started the state's first "Pearl Harbor Club." According to the *Franklin Favorite*, members pledged to purchase "one 25¢ Defense Stamp each week to help in Defense Work." Close to two hundred women worked at the shirt factory. Club organizers hoped to sign everybody up; by noon on December 16, sixty-four had enrolled. By late January "practically every woman employee [was investing] . . . a certain sum in defense bonds or stamps each week," the *Favorite* reported. Plant management agreed to permit employees to sew for the Red Cross for two hours on Saturdays starting January 31: "A finer thing than the Company's proposal could scarcely be conceived, and likewise, too much in praise cannot be said of the patriotic women, who not only invest a portion of their wages in defense stamps, but now propose to give a portion of their time to the work of aiding the Angels of Mercy who minister through the agency of the Red Cross to wounded soldiers and sailors."[84]

Allen was typical of many Kentucky firms that switched to war production. The "shirt factory" was remodeled so that employees could make mattress covers for the military. "The government now has thousands of soldiers in camps, in the field and in barracks scattered all over America," said Norris Boaz, who was brought in to supervise the war work. "Not only is the best of food provided for the fighting forces, but sleeping quarters, as well, are given primary consideration." Boaz intended for Allen "to provide a finished mattress that will measure up to the fullest government restrictions."[85]

Franklin is in south-central Kentucky. Some patriotic northern Kentucky belles organized the "Kenton-Campbell County Battalion Dancers for Democracy." Their mission was boosting the morale of local servicemen home on leave and Fort Thomas soldiers. The young women were posted to the Covington YMCA nightly during the holidays with orders to entertain servicemen "with a program of dancing, bridge and musical numbers." Battalion "captains and chaperones" were on watch to head off any potential hanky-panky.[86]

Ashland blazed with patriotism on the one-week anniversary of Pearl Harbor. Over five hundred hardy folks "braved a northwest wind" to watch "about $2,000 worth of trinkets, merchandise, and articles labeled 'Made in Japan'" burned up in a big bonfire. The city thus "whipped up a brand-new American war-time slogan today, contrasting in meaning with 'Bundles for Britain,'" reported the December 15 *Cincinnati Enquirer* Kentucky edition. "It is 'Ashes for Japan.'" The blaze lasted for an hour in Central Park with merchants from Ashland, Catlettsburg, and other eastern Kentucky towns furnishing the special fuel.[87]

Sponsored by Ashland's Clarence Fields American Legion Post, the conflagration was kindled at 2:45 P.M. That was about the time the Japanese air raid had begun in Hawaii on December 7, the *Ashland Daily Independent* explained. When plans for the fire were announced, more than a few store owners had been unsure about what goods would be consigned to perdition. After meeting with merchants, the post commander E. C. Downs told the *Independent* that some of the store owners and numerous newspaper readers thought that everything made in Japan was to go up in smoke. Only "certain Christmas decorations" should be incinerated "as a symbolic gesture of American feeling toward the Japanese," he advised.[88]

Evidently, nobody saw a possible parallel with the Nazis burning books, some of them by American writers. Nonetheless, patriotism would not entirely trump profit on the "anti-Axis" pyre. Downs said that store owners told him that "no good could be accomplished by merchants taking substantial losses on their merchandise by destroying it." Besides, the proprietors pointed out, the now offending stock was bought before the day of infamy. Meanwhile, some merchants were letting shoppers in on where their prospective purchases were manufactured. "This will enable the customer to make the decision as to whether it is wanted or not," the paper suggested.[89]

In Ashland, as elsewhere in Kentucky and the nation, war production would wipe out the last lingering joblessness from the Great Depression. But Kentuckians who wanted work closer to the war got a chance in late December when papers put out the word that civilian employees were badly needed at Pearl Harbor. "The navy department furnishes transportation," reported the *Madisonville Messenger* on New Year's Eve. Prospective workers had to pay only for meals on the way, but they would be reimbursed at the rate of $4.00 a day when they got to Hawaii. According to the paper, the navy needed boxmakers, packers, enginemen, molders, punchers and shearers, riveters, sheet-metal workers, blacksmiths, coppersmiths, ship and shop electricians, instrumentmakers, machinists, riggers, radio, aircraft, bombsight, and motor mechanics, toolmakers, watch and chronometer repairers, boilermakers, and rigger and shipfitter helpers.[90]

The *Messenger* said that the navy wanted skilled civilians to keep the fleet and its air arm "ready and fit for action." But, from the jobs listed, it was obvious that the civvy street workers were needed to help repair and salvage ships and aircraft damaged or lost in the attack. A cantonment had been built near the navy yard for the workers, who were promised low rent and inexpensive meals at the cafeteria. More information was available at the Madisonville post office.[91]

It was white workers the navy wanted. The marines did not want black recruits, and opportunities for blacks in the Jim Crow army and navy were limited. Nonetheless, on December 8, the Louisville Ministers and Deacons, an organization of African American Baptist pastors, met and pledged support to FDR "in the national emergency." The group, which represented about sixty thousand church members, telegraphed the pledge to the president, according to the Reverend W. P. Offutt, the pastor of Calvary Baptist Church.[92]

Seven days later, with patriotism surging in the segregated city, officials of the downtown Louisville Free Public Library invited the public to come and hear a nationally broadcast radio program celebrating the sesquicentennial of the Bill of Rights. "White public" was implied, but Offutt and a group of African Americans came. They were denied admission, "although they pointed out, with considerable irony, that they merely wished to hear the program which ended with an address by President Roosevelt," the *Courier-Journal* reported.[93]

Offutt and his group persisted. "We pushed our way in and were permitted to remain until the program was over," he said. The librarian Harold F. Brigham said that Offutt and the other blacks were told: "Negro branches [of the library] were also open so that Negroes could hear the program." He added that "the Negroes asked to stay at the main library" and that "since they were already there . . . they were granted that right."[94]

Brigham predicted: "This question will continue to keep coming up. It has never been settled legally whether Negroes have a right in the public libraries used by whites; that is, whether the Kentucky School Law [i.e., segregation] applies to libraries. There is no specific mention in the state library law relating to Negroes."[95]

The *Courier-Journal* story did not say whether Offutt or anybody who came with him was a World War I veteran. But thousands of Kentucky blacks served in the war that was supposed to make the world safe for democracy and end all war—and failed on both counts. African Americans "found few new freedoms as a result" of the war, the historians Lowell H. Harrison and James C. Klotter wrote. "One decorated black soldier [Rufus Ballard Atwood, who became the longest-serving president of Kentucky State University] was warned not to return to his Hickman hometown in the uniform he had honored, because the police chief did not like blacks in uniform." They added: "This soldier's experience was not uncommon. Improved race relations would not be an outcome of this war." Indeed, the color bar remained rigid. White supremacy continued virtually unabated across Kentucky and the country.[96]

Even so, many blacks again volunteered to fight, again did their part on the home front, and again shared in the national sacrifice for victory. Yet African Americans "understood Pearl Harbor as a watershed in the history of race relations," wrote the historian Chris Dixon. "Remember Pearl Harbor" had different meanings for whites and blacks: "African Americans invested the phrase with a racially distinct meaning that merged calls for victory over Japan with the demands that the United States fulfill its democratic promises—to all its citizens." Whites, on the other hand, took the phrase to mean that winning the war "would restore the nation." Blacks demanded, "not restoration, but change."[97]

On December 20, the *Louisville Leader,* a leading African American paper in Kentucky, editorialized for victory and racial equality. It quoted a statement from Walter White, the executive secretary of the National Association for the Advancement of Colored People (NAACP): "Declaration of war by Germany, Italy and Japan, with the collaboration, willing or otherwise, of their satellite nations brings thirteen million American Negroes sharply to a decision which is more critical than any they or any other American has been forced to face."[98]

In World War I White noted: "[Blacks] were taken up to a mountain-top and promised that if we gave without stint of our lives and resources we would enjoy after the war democracy in full measure." Instead, some African American veterans "were lynched for wearing the uniform which they had worn in France fighting to preserve democracy": "The Ku Klux Klan was revived and I need not list what it and other fiendishly anti-Negro organizations and individuals did in an effort to give less, rather than more, opportunity to Negro Americans."[99]

White urged African Americans to remember "that the declarations of war do not lessen the obligation to preserve and extend civil liberties here while the fight is being made to restore freedom from dictatorship abroad." No easy task, he acknowledged. But he warned: "If we fail we shall contribute to dictatorship after, as well as during, the war." He said that lines in World War II were more sharply drawn than they were in the First World War, which was known as the *Great War* until 1939: "The Nazi philosophy crystalizes all and every anti-Negro, anti-Jewish, anti-liberal and anti-freedom principle." Yet he cautioned: "We all know that the attitude towards the Negro of the nations fighting Hitler, Mussolini and Hirohito leaves much to be desired." The statement said: "We Negroes are faced with a Hobson's choice. But there *is* a choice. If Hitler wins, every single right we now possess and for which we have struggled here in America for more than three centuries will be instantaneously wiped out. . . . If the allies win, we shall at least have the right to continue fighting for a share of democracy for ourselves."[100]

The editorial concluded by reprinting part of a December 13 *Leader* editorial: "The Negro stands today as the most dependable American citizen to whom the President of the United States may appeal." Even so, the paper promised: "Negroes and great Americans like Pearl Buck will not cease to remind the ministers of the government that charity should first begin at home, and that the foundation upon which American democracy was built needs strengthening, that the war in which we are involved may not be prolonged, and that more confidence may be enhanced in the victory."[101]

Meanwhile, from Jordan to Jenkins, Kentuckians huddled around radios listening to bulletins from Hawaii. In larger towns, they expected to learn more from anticipated extra editions of their hometown papers.

As the news rolled in, they were "changing the World War's slogan of 'to Hell with the Kaiser,' to one of 'To Hell with Hirohito and Hitler,'" reported the *Owensboro Messenger* extra, explaining that Hirohito was Japan's emperor.[102]

Most locals who remembered April 6, 1917, when Congress approved President Woodrow Wilson's declaration of war against imperial Germany, "realized the contrast between that spring day twenty-four years ago and the bleak Sunday afternoon when the entire nation became a sounding board for the word that 'Japan has declared war on the United States,'" reported the *Messenger* extra, which appeared early on December 8. As in most other communities nationwide, Owensboro townsfolk first heard about Pearl Harbor from radio bulletins. Shortly after broadcasting the first news flash, WOMI, a local station, announced that all other programs would be interrupted for more bulletins "as they were received." WOMI kept broadcasting long after it usually signed off.[103]

While *Messenger* staffers worked on the extra, clergy modified their Sunday night services, "offering prayers for the members of the American military forces who will be thrown into combat with the Japanese." Hundreds of worshipers joined the supplications. Many local young men were already in service, including several sailors at Pearl Harbor whose ships "will carry the brunt of the first fighting of the war," the extra said. More than 250 men from Owensboro and Daviess County had been drafted since November 16, 1940, when the first of them were called to the colors under the Selective Service System.[104]

The extra also cited a famous native of nearby Henderson, reporting that Admiral Kimmel's "present whereabouts are unknown to his brothers, S. H. and Lambert Kimmel who suppose he is aboard his flagship, the Pennsylvania." The *Messenger* told its readers that Kimmel's wife was in Long Beach, California, and that their two sons were both submarine officers. The paper included an AP report that described Kimmel as "a two-fisted naval officer with the reputation of being one of the toughest in the service."[105]

In *Day of Infamy,* Walter Lord wrote that almost everybody in an American uniform on Oahu "went through successive stages of shock, fear, and anger." The news from Pearl Harbor triggered similar emotions among adults stateside. Even five-year-old John Ewing Roberts of

Louisville, who was probably typical of most kids, sensed that something was terribly wrong but had no idea what it might be.[106]

"On Sunday afternoon and evening, we'd always listen on the radio to a series of comic shows—comedians like Jack Benny, Fred Allen and Edgar Bergen and Charlie McCarthy," said Roberts, a retired Baptist pastor in Baltimore when I spoke to him. He was home with his mother and grandmother; his father, a traveling salesman, was on the road. The program they were enjoying was "interrupted by the announcement about the attack Pearl Harbor."[107]

Roberts did not understand what the interruption meant: "But Mother and Grandmother were clearly upset, and they went out of the room and talked to each other. When they came back, I said, 'Well, what's wrong?' They said, 'Our country's been attacked, and it looks like we're going to be in a war.' They explained to me a little bit about what that was, and they could tell I was worried as well as, I guess, puzzled, confused. They said, 'Well, don't worry. We have a good country, and we have a good God. It's going to be hard, but it's going to be OK.'"[108]

While the Roberts family was at home, fifteen-year-old Mildred Schofield and other congregants were still in the pews at Allen Chapel African Methodist Episcopal Church, a tiny meetinghouse in tiny Wingo in Graves County, an hour behind Louisville time. "I don't remember how we heard it," said the ninety-three-year old Schofield of Mayfield, the county seat. "I didn't know what to think. I was a little bit scared, numb—I didn't know what was happening.[109]

The Robertses went to Highland Baptist Church, established in 1893. Congregants at Hillcrest Baptist Church in Lexington were enjoying their first Sunday service. They had no house of worship, so they met in the basement of J. B. Day's grocery. Day, who had a radio on upstairs, rushed in and announced that Pearl Harbor had been bombed. Many worshipers had never heard of it. But Brother R. D. Aubrey, the brand-new pastor, stopped the services to pray for the dead and for those who would have to fight.[110]

Fourteen-year-old Ella Ritchey Flynn bowed her head. "It was quite a Sunday," she told the *Lexington Herald-Leader* seventy years later. "Everybody was shocked because the Japanese were actually in Washington at the time. Two boys that I grew up with were at Pearl Harbor that day." She added: "It was frightening, but if you were young, it was also a sort of romantic time, a very exciting time. In my sophomore and junior years at Lafayette [High School], I worked in a parachute factory out where Pepsi-Cola is today. Sometimes it scared me. I hoped I didn't overlook something that might cause someone to plunge to their death. But I felt like I was doing something wonderful for the servicemen."[111]

Something wonderful happened to Christine and Hugh Benjamin Hall Sr. of Pikeville on December 7, 1941. Hugh Benjamin Hall Jr. was born. Just before the couple left for the Methodist Hospital, Hugh Sr. answered the phone. "Turn your radio on. All hell has broken loose!" the caller yelled. Christine's condition took priority, and off to the hospital they sped. Despite "complete bedlam with doctors and nurses rushing everywhere," Hugh Jr. arrived around 7 P.M.[112]

Four hours earlier, the brothers Richard D. and Charles Howard of Clover Bottom in Woodford County had walked home from a pickup football game in a nearby cow pasture. When they got back, they saw several neighbors gathered by the family radio. The guests, Richard recalled, "were upset and nervous." His folks, John and Lena Howard, "were very silent and calm."[113]

The oldest Howard brother, John Allen, was at Pearl Harbor on the *Bach,* a destroyer. Elmo, another brother, was on the *Arizona.* "Needless to say, our family was very worried about their safety," Richard told the *Herald-Leader* in 2011. "Friends and neighbors would stop by the farm or see us in town and ask about the boys. Our school teacher asked about them every day."[114]

The feared telegram arrived in mid-January. The navy said that Elmo "was missing in action and presumed dead." Richard added: "John Allen finally got a letter out later that month, but it was so censored that all we were able to find out was that he was OK. It would be after the war was over that he was finally able to tell us what happened that day." The *Bach* was with the *Enterprise,* whose arrival at Pearl Harbor was delayed by stormy weather and related problems with refueling the escorting destroyers.[115]

"My mother believed for over 20 years that Elmo was alive," Richard said. "John Allen looked for him at every hospital he could get to for the remainder of the war. John Allen served in the Navy from 1939 to 1946. Our brother Jim joined the Army in 1943 and served until 1946. I joined the Army in 1944 and served until 1946. Charles served in the

Navy from 1945 to 1946 and was recalled to serve in the Korean War from 1951 to 1956. And Joe served in the Navy from 1952 to 1956."[116]

Darrell Bruner was an Owensboro first grader on Pearl Harbor Day. "We heard a commotion out in the yard, so we go out to see what's wrong," the Owensboro *Messenger-Inquirer* quoted him saying in a December 7, 2016, story. "Somebody was saying, 'The Japanese bombed Pearl Harbor! The Japanese bombed Pearl Harbor!' And then my dad and some others who were standing there said, 'Where in the hell is Pearl Harbor?' It took a few minutes before we found out it was in Hawaii. . . . Everybody was upset and angry. And back then, nobody knew much about Japan or the war going on."[117]

Gradie Wayne Jackson, who was born near Oil Springs in Barren County, said that he had been following the war news and thought that the United States should have joined the conflict on the Allied side "long . . . before" it did: "We'd a saved a lot of boys' lives and saved the taxpayers money." When Pearl Harbor was bombed, he was working at the Curtiss-Wright aircraft factory in Columbus, Ohio, helping build planes for the navy. He said that the news from Hawaii was something that he had "been expecting for some time." Jackson, twenty-six at the time, said: "I tried to enlist in every branch of service there was except the infantry." He explained why he stayed stateside in civvies: "They thought I was needed, with the family that I had, more in the defense plant [than] . . . in the Army or service."[118]

Pearl Harbor made the Perry Countian Lela Sizemore Byrd a real-life "Rosie the Riveter." After she graduated from Hazard High School, she went north and got a job assembling B-24 bombers for the army air force at Ford's Willow Run plant near Detroit. She was seventeen and visiting her father's Leslie County sawmill when she heard about the attack from a relative.[119]

"I was outside with a brother when somebody came out and told us Pearl Harbor had been bombed," Byrd remembered. She said that, because she knew Japanese diplomats were in Washington, she had "no idea there was going to be a war."[120]

Mary Francis Richards, who taught geography at Eastern Kentucky State Teachers College in Richmond, was home and looking forward to listening to an opera on the radio when "out poured this Pearl Harbor business." The next morning, she said, President Lee Donovan called a campus assembly: "Everybody went and I sat by Nancy Loman and we held hands and listened [on a radio hookup] to president Roosevelt go before Congress and ask for a declaration of war."[121]

In Paducah, Joanne Thomis Golden, age twelve, went to Sunday school, had lunch, and headed downtown with her friend Jane to catch a movie. "It wasn't too cold and we enjoyed walking the three miles," she jotted in her diary. "At 17th and Broadway, a car stopped and someone inside rolled down the window and shouted, 'The Japs bombed Pearl Harbor.'" The next day, she went to classes at Adah Brazelton Junior High School. She added: "Today Carrie Hale [her teacher] took her duster and wiped off the rolled-up maps. She showed us where Pearl Harbor was located."[122]

The Louisvillian William M. Dorr, a year older than Joanne, was enjoying *The Adventures of Daniel Boone* on the family radio when he heard a news bulletin that the Japanese had attacked Pearl Harbor. "Although I knew that this meant we were at war, I was not really sure where Pearl Harbor was," he remembered.[123]

Dorr had no time to ponder geography: "I had a job to go to. For three months I had been walking the English bulldog that belonged to Col. Harry Hutchings for the salary of 50 cents a week. . . . In 1941 it would pay for three trips to the neighborhood movie house plus a box of chocolate-covered peanuts." Hutchings was in the Army Corps of Engineers; he and his family had moved to the Falls City after the 1937 Ohio River flood. The corps was helping build the city a floodwall.[124]

Dorr rode his bicycle to the colonel's house. He related: "When I reached his front door, it was obvious something was very wrong. The front door was wide open and there was no one in the house." Dorr dutifully walked the dog in Cherokee Park. "To each person we met, I told of the Japanese attack," he said. But there was still no one at home when he got back with the dog. The next afternoon, Dorr returned to walk the dog again. Again, nobody was home: "Even the dog was gone. Tuesday . . . Col. Hutchings, his family and dog had moved away. I was never to see any of them again." Dorr added: "With all the changes that World War II would eventually bring to our lives, Pearl Harbor had brought an immediate one to mine. I lost my very first job. I still feel that the Japanese 'stiffed' me out of my final pay. In his rush to his first war duty, Col. Hutchings had neglected to pay me my final 50 cents."[125]

Sixteen-year-old Leonard Ferrell of Madisonville was also home and glued to the family radio when he heard a news flash from Pearl Harbor. "I was ready to go into the service right then if my mother would've signed my papers," he told the *Messenger-Inquirer.* "But I was an only child, so I can see now why my mother didn't want me to go."[126]

Ferrell added that it was difficult watching his buddies volunteer and go off to war. "All my friends, who I ran with, were all leaving," he said. "I thought it was my duty, too. . . . But on the day I turned 18, I signed up with the Navy to go." He served aboard the destroyer escort *Martin H. Ray,* helping shepherd convoys across the U-boat-infested Atlantic Ocean to the European theater. He said that he ultimately forgave the Japanese for bombing Pearl Harbor: "I changed. And it was because of my Christian faith."[127]

While Roberts's family seemed to have faith in eventual victory, other godly Kentuckians feared fifth columnists and assorted other godless subversives. Even before Pearl Harbor, G-men were quietly and systematically investigating "un-American activities" in Cincinnati. The probe purportedly peaked on December 10 when "special FBI agents working in conjunction with local police agencies" seemed set to apprehend "dangerous aliens." Agents sent to northern Kentucky from the Louisville FBI office declined to comment, according to the *Kentucky Post.* Nor would they say whether they had arrested anybody. Mum was also the word from local police chiefs. But the *Post* suspected that persons taken into custody would be locked up at Fort Thomas. Ten alleged "dangerous aliens," arrested in Cincinnati, were already behind bars at the post in Kentucky.[128]

Local FBI men and police were following the president's orders to arrest Japanese, German, and Italian aliens who were considered "enemies of the United States," the *Post* said. Police cautioned citizens "against becoming alarmed or 'taking matters in their own hands.'" Rather, they were to report suspicious activity to the local police. Tips would be strictly confidential.[129]

At Frankfort, the Legislative Council also approved bills that would coordinate Kentucky's defenses and authorize heavy penalties for sabotage. The measures were to be recommended to the General Assembly for consideration when it met in January. The council wanted both measures passed on an emergency basis, to take effect as soon as the governor signed them. The legislation would create a five-member defense board, with Governor Johnson as chairman, and mandate prison sentences of up to ten years and fines of up to $10,000, or both, for anyone found guilty of committing "any act of sabotage against a thing of substance used directly or indirectly in the war effort."[130]

Later, the council unanimously voted to broaden the bill to include the death penalty for anyone who killed or endangered the life of a defense plant worker or a soldier. "That's the only way to stop this sabotage," said the finance commissioner, J. Dan Talbott, a council member. "This is a tough time. It would be pitiful to send out boys to fight for us and let some paid agent of a foreign country kill 20 or 30 people. If they commit sabotage take them out and shoot them." The bill eschewed firing squads and ordered execution via the electric chair.[131]

The first Kentuckian arrested for sabotage was a twenty-two-year-old Louisville army veteran who was neither an enemy agent nor a Japanese, German, or Italian sympathizer. Evidently, he was just mad because he had to work the night before Christmas. Apparently, he tossed a piece of steel into a rolling machine to shut it down so he could go home. He might have been drunk, to boot. Anyway, the Hoosier native Wandell Virgil Skelton confessed that he sabotaged the machine at the Reynolds Metals plant. FBI agents arrested him, and he was arraigned before Commissioner Ray H. Kirchdorfer. When Kirchdorfer read the charges and asked for a plea, Skelton mumbled: "Guilty."[132]

The case was as strange as it was unprecedented. "At Skelton's home and in the surrounding neighborhood everyone expressed surprise at his arrest and all were unanimous in pointing out that Skelton 'couldn't have been more patriotic than he was,'" the *Louisville Courier-Journal* reported. The paper also said that Skelton had been in the army field artillery and had tried to "rejoin some military or naval unit." A hand injury disqualified him.[133]

Skelton was married but estranged from his wife and living with his parents. They said that their son had been behaving oddly and wondered whether an old "spinal operation . . . had affected his mind." The Skeltons claimed that Wandell "had a kind of 'don't care' attitude.'" They said that he acted particularly strangely on Christmas Eve after appearing "depressed and 'jumpy' for some months." He gave his friends $25.00 he had been saving up. Several neighbors who saw him after he left work that night said he had been drinking: "One neighbor who declined to be quoted by name said she had heard about 'some horseplay down there—something about the shift Skelton was in not wanting to work on Christmas Eve and maybe throwing some steel into the machine to knock it out so they could go.'"[134]

Skelton was jailed on $25,000 bond. He faced a federal sabotage charge that could have landed him in prison for up to thirty years and cost him a fine of up to $10,000, or both. He got off with only a year and a day behind bars. "Boy was I lucky!" he exclaimed after he was sentenced in federal court in Louisville. The *Owensboro Messenger* was not so sure, editorializing that the sentence, however light, might have been "only the lesser of two exceedingly evil alternatives confronting the accused." The paper suggested: "Men who serve prison sentences have a hard enough time getting along when they leave if confined for ordinary infractions of the criminal laws of society." It predicted that a convicted saboteur "will be even more of a social outcast when he is set free": "Skelton will learn this when he gets out of prison." The editorialist suspected that Skelton got off easy because he tried to break the machine "more on drunken impulse than from any disloyalty." Even so: "The law applies just the same." Still: "It was a very unlucky moment when he committed the crime for which he was convicted."[135]

Lexington, too, braced for saboteurs, whatever their motives. Except for the downtown office, all waterworks property was to be off-limits to the public and patrolled by armed guards as "a precautionary war measure suggested by the federal government." No visitors were allowed at the reservoir, pumping station, or filtration plant. Angling was prohibited at the reservoir until the war emergency was over. There were no exceptions, not even for the Lake Ellerslie Fishing Club. Picnicking was prohibited, too. The property was similarly restricted in World War I.[136]

Danville police were also on the lookout for Japanese. The police chief, R. E. Dunham, assured the *Advocate-Messenger* that there were none in town. He had promised the FBI that he and his officers "would work in close co-operation" with agents to prevent sabotage. To that end, he said, FBI officials had asked him to comb the town for anybody from Japan, including students at Center College. Though the police turned up nobody, he pledged that his department would remain "on the alert more than ever." Still, he confessed that he did not know what the Danville police would be "called upon to do" but revealed that plans were in the works "to guard more closely the Southern Railroad property" in town. He also promised the paper that the city waterworks and the Dix River Dam had "been under close guard for some time." The dam, which Kentucky Utilities owned and operated, was closed to the public.[137]

Most Kentuckians, like most Americans, were not counting on a happy new year in 1942. The war news seemed uniformly bad. Though the Soviets had stopped the Germans just short of Moscow, the invaders were still hundreds of miles inside the Soviet Union, having captured Minsk and Kiev, and were besieging Leningrad. On the other side of the globe, Japan seemed on schedule to push the Americans and Europeans out of East Asia. British Hong Kong had fallen, British forces were retreating in Malaya, and Japanese forces were threatening the Dutch East Indies, New Guinea, and even Australia. America had lost Guam and Wake islands and was soon to lose the Philippines. About the only thing the Americans could cheer was the Stars and Stripes still flying over Oahu.

Not surprisingly, many Americans were praying for divine intervention. FDR proclaimed New Year's Day a national day of prayer. Cities and towns across the country responded. "Mayfield and Graves County knelt at the altar of peace and victory," the hometown *Messenger* reported. Everything closed from 1:30 to 2:30 that afternoon. The town's two big clothing factories also shut from 11:00 A.M. to noon. The First Baptist and First Christian churches held services throughout the day and into the night.[138]

Peace and victory would not come until 1945 when Germany and Japan surrendered (Italy had given up and switched sides in 1943). The Japanese formally capitulated aboard the battleship *Missouri*. After service in the Korean conflict and the Gulf War, the *Mighty Mo* ended up as a museum ship at Pearl Harbor, the alpha and the omega, the beginning and the end, of American involvement in World War II. The *Missouri* is permanently berthed about where the *Maryland* was moored on December 7, 1941, and close to where it joined the Pacific Fleet on Christmas Eve 1944. The battlewagon points toward the *Arizona* Memorial.[139]

The USS *Missouri* Memorial opened in 1999. Guides show a steady stream of tourists, many of them Japanese, around the old battlewagon. They show visitors a small dent aft where the steel hull meets the teakwood main deck. A plaque explains that a kamikaze pilot crashed his plane here on April 11, 1945. He was the only casualty.

But probably the most photographed part of the ship is forward, near the two big gun turrets: a round, gold-colored plaque set in the deck. "Over this spot on 2 September 1945 the instrument of formal surrender of Japan to the Allied powers was signed thus bringing to a close the Second World War," the inscription reads. The *Mighty Mo*, the plaque explains, was anchored in Tokyo Bay, a little more than twelve hundred miles southwest of Hitokappu Bay, from which the Japanese fleet left for Pearl Harbor. "We had thought that we would never be able to come back from that attack," a Japanese sailor admitted on the way home. "But miles behind us, Oahu was in flames. The sun was already out but darkened by the smoke. I felt from the bottom of my heart that this successful attack was made possible only through the glory of our Imperial power and to the kind hand of Providence." General Douglas MacArthur also invoked the almighty when he concluded the surrender ceremony: "Let us pray that peace now be restored to the world, and that God will preserve it always."[140]

Hinako Regier, who was living with her parents near Osaka, did not feel glorious when she heard about Pearl Harbor the day after the attack. She was nine years old and scared. "I understood what was happening," she said. "I still remember the expression on my father's face. He was so grim and ashen. I thought we all were going to die."[141]

They nearly did. American B-29s, dropping firebombs, destroyed her family's home on the night of August 5, 1945. The next day, another B-29 dropped an atomic bomb on Hiroshima.[142]

Regier moved to the United States in 1957 to go to college. She stayed, became an American citizen, got married, was widowed, remarried, and ended up in Lexington. She worked at the Toyota car and truck plant in nearby Georgetown. She said that, years ago, she heard that a Pearl Harbor survivors group was having a meeting in Lexington. "I met these gentlemen and apologized for what happened," she said. "Ever since I came to the States, I felt like I was a goodwill ambassador for Japan. Any time I had a chance to talk to a church group or any group, I went and told about my experiences and how I wished there was no war."[143]

Epilogue

Survivors Post–Pearl Harbor

"Most Americans caught in the Japanese attack on Oahu went through successive stages of shock, fear and anger," Walter Lord wrote of Pearl Harbor. Most who survived the attack experienced anew the awe, terror, and rage of combat at Midway, Guadalcanal, Tarawa, Kwajalein, Saipan, Iwo Jima, Okinawa, Leyte Gulf, and other Pacific battle sites. Some also fought the Germans in the European theater.[1]

The Sailors

James Allard Vessels was an exception among Pearl Harbor survivors. The air raid was his only battle. After the attack, he helped supervise shore batteries on Oahu and served in an honor guard at burial rites for sailors and marines killed in battle elsewhere and interred on Oahu. He also served aboard a floating dry dock that was towed from Pearl Harbor to Australia. After the war, he came home to Paducah, worked as a mechanic for the Colonial Baking Company, and died in 1981 at age sixty. He and his wife, Anita, had two daughters and five sons, four of whom were sailors.[2]

In his youth, James Allard's son Kenneth played in a local rock-and-roll band. "I was like a hippie," he recalled with a chuckle. He said the group "decided to get these Maltese Crosses [pendants] because we thought it was cool, you know, hip." Unaware that the German Iron Cross medal is a variant of the Maltese Cross, he wore his home one night: "Dad looked at it, and it was like I'd punched him in the gut."[3]

James Allard asked Kenneth whether he knew what the cross represented; Kenneth confessed that he did not. James Allard said: "I fought against what that stands for." Then he gently admonished his son: "You have no idea what it's like to be talking to one of your buddies and, two seconds later, you don't know where they are."[4]

Vessels promised not to rip the pendant away or forbid his son from wearing it in public. He said: "I'm just going to ask you not to wear it in front of me." Kenneth took it off on the spot and threw it away.[5]

Kenneth's siblings, Donald, Chuck, Jay, and Mike, were all in the navy. Mike was on the East Coast bound for Vietnam aboard the *Power*, a World War II–vintage destroyer when he became seriously ill and had to be hospitalized. After he recovered, he asked to be returned to his ship, and the navy flew him to Pearl Harbor, where the *Power* was then headed. Mike got there first. "They were flabbergasted when I walked up the gangplank and asked for permission to come aboard," he said, chuckling.[6]

But Mike, a gunner's mate like his father, had been astonished at what he saw after his plane landed: the filming of the Pearl Harbor movie *Tora! Tora! Tora!* which came out in 1970. He remembered: "I was standing on the pier when these Japanese torpedo planes were flying over, dropping torpedoes, and they were setting off explosions in the water. So I'm here watching what dad really went through." He also had time to visit the *Arizona* Memorial. "It was mind-boggling," he said.[7]

Mike paid for his parents' trip to Pearl Harbor for the thirtieth anniversary of the attack. James Allard Vessels said that the memorial straddled the *Arizona* at the base of the mainmast. Reading the roll of the dead, Vessels found the name he was looking for, Gunner's Mate Third Class Ross Worth Lightfoot.[8]

Herbert Buehl, who narrowly escaped death on the *Arizona*, retired to Louisville after working for a telephone company in his native Wisconsin. He was featured in the *Honolulu Star-Bulletin* on the fiftieth anniversary of the Pearl Harbor attack. His brief reminiscence included a photograph of him holding a souvenir Japanese sword. He was eighty when he died in the Falls City in 2002. He was survived by his wife, Helen Voss Buehl, two sons, and a daughter. He and his wife made four trips to Pearl Harbor for memorial services, the first time in 1986. That visit was the first time he had been back since the war.[9]

Jim Hamlin was probably reported missing from the *California* because he joined the crew of the heavy cruiser *Chicago*, which steamed out of Pearl Harbor on December 16. The *California* was still on the harbor bottom, and the navy must have figured he was dead somewhere inside the battleship. Based at Pearl Harbor, too, the *Chicago* had been at sea during the attack. It returned afterward, then left again. After the Japanese sank the *Chicago* at the battle of Rennell Island in January 1943, Hamlin was transferred to the *La Salle,* a troopship. In November 1943, it landed marines at Tarawa, the opening assault in the US central Pacific campaign. "I remember singing 'I'll Be Home for Christmas' when we put them ashore," he said. "A lot of them didn't make it, though."[10]

The *La Salle* also landed troops at Saipan in 1944. Hamlin wound up the war as a master-at-arms at shore patrol headquarters in Chicago. Back on Civvy Street, he was the sports editor of the *Jackson (TN) Sun* before he and his wife, Almyra, returned to Lone Oak, her hometown, and he went to work for the Tennessee Valley Authority. He retired after twenty-three years with that agency. Jim and Almyra married in 1943 and reared a trio of sons. She preceded him in death; he died in 1999 at age eighty-six.[11]

V. C. Kidd was nearly killed twice in the war. The Japanese failed to sink the *Tucker* at Pearl Harbor, but an American mine sent the destroyer to the seafloor off Espiritu Santo on August 4, 1942. The captain steamed into the minefield unaware it was there. Kidd was the only sailor from the engine room crew who did not die in the blast. He ended up on another ill-fated tin can, the *Nelson,* which the navy dispatched to the European theater to help cover the Allied invasion of Normandy on June 6, 1944. Seven days later, a German motor torpedo boat torpedoed and heavily damaged it. Kidd was not hurt, but two dozen of his shipmates were killed or listed as missing, and nine more were wounded. Kidd made chief petty officer before he was discharged after World War II. He owned a heating and air conditioning business in Mayfield, his hometown (about twenty-seven miles south of Lone Oak on US Highway 45), and died in 1998 at age seventy-six. He and his wife, Lillie Ann Kidd, reared a son and a daughter.[12]

Another tin-can sailor, **J. C. Riley** of Benton, about twenty-six miles northeast of Mayfield, retired from the Illinois Central Railroad. The *Paducah Sun* interviewed him after he took in the 2001 movie *Pearl Harbor* at a city theater. He joshed that he wanted an aisle seat: "If they start shooting at me, I can get up and leave." Though more than a few critics panned the film, Riley said it was accurate and "brought back a lot of eerie memories." Riley rated it an "A," though he did not like the foul language. He also faulted the moviemakers for failing to show "as much devastation as actually happened": "They confined it to Battleship Row. There was a lot around it they didn't show." Riley died in 2006 at age eighty-four and was survived by his wife, Mildred Jones Riley—who had watched *Pearl Harbor* with him—and a stepdaughter.[13]

Joe Sanders, Kidd's fellow Mayfield resident, stayed on the *St. Louis* until 1943, when he was transferred to a troopship, and afterward spent the rest of the war stateside. He returned to Mayfield, where he and his wife opened Joe and Claudine's, a popular restaurant. The couple reared two sons and a daughter. Sanders died in 1992 at age sixty-nine.[14]

Chaplain **Howell Forgy** was aboard the *New Orleans* when the cruiser was torpedoed on the night of November 30, 1942, in the Battle of Tassafaronga. The blast tore away *NO Boat*'s bow. The navy did not list Forgy as among the dead, but his wife believed that he perished, according to a January 6, 1943, story in the *Madisonville Messenger.* Louise Morgan Forgy said unofficial information she got "from the west coast . . . indicated he was among several killed or lost when his ship was hit." But, in the same story, she said she subsequently got a let-ter from her husband assuring her he was "safe and unhurt."[15]

Meanwhile, *NO Boat* steamed backward to Sydney, Australia, for temporary repairs. After work crews fitted the ship with a stub bow, it crossed the Pacific to Puget Sound, Washington, Navy Yard for perma-nent repairs. It was Forgy's last port of call. Before work could start, the crew had to offload the ship's ammo onto barges. Forgy wrote that, as he exited the *New Orleans,* "the men were singing . . . a song about passing the ammunition": "They looked up at me, waved, and smiled. There were tears in my eyes, for somehow I could not help thinking that when enough people really praise the Lord, it will no longer be necessary to pass the ammunition."[16]

In 1946, Forgy was discharged with the rank of lieutenant com-mander. After he retired from the ministry, he and his wife, who were the parents of a daughter and three sons, settled in Glendora, California, where he died in 1972 at age sixty-four. Forgy's death notice in the *Pomona Progress Bulletin* must have chagrined his widow. "Mr. Forgy was helping load guns on the U.S.S. *New Orleans* during the attack on Pearl Harbor when he bellowed the now famous phrase," the paper wrongly reported. The actor Gregory Scott played Forgy in the 1970 Pearl Harbor movie *Tora! Tora! Tora!* In the last years of his life, Forgy was confined to a wheelchair, having suffered a stroke and crippling arthritis, according to the *Progress Bulletin.* Western Kentucky papers also reported his death. The *Paducah Sun-Democrat* said that Jessie Rogers, the only living charter member of the Murray church, remembered him as a "dynamic minister, elegant in his speaking." She said that he "became well known and well liked in his associations not only with his congregations but with the other churches and ministers in the city." She was evidently the "Mrs. Rogers" he cited in his autobiography for producing tasty "tomato and red pepper relish."[17]

Vance Leneave spent the rest of the war on the *Medusa* and other ships. Back in Golden Pond after the Japanese surrendered, he ran a store before the tiny town was removed to make room for the Land between the Lakes National Recreation Area. He was also an Edsel-driving rural mail carrier and president of the Kentucky chapter of the national Pearl Harbor Survivors Association. He and his wife, Nell Upton Leneave, had a son and a daughter. He was seventy-three when died in 1993.[18]

Clarence Gunther Jr. stayed in the navy until 1946. He reenlisted in August 1950 and served until 1952. Besides the *Farragut,* he also served on the carrier *Yorktown* and the battleship *Missouri,* the latter apparently in the Korean War. His dress blues are on display at the Kentucky Military Museum in Frankfort. His Pacific and European theater ribbons are studded with battle stars; he earned fourteen all told. Married to Beulah Blackwell Gunther, he died at eighty-two in 2003.[19]

Eddie Klusmeier, reported dead at Pearl Harbor like his shipmate Jim Hamlin, married, fathered a son and a daughter, and died in Louisville in 1995, at age seventy-four, according to his obituary in the August 1, 1995, *Courier-Journal.* He was a retired gear inspector at the city's International Harvester plant. **Perry Calhoun** made it home to Eddyville. He retired after working as a lockmaster at nearby Barkley Dam and Kentucky Dam. He and Edna Lois Duncan Calhoun had two sons and a daughter. He died in 2011 at age ninety-nine.[20]

Eugene B. Hayden of the *Curtiss* and the *San Francisco* sailor **John Locker** made careers of the navy. Hayden retired as a commander and died in Owensboro in 1993 at age eighty-two. He was survived by his wife, Julia Payne Hayden, and daughter, Sue Gene Hayden Baker, who were with him on Oahu on December 7, 1941. Locker left the navy as a lieutenant; he was in uniform for thirty years. He and his wife, Willa Pace Locker, had two daughters. He was seventy-seven when he died in Paducah in 1993.[21]

John W. Hamlet of Hartford, the Ohio County seat, stayed in the navy for thirty years, retiring in 1970. Following the Pearl Harbor attack, he served on the destroyer *Worden,* the destroyer escort *Thomas,* and the *Neshoba,* an attack transport. He studded thirteen battle stars on his Asiatic and Pacific campaign ribbon. After he left the navy, he was a pilot and master on a cruise boat in New York, a firefighter in Washington State, and a foreign duty contractor in the Marshall Islands. He died in Sedro-Woolley, Washington, at age eighty-two in 2006. He was cremated, and his ashes were scattered at Pearl Harbor.[22]

Many Pearl Harbor survivors were featured in their local papers, especially on anniversaries of the attack. But few, if any, got as much year-round ink as **Lee Philip Ebner** of Louisville. After he was discharged in 1946, Ebner enrolled in the Louisville Art Center and the Chicago Academy of Fine Arts. His schooling landed him his dream job: staff artist for the *Louisville Courier-Journal* and the *Louisville Times.* He held the post for thirty-two years. He also taught cartooning at Bellarmine University and was "always available to give cartooning demonstrations or interviews about Pearl Harbor to students at Louisville area high schools." Preceded in death by his wife, Wanda Rhea Jenkins Ebner, he died in 2014 at age ninety-four.[23]

The *Maryland* mail clerk **Jack Roberts** stayed in the navy until 1959, after which he worked for the Sweetwater School District in Chula Vista, California. He and his wife, D. Loretta Roberts, retired to Bowling Green, the Warren County seat, in 2003. He died in 2015 at age ninety-three. He was the last Pearl Harbor survivor in the county, according to his obituary in the *Bowling Green Daily News.*[24]

George Callahan of the *Nevada* remained a sailor until 1960. He and his wife, Lois June Jenkins Callahan, ended up in Danville, where he retired from the post office after twenty-two years. George and Louis had four sons and three daughters. He was ninety-two when he died in 2015 at ninety-two.[25] Despite his horrific wounds, **Earl Emery Davis**, Callahan's shipmate, lived to age ninety-seven. His life ended in Owensboro, where he retired as a Tennessee Valley Authority engineering aide. Davis and his wife, Loeran M. Ball Davis, had a daughter.[26]

The Marines

The marine **Thomas B. Crump** was a lifer who fought at Guadalcanal, Bougainville, Pileliu, and Okinawa and in the Korean War. He died in Louisville in 2014 at age ninety-three and was survived by his wife, Ida Amy DeAngelo Crump, and a granddaughter.[27]

John Edwards Wood died in Glasgow on the seventy-fourth anniversary of the Pearl Harbor attack. He was ninety-five. Wood never made it to Wake Island, which fell to the Japanese on December 23, 1941. But he joined the successful defense of Midway in June 1942, helping win the turning-point battle in the Pacific theater. In 1943, the marines sent him stateside to Camp Lejeune, in North Carolina. Following his discharge, he spent more than forty-one years as a broadcast engineer for WKAY and WGGC radio stations in Galesburg, Illinois. Back in Kentucky, he was president of his Pearl Harbor Survivors chapter. A widower, when he died in 2015 at ninety-five, he was survived by a son and two daughters.[28]

The Army Men

Dr. Leonard D. Heaton earned brigadier general's stars in 1950 and three years later became the tenth commander of Walter Reed Army Medical Center in Washington. He made lieutenant general—the first physician to earn three stars—and was the surgeon general of the army from 1959 until he retired in 1969. At Walter Reed, his patients included President Dwight D. Eisenhower, Secretary of State John Foster Dulles, and Generals Douglas MacArthur and George C. Marshall. He died in 1983 at age eighty, leaving behind his wife, Sara Richardson Heaton, and their daughter, Sara Heaton Mason, Pearl Harbor survivors like the general.[29]

E. C. Mitchell practiced what he preached about the rewards of army air force life. In 1962, he retired from the army as a captain. Afterward, he moved back to Paducah, where he was in business. E. C. and Jeanne League Mitchell had two sons.[30]

Philip C. Sprawls was said to be the first American casualty in the 1942 Solomon Islands campaign. He earned a Purple Heart on a bombing run when antiaircraft fire hit him in the leg; shrapnel also blew the onyx stone out of his 1938 Clemson class ring. After he recovered, Sprawls flew more than twenty-five combat missions. His bravery and flying skill did not go unnoticed; Fleet Admiral William F. Halsey pinned a Distinguished Flying Cross on his uniform. Sprawls stayed in the army air force/air force and came to the Falls City in 1959 to head the Air Force Reserve Officer Training Corps program at the University of Louisville. He retired in 1966 as a lieutenant colonel but returned to the university as the placement director, a job he held until he retired again fifteen years later. He and his wife, Helen M. Pyle Sprawls, had three sons and a daughter. He died in 2014 at age ninety-eight.[31]

Raymond Turley was ninety and retired from the post office when he died in Mount Sterling in 2011. He and his wife, Millie Chester Turley, reared two sons and two daughters.[32]

As of May 2019, **Albert Patrick,** going on 101, was in a nursing home in Salyersville, the Magoffin County seat. After Pearl Harbor, he fought in the Pacific campaign, earning a Bronze Star and Purple Heart. Students at Magoffin County High School in Salyersville threw him a one hundredth birthday party in the gym. After Heather French Henry, a former Miss America, sang to him, she kissed him on his cheek. Route 1888, Old Burning Fork Road, was to be renamed "Sgt. Albert Patrick Highway."[33]

Luby Saxon returned to Graves County after he was discharged and helped spruce up houses for real estate agents. He died in 1986 at age seventy, said Taira McAfee, his great-nephew.

Richard Don Lay died in 1995 at age sixty-eight. He obviously saw combat because he earned a Silver Star and a Purple Heart, according to his military footstone in Monhollen Cemetery in Corbin.[34] **Frank Weise** moved to Louisville and married Mary Edwina Bell in 1944. They were the parents of a daughter. He was sixty when died in 1977.[35]

John D. Barker retired as a Morehead insurance agent in 1972 and died in a local hospital on December 6, 2010, at age ninety-three. Survivors included his wife, Pearl Dean Lewis Barker, and a son. Barker fought across the Pacific, earning a Bronze Star "for meritorious service in action" on Bougainville in 1944.[36]

The Civilians

Robert Coleman graduated from Paducah Lincoln High School in 1950, then joined the air force during the Korean conflict. A civil rights and union leader, he was elected to the city commission in 1974 and served for twenty-eight years—six years as mayor pro tem. He helped push Paducah to hire its first black police and fire chiefs. A lifelong member of the Paducah–McCracken County NAACP branch, he was the first African American elected president of Paducah Branch 383 of the National Association of Letter Carriers union. He was also the first black chairman of the letter carriers association's Kentucky State Association. In addition, he is a member of the Kentucky Commission on Human Rights Hall of Fame. He is married to Connie Coleman.[37]

The Louisville native **John Roberts** of Baltimore earned a bachelor of divinity degree from Yale University in 1960, taught Latin at Wake Forest University, and was pastor at Woodbrook Baptist Church in Baltimore for thirty-one years. He was on the board of the city's Institute for Islamic, Christian and Jewish Studies and helped start the Alliance of Baptists, "a faith community comprised of male and female laity and clergy, people of diverse sexual orientations, gender identities, theological beliefs, and ministry practices," according to the group's website. He and his wife, Marylynn, reared a son.[38]

Ben Fritz died in Cynthiana in 1996 at age eighty-seven. He belonged to the Unity Christian Church, the Harrison County Beef Cattle Association, and the Pearl Harbor Survivors Association. He worked for twenty-eight years as district supervisor of the Harrison County Conservation District. He and his wife, Cynthia Mary McCauley Fritz, were the parents of a son and a daughter.[39]

Kenneth Huff taught at the Kentucky School for the Deaf from 1942 to 1945, when he became principal at the Arkansas School for the Deaf in Little Rock. He retired as superintendent of the Wisconsin

School for the Deaf in Delavan. He married Anna Hoagland in 1938 and died in 1975 at age sixty-three.[40]

Nancy Brinton Shea wrote *The Army Wife, The Navy Wife, The Marine Wife,* and *The WAACS.* Born in 1897, she died in 1963 and is buried in Lebanon, Kentucky.[41]

All the Pearl Harbor veterans I interviewed are dead. The ranks of survivors will be thinner by December 7, 2021, the eightieth anniversary of the attack. The media is fond of milestone anniversaries: twenty-fifth, fiftieth, seventy-fifth, and so on. The stories of Pearl Harbor Day will be retold. Most Americans who hear them—many for the first time—will be far removed, agewise, from these men and women, military and civilian, of Tom Brokaw's "Greatest Generation." "I grew up thinking everybody's dad fought in War II," I would tell my community college students. Toward the end of my twenty-four-year career in the classroom, Vietnam had become students' grandfathers' war.

Vietnam was among our most divisive wars. But all our wars have divided us to one degree or another, save World War II. The tide of patriotism that surged after Pearl Harbor swept away almost all isolationist and antiwar sentiment. Never before—or since—have we been *e pluribus unum* during an armed conflict.

"Be careful how you shake your family tree," I used to warn students interested in genealogy. "A patriot might fall off one limb and a loyalist off the other." I meant the Revolutionary War. While many Americans fought for independence, many others fought along the Redcoats to remain British.

Many New Englanders were against the War of 1812. Abolitionists in the northern free states condemned the Mexican-American War, arguing that it was wanton aggression against Mexico and a proslavery southern president's blatant land grab for more potential slave territory. The Civil War was the most divisive—and bloodiest—of all our wars, riving the country into North and South, and, in border states like Kentucky, splitting family, friends, neighbors, and communities.

Though short and uniformly successful, the Spanish-American War triggered a wave of anti-imperialism in the country. By no means did everybody back World War I; a half dozen senators and fifty representatives—including the Montana Republican Jeanette Rankin—

rejected President Woodrow Wilson's war declaration. The federal government had to create what amounted to a propaganda ministry to get everybody fired up against the Hun. "Hamburgers," named for the German city, became "Liberty Steaks," German Shepherds were "Liberty Pups," and the German Measles was, you guessed it, the "Liberty Measles." Uncle Sam did not have to get John and Jane Q Citizen riled against the Japanese, Germans, and Italians in World War II. "Remember Pearl Harbor!" was anything but empty sloganeering.

After World War II came the era of undeclared wars—in Korea, Vietnam, and the Middle East. All had skeptics stateside, none more so than the Vietnam "quagmire," which has been eclipsed by the Middle East "quagmire."

Brokaw wrote that the World War II generation "answered the call to help save the world from the two most powerful and ruthless military machines ever assembled, instruments of conquest in the hands of fascist maniacs": "They faced great odds and a late start, but they did not protest."[42] Almost nobody did. (Representative Jeannette "Japanette" Rankin, pacifist to the end, was the only lawmaker to vote no on FDR's war declaration.) For nearly every other American, Pearl Harbor was a clear-cut entry to a clearly righteous war, the "Good War," as Studs Terkel dubbed it.[43] America, John and Jane Q Public were certain, was the blameless victim of a sneak attack that claimed almost twenty-four hundred innocent lives. Citizens who tuned into FDR's message on the radio were reminded of their country's "other historic days of infamy: the Alamo massacre and Custer's Last Stand. In those two instances, terrible setbacks were followed up by heroic victories, and the Texas cry of 'Remember the Alamo' soon became 'Remember Pearl Harbor,'" Nelson wrote.[44]

On the fiftieth anniversary of Pearl Harbor, Japan had been our reliable ally for forty-six years. Hence, the *Louisville Courier-Journal* tried to add perspective in an editorial: "Yes, the Japanese strike at the US fleet in Hawaii came after Washington had embargoed oil shipments to Japan, shipments upon which Japanese industry and the Japanese military depended. But the embargo, in turn, was in response to Japan's forcible annexation of Manchuria a decade earlier, its subsequent war against China, and its invasion of French Indo-China in July of '41.

If Japan's leaders felt encircled and isolated by the end of 1941, it was because they had chosen an imperialist course that required their country's isolation."[45]

On the attack's seventy-fifth anniversary, the *Courier-Journal* editorialized: "What always seems clearer in the years following wars and military action is that rhetoric and failed diplomacy leads [*sic*] to dangerous brinksmanship and ultimately the exercise of military might. That same story applied to England and European countries while trying to contain and appease Hitler's Nazi Germany and his scheme to create the Third Reich—the Thousand-Year Reich. What also can't be forgotten is that now both Japan and Germany are staunch allies." (Russia, on the other hand, is our enemy.)[46]

On December 7, 1941, most of Oahu's defenders had never heard a shot fired in anger. Those who survived got to pin a tiny bronze battle star on their yellow American Defense Service medals and ribbons, decorations awarded to sailors, marines, soldiers, and airmen who were in service before the United States joined the war. Many ended the war with multiple stars attached to their also yellow Asiatic and Pacific campaign medals and ribbons. Many earned medals for individual bravery to boot.

"This book, I hope, will in some small way pay tribute to those men and women who have given us the lives we have today," Brokaw wrote. That is my hope, too, for this book. Brokaw added: "I am in awe of them, and I feel privileged to have been a witness to their lives and their sacrifices."[47] So do I. On December 8, 1977, the day after my story on Jim Hamlin appeared in the *Paducah Sun-Democrat*, the ex-sailor showed up in the newsroom. "Thank you," he said, handing me a small Christmas fruitcake and shaking my hand. "No, sir," I replied. "Thank you."

Acknowledgments

"No man is an island entire of itself," John Donne famously wrote. No author is either. My byline is on this book, but I could not have written it alone. I am indebted to many helpers, starting with Melinda Anne Hocker Craig, my wife and best friend and a retired senior English teacher at Mayfield High School. She spent hours proofreading the manuscript and offering suggestions and comments that greatly improved the product. I am especially grateful to Daniel Martinez, the chief historian at the Pearl Harbor National Memorial. Not only did he consent to a lengthy interview; he drove Melinda and me around parts of Pearl Harbor and Ford Island that are still navy country and not on the beaten tourist path. He also reviewed the manuscript for accuracy and completeness and supplied additional information that greatly improved the product. Others who came to my aid included Charlotte Beahan, professor emeritus of history at Murray State University, my alma mater, who also reviewed parts of the manuscript; Dieter Ullrich, special collections librarian at Morehead State University; Jennifer Cole of the Filson Historical Society; staff at the Kentucky Historical Society, the Lexington Public Library (especially J. P. Johnson and Bobby Webb), and the libraries at the University of Kentucky and Georgetown College; Skylar Phaup, the director of customer service and public relations of the city of Madisonville; the historian Russ Hatter, Frankfort; Wanda Stubblefield, Mayfield; Penny Baucum Fields, Paducah Market House Museum; Kenneth and Mike Suttles and Margaret Shoulta, three of the late James Allard and Anita Vessels's children; Stanley and Jamie Hamlin, the son and grandson of the late Jim Hamlin; JoAnn Hamm, Kentucky School for the Deaf; and Taira McAfee, Mayfield.

Notes

Introduction

1. Walter Lord, *Day of Infamy* (New York: Holt, Rinehart & Winston, 1957), ix, 219.

2. "USS *Arizona* Casualties, Pearl Harbor, December 7, 1941," Pearl Harbor, n.d., http://pearl-harbor.com/arizona/casualtylist.html; James Vessels, interview by the author, December 3, 1976, Paducah, KY; *Paducah Sun-Democrat,* December 7, 1976. Shortly after my interviews with James Vessels, James Hamlin, Joe Sanders, J. C. Riley, Vance Leneave, Perry Calhoun, H. S. Reeves, Clarence Meece, Tommy Lewis, V. C. Kidd, and John Locker were conducted, they appeared in the *Paducah Sun-Democrat* in extracted form. All quotations are taken from the original interview transcripts, but, for the reader's convenience, interview citations are paired with the published versions.

3. James Vessels interview (December 3, 1976); *Sun-Democrat,* December 7, 1976; "USS *Arizona,* Report of Pearl Harbor Attack," December 13, 1941, Naval History and Heritage Command, https://www.history.navy.mil/research /archives/digitized-collections/action-reports/wwii-pearl-harbor-attack/ships -a-c/uss-arizona-bb-39-action-report.html.

4. James Hamlin, interview by the author, December 2, 1977, Lone Oak, KY; *Paducah Sun-Democrat,* December 7, 1977.

5. Joe Sanders, interview by the author, December 1, 1978, Mayfield, KY; *Paducah Sun,* December 7, 1978.

6. *Owensboro Messenger-Inquirer,* December 7, 1999; *Glasgow Times,* December 6, 2012.

7. J. C. Riley, interview by the author, December 5, 1979, Benton, KY; *Paducah Sun,* December 7, 1979.

8. *Lexington Herald-Leader*, December 6, 2016.

9. *Louisville Courier-Journal,* December 3, 2016; *USA Today,* December 5, 2016.

10. Clarence Meece, interview by the author, December 5, 1981, Hopkinsville, KY; *Paducah Sun,* December 6, 1981.

11. Perry Calhoun, interview by the author, December 4, 1981, Eddyville, KY; *Paducah Sun,* December 6, 1981.

12. John E. Kleber, ed., *The Kentucky Encyclopedia* (Lexington: University Press of Kentucky, 1992), 483, 779.

13. *Paducah Sun-Democrat,* August 6, 1940; *Louisville Courier-Journal,* December 21, 1941.

14. *Paducah Sun-Democrat,* December 7, 1977.

15. *Louisville Courier-Journal,* December 8, 1941.

16. Oliver Gramling and Associated Press Correspondents around the World, *Free Men Are Fighting* (New York: Farrar & Rinehart, 1942), 271; *Owensboro Messenger,* November 19, 1938.

17. *Paducah Sun-Democrat,* December 7, 9, 1941.

18. *Paducah Sun-Democrat,* December 9, 1941; Gordon W. Prange with Donald M. Goldstein and Katherine V. Dillon, *Pearl Harbor: The Verdict of History* (New York: Anne Prange/Prange Enterprises, 1986), 346.

19. *Louisville Courier-Journal,* December 8, 1941.

20. Lowell H. Harrison and James C. Klotter, *A New History of Kentucky* (Lexington: University Press of Kentucky, 1997), 372.

21. Prange, Goldstein, and Dillon, *Pearl Harbor,* 533.

22. Craig Nelson, *Pearl Harbor: From Infamy to Greatness* (New York: Scribner, 2016).

23. Chris Dixon, *African Americans and the Pacific War, 1941–1945: Race, Nationality, and the Fight for Freedom* (Cambridge: Cambridge University Press, 2018), 22–23.

24. *Louisville Leader,* December 20, 1941.

25. Todd South, "First Black Marines Mark the 75th Anniversary of the Segregated Boot Camp," *Marine Times,* August 26, 2017, https://www.marinecorpstimes.com/news/your-military/2017/08/26/first-black-marines-mark-75th-anniversary-of-the-segregated-boot-camp.

26. *Louisville Courier-Journal,* December 7, 1991.

27. Hillel Italie, "Robert Caro Shares Tips about His Craft in 'Working,'" AP News, April 3, 2019, https://apnews.com/ef09306fa6c34d9f8be4105a8da8a24c; Daniel Martinez, interview by the author, April 2, 2019, Pearl Harbor, HI.

28. Martinez interview.

29. Martinez interview.

30. Hamlin interview; *Paducah Sun-Democrat,* December 7, 1977.

31. Riley interview; *Paducah Sun,* December 7, 1979.

32. *Louisville Courier Journal,* October 6, 2019.

33. *Louisville Courier Journal,* October 6, 2019.

1. America and Japan

1. *Louisville Courier-Journal,* December 7, 1941.

2. *Louisville Courier-Journal,* December 7, 1941.

3. *Louisville Courier-Journal,* December 7, 1941; Lord, *Day of Infamy,* 126.

4. *Louisville Courier-Journal,* December 7, 1941.

5. *Louisville Courier-Journal,* December 7, 1941.

6. *Louisville Courier-Journal,* December 7, 1941.

7. *Louisville Courier-Journal,* December 7, 1941.

8. *Louisville Courier-Journal,* March 16, 1941.

9. *Louisville Courier-Journal,* March 16, 1941.

10. *Louisville Courier-Journal,* March 16, 1941.

11. *Louisville Courier-Journal,* March 16, 1941.

12. *Louisville Courier-Journal,* March 16, 1941.

13. *Louisville Courier-Journal,* March 16, 1941.

14. *Paducah Sun-Democrat,* August 6, 1940.

15. *Paducah Sun-Democrat,* August 6, 1940.

16. *Paducah Sun-Democrat,* August 6, 1940.

17. *Paducah Sun-Democrat,* August 6, 1940.

18. *Paducah Sun-Democrat,* May 26, 1941.

19. *Paducah Sun-Democrat,* May 26, 1941. Zeiss was at Hickam during the attack. He was wounded, hospitalized, earned a Purple Heart, and returned to duty. See *Paducah Sun-Democrat,* April 19, 1942. Zeiss was commissioned a lieutenant and became a pilot. He was killed on July 7, 1944, when his B-29 crashed in a training flight in Kansas. He is buried in Paducah.

20. *Louisville Courier-Journal,* December 21, 1941.

21. *Louisville Courier-Journal,* December 21, 1941.

22. *Louisville Courier-Journal,* August 3, 1941.

23. *Louisville Courier-Journal,* August 3, 1941.

24. *Louisville Courier-Journal,* August 3, 1941.

25. *Louisville Courier-Journal,* August 3, 1941.

26. *Louisville Courier-Journal,* August 3, 1941.

27. Pearl Harbor National Memorial Hawai'i, "Pearl Harbor," National Park Service, updated April 12, 2019, https://www.nps.gov/valr/learn/historyculture/pearl-harbor.htm.

28. Julia Flynn Siler, *Lost Kingdom: Hawaii's Last Queen, the Sugar Kings, and America's First Imperial Adventure* (New York: Grove, 2012), xxii–xxiii.

29. Pearl Harbor National Memorial Hawai'i, "Pearl Harbor"; Siler, *Lost Kingdom,* xxiv; Nelson, *Pearl Harbor,* 8.

30. Siler, *Lost Kingdom,* 66; Tom Coffman, *Nation Within: The Story of America's Annexation of Hawai'i* (Kāne'ohe, HI: Tom Coffman/Epicenter, 1998), 62. See also Julius W. Pratt, *Expansionists of 1898: The Acquisition of Hawaii and the Spanish Islands* (Chicago: Quadrangle Paperbacks/Quadrangle Books, 1964), 35.

31. Siler, *Lost Kingdom,* 144–46.

32. Siler, *Lost Kingdom,* 165; Pratt, *Expansionists of 1898,* 35; Coffman, *Nation Within,* 93.

33. Siler, *Lost Kingdom,* xxx; Pratt, *Expansionists of 1898,* 113; Nelson, *Pearl Harbor,* 9.

34. Steve Twomey, *Countdown to Pearl Harbor: The Twelve Days to the Attack* (New York: Simon & Schuster, 2016), 4.

35. Pearl Harbor National Memorial Hawai'i, "Pearl Harbor." It became US naval custom to name battleships for states and cruisers for cities.

36. The United States paid Spain $20 million for the Philippines, a fraction of what the islands were worth.

37. Nelson, *Pearl Harbor,* 25, 27.

38. Nelson, *Pearl Harbor,* 27.

39. Nelson, *Pearl Harbor,* 27.

40. Nelson, *Pearl Harbor,* 27–28.

41. Nelson, *Pearl Harbor,* 28.

42. Alfred Thayer Mahan, *The Influence of Sea Power upon History, 1660–1783* (Boston: Little, Brown, 1890); Nelson, *Pearl Harbor,* 30.

43. Nelson, *Pearl Harbor,* 30–31.

44. Gordon W. Prange with Donald M. Goldstein and Katherine V. Dillon, *At Dawn We Slept: The Untold Story of Pearl Harbor* (New York: Penguin, 1991), 5.

45. Prange, Goldstein, and Dillon, *At Dawn We Slept,* 4.

46. John Toland, *The Rising Sun: The Decline and Fall of the Japanese Empire, 1936–1945* (New York: Modern Library, 2003), 56. See also Prange, Goldstein, and Dillon, *At Dawn We Slept,* 5.

47. Prange, Goldstein, and Dillon, *At Dawn We Slept,* 4.

48. Prange, Goldstein, and Dillon, *At Dawn We Slept,* 5.

49. Prange, Goldstein, and Dillon, *At Dawn We Slept,* 5.

50. Prange, Goldstein, and Dillon, *At Dawn We Slept,* 5–6.

51. Nelson, *Pearl Harbor,* 94.

52. Samuel Eliot Morison, *The Two-Ocean War: A Short History of the United States Navy in the Second World War* (Boston: Little, Brown, 1963), 3, 14–15.

53. Nelson, *Pearl Harbor,* 60. See also Morison, *The Two-Ocean War,* 14.

54. Morison, *The Two-Ocean War,* 44; Daniel Martinez to Berry Craig, email, May 4, 2020.

55. Prange, Goldstein, and Dillon, *At Dawn We Slept,* 11; Martinez to Craig, May 4, 2020.

56. Nelson, *Pearl Harbor,* 101.

57. Morison, *The Two-Ocean War,* 46–47.

58. Morison, *The Two-Ocean War,* 47.

59. Nelson, *Pearl Harbor,* 171–72.

60. Nelson, Pearl Harbor, 177–78.

2. "We Are Too Big, Too Powerful, and Too Strong."

1. Nelson, *Pearl Harbor,* 190, 197; *Lord, Day of Infamy,* 219.

2. Daniel Martinez to Berry Craig, message, May 4, 2020.

3. Ronald H. Spector, *Eagle against the Sun: The American War with Japan* (New York: Vintage, 1985), 4.

4. Spector, *Eagle against the Sun,* 3–4; Martinez to Craig, text message, May 4, 2020.

5. Nelson, *Pearl Harbor,* 173; Martinez to Craig, text message, May 4, 2020.

6. Nelson, *Pearl Harbor,* 83; Martinez to Craig, text message, May 4, 2020.

7. Lord, *Day of Infamy,* 53–54.

8. Lord, *Day of Infamy,* 219; Martinez to Craig, text message, May 4, 2020.

9. Spector, *Eagle against the Sun,* 1–2; Twomey *Countdown to Pearl Harbor,* 6–8; Nelson, *Pearl Harbor,* 12.

10. Prange, Goldstein, and Dillon, *At Dawn We Slept,* 44.

11. *Owensboro Inquirer,* January 9, 1941. See also Prange, Goldstein, and Dillon, *At Dawn We Slept,* 50–51.

12. Kleber, ed., *The Kentucky Encyclopedia,* 517; Prange, Goldstein, and Dillon, *At Dawn We Slept,* 50–51.

13. *Owensboro Inquirer,* January 9, 1941. See also Kleber, ed., *The Kentucky Encyclopedia,* 517; Prange, Goldstein, and Dillon, *At Dawn We Slept,* 51.

14. *Louisville Courier-Journal,* January 26, 1941.

15. *Louisville Courier-Journal,* January 26, 1941.

16. *Louisville Courier-Journal,* January 26, 1941.

17. *Louisville Courier-Journal,* January 26, 1941.

18. Prange, Goldstein, and Dillon, *At Dawn We Slept,* 50.

19. Twomey, *Countdown to Pearl Harbor,* 9–10. See also Nelson, *Pearl Harbor,* 261.

20. Lord, *Day of Infamy,* 7.

21. *Owensboro Messenger,* May 18, 1941.

22. *Owensboro Messenger,* May 18, 1941.

23. *Owensboro Messenger,* May 18, 1941.

24. Twomey, *Countdown to Pearl Harbor,* 277.

25. Twomey, *Countdown to Pearl Harbor,* 277; Nelson, *Pearl Harbor,* 261.

26. *Louisville Courier-Journal,* July 14, 1941.

27. *Louisville Courier-Journal,* July 14, 1941. See also Bill McWilliams, *Sunday in Hell: Pearl Harbor Minute by Minute* (New York: Open Road Integrated Media, 2011), 213.

28. Prange, Goldstein, and Dillon, *At Dawn We Slept,* 52.

29. Daniel Martinez to Berry Craig, email, May 14, 2020.

30. Pamela G. Wood, ed., *Pearl Harbor Survivors* (Paducah, KY: Turner, 1992), 154; Martinez to Craig, May 14, 2020.

31. Martinez to Craig, text message, May 14, 2020.

32. Martinez to Craig, May 14, 2020.

33. *Louisville Courier-Journal,* December 18, 1941. See also Prange, Goldstein, and Dillon, *At Dawn We Slept,* 592–95.

34. *Louisville Courier-Journal,* December 18, 1941. See also Prange, Goldstein, and Dillon, *At Dawn We Slept,* 594–95.

35. Prange, Goldstein, and Dillon, *At Dawn We Slept,* 599–600.

36. Prange, Goldstein, and Dillon, *At Dawn We Slept,* 600; Nelson, *Pearl Harbor,* 437–38; *Louisville Courier-Journal,* April 7, 1942. For the rest of their lives, Kimmel, Short, and their military and civilian sympathizers maintained that the duo was railroaded. Some anti-FDR Republican politicians and newspaper publishers and pundits even charged—without evidence—that the president deliberately kept Short and Kimmel in the dark so that he could drag the country into the war on Britain's side. After Pearl Harbor, Short and Kimmel became martyred heroes, especially to conservatives. At any rate, Kimmel is still a hero in Henderson, where a bronze statue of him in uniform—with four-star shoulder boards—stands next to the Ohio River near where he almost lost his life in his youth.

37. *Louisville Courier-Journal,* April 7, 1942. See also Prange, Goldstein, and Dillon, *At Dawn We Slept,* 722–23.

38. *Louisville Courier-Journal,* April 15, 1942.

39. *Louisville Courier-Journal,* April 8, 1942.

40. *Danville Advocate-Messenger,* April 15, 1942; *Paducah Sun-Democrat,* April 20, 1942.

41. *Louisville Courier-Journal,* April 14, 1942.

42. *Louisville Courier-Journal,* April 14, 16, 1942.

43. *Louisville Courier-Journal,* April 14, 26, 1942.

44. *Louisville Courier-Journal,* April 29, 1942.

45. *Louisville Courier-Journal,* January 26, 1942.

46. *Louisville Courier-Journal,* January 26, 1942.

47. *Madisonville Messenger,* February 18, 1942.

48. Don Keith, *War beneath the Waves: A True Story of Courage and Leadership aboard a World War II Submarine* (New York: NAL/Caliber, 2010), 10–11.

49. *Owensboro Messenger,* March 4, 1942. See also Prange, Goldstein, and Dillon, *At Dawn We Slept,* 608.

3. The *Arizona* and the *Oklahoma*

1. Captain Mitsuo Fuchida, "I Led the Air Attack on Pearl Harbor," ed. Roger Pineau, *U.S. Naval Institute Proceedings,* vol. 78, no. 9 (September 1952), https://www.usni.org/magazines/proceedings/1952/september/i-led-air-attack-pearl-harbor.

2. Fuchida, "I Led the Air Attack on Pearl Harbor."

3. Fuchida, "I Led the Air Attack on Pearl Harbor."

4. Nelson, *Pearl Harbor,* 283–85. See also T. J. Cooper, *The Men of the USS Arizona (BB-39)* (n.p., 2008), 18; Pearl Harbor National Memorial Hawai'i, "Frequently Asked Questions," National Park Service, n.d., https://www.nps.gov/valr/faqs.htm; Martinez interview; Philip J. Hilts, "Divers Report USS Arizona Blown in Two in Pearl Harbor Raid," *Washington Post,* September 21, 1983; and "USS Arizona during the Attack," Naval History and Heritage Command, n.d., https://www.history.navy.mil/our-collections/photography/wars-and-events/world-war-ii/pearl-harbor-raid/battleship-row-during-the-pearl-harbor-attack/uss-arizona-during-the-pearl-harbor-attack.html.

5. Herbert Buehl, interview by Michael Stucky, December 4, 1996, Pearl Harbor National Memorial Hawai'i, Oral History Interviews, https://www.nps.gov/valr/learn/historyculture/upload/HerbertBuehl.pdf.

6. Buehl interview.

7. Buehl interview. See also "USS *Arizona,* Report of Pearl Harbor Attack." There are discrepancies about when general quarters sounded. One report said around 7:45 A.M. Others said 7:55, "about two or three minutes before 0800," and "about 8 o'clock." Don Keniston was also killed. His and his brother's remains are still on the *Arizona.* Their names are enshrined in the Gardens of the Missing, a series of eight gleaming white marble monuments that flank the similarly hued marble steps leading to the Honolulu Memorial in the National Memorial Cemetery of the Pacific in Honolulu.

8. Buehl interview.

9. Buehl interview.

10. Buehl interview.

11. Buehl interview.

12. Buehl interview.

13. Buehl interview.

14. Buehl interview.

15. Buehl interview.

16. Buehl interview.

17. Buehl interview.

18. Buehl interview.

19. Buehl interview.

20. Buehl interview.

21. Buehl interview.

22. Buehl interview.

23. Buehl interview.

24. Buehl interview.

25. Buehl interview.

26. Buehl interview.

27. Buehl interview.

28. Buehl interview.

29. Buehl interview; *Louisville Courier-Journal,* December 7, 1999. See also "Pearl Harbor Survivors, Herbert V. Buehl, USS Arizona, US Navy," Homestead.com, n.d., http://pearlharborsurvivors.homestead.com /BuehlHerbert.html. Buehl died in Louisville in 2002. He was eighty-six.

30. James Vessels interview (December 3, 1976); *Paducah Sun-Democrat,* December 7, 1976. See also Berry Craig, "Old Time Kentucky: Christmas Report of Pearl Harbor Soldier's Demise Was Greatly Exaggerated," *Kentucky Forward,* December 23, 2016, https://www.kyforward.com/old-time-kentucky -christmas-report-of-soldiers-pearl-harbor-demise-was-greatly-exaggerated.

31. James Vessels, interview by Susan Hodge Hackett, Pinson, AL, 1975. The original is in the possession of Susan Hodge Hackett, Pinson, AL.

32. James Vessels interview (December 3, 1976); *Paducah Sun-Democrat,* December 7, 1976; Martinez interview; Paul Stillwell, *Battleship Arizona: An Illustrated History* (Annapolis, MD: Naval Institute Press, 1991), 370–71.

33. Edward J. McGrath and Craig O. Thompson, *Second to the Last to Leave: USS Arizona: The Lauren F. Bruner Story—Memoir of a Sailor* (Honolulu: RMR, 2017), 198–99. See also James Vessels interview (December 3, 1976); *Paducah Sun-Democrat,* December 7, 1976; and Martinez interview.

34. Paducah *Sun-Democrat,* December 7, 1976; *Paducah Sun,* December 7, 1991; Margaret Vessels Shoulta, interview with the author, November 19, 2019, Paducah, KY.

35. *Paducah Sun-Democrat,* December 7, 1976; Shoulta interview.

36. *Paducah Sun-Democrat,* December 7, 1976; "USS *Arizona,* Report of Pearl Harbor Attack."

37. *Paducah Sun,* December 7, 1991.

38. James Vessels interview (December 3, 1976); *Paducah Sun-Democrat,* December 7, 1976.

39. Shoulta interview.

40. Shoulta interview. Fancy Farm is famous for hosting Kentucky's largest political picnic. The festivities are always the first Saturday in August.

41. Shoulta interview.

42. *Louisville Courier-Journal,* December 13, 1941; Cooper, *The Men of the USS Arizona,* 225.

43. *Louisville Courier-Journal,* December 13, 1941.

44. *Louisville Courier-Journal,* December 13, 20, 1941, July 28, 1942.

45. *The Cardinal,* January 16, 1942.

46. *Louisville Courier-Journal,* December 21, 1942.

47. William Marshall Bullitt to Maj. Gen. Frank M. McCoy, December 20, 1941, copy, Bullitt Family Papers, Oxmoor Collection, Filson Historical Society, Louisville.

48. Bullitt to McCoy, December 20, 1941.

49. Bullitt to McCoy, December 20, 1941.

50. Sara D. Porter to Bullitt, December 26, 1941, and Bullitt to Norman H. Davis, December 31, 1941, copy, Bullitt Papers. See also Pearl Harbor National Memorial Hawai'i, "U.S. Navy Casualties," National Park Service, updated November 14, 2018, https://www.nps.gov/valr/learn/historyculture/navy-casualties.htm.

51. Davis to Bullitt, January 5, 1942, A. W. Johnston to Elsie K. Mantle, January 9, 1942, copy, and Mantle to Bullitt, January 14, 1942, Bullitt Papers.

52. McCoy to Bullitt, January 28, 1942, Bullitt Papers; National Park Service, "Frequently Asked Questions," https://www.nps.gov/valr/faqs.htm; American Battle Monuments Commission, "Robert L. Leopold" https://www.abmc.gov/node/482383. On the Gardens of the Missing, see n. 7 above.

53. *Louisville Courier-Journal*, March 26, 1942. See also *Louisville Courier-Journal*, January 5, February 20, 1942.

54. *Louisville Courier-Journal*, June 9, 1943, July 2, 1979.

55. *Paducah Sun*, December 7, 1988. See also *Louisville Courier-Journal*, December 18, 1941.

56. *Louisville Courier-Journal*, December 18, 1941.

57. *Paducah Sun*, December 7, 1988.

58. *Paducah Sun*, December 7, 1988.

59. *Paducah Sun*, December 7, 1988; *Louisville Courier-Journal*, December 18, 1941.

60. *Paducah Sun*, December 7, 1988.

61. *Paducah Sun*, December 7, 1988.

62. *Paducah Sun*, December 7, 1988.

63. *Owensboro Messenger-Inquirer*, December 24, 2000.

64. *Owensboro Messenger*, January 2, 1929.

65. *Owensboro Messenger*, January 29, 1928.

66. *Louisville Courier-Journal*, December 1, 1957; *Owensboro Messenger*, February 11, 1942.

67. *Louisville Courier-Journal*, December 1, 1957.

68. *Louisville Courier-Journal*, December 7, 1971.

69. *Harrodsburg Herald*, December 26, 1941, January 2, 1942.

70. *Harrodsburg Herald*, January 9, 16, 1942.

71. "Pacific Fleet Band #22: Story of USS Arizona's Last Band," USSArizona.org, January 23, 2000, http://www.ussarizona.org/index.php/history/band. See also "Frederick W. Kinney," American Battle Monuments Commission, n.d., https://www.abmc.gov/node/481907; "Emmett Isaac Lynch," American Battle Monuments Commission, n.d., https://www.abmc.gov/node/482707.

72. Lord, *Day of Infamy*, 66.

73. *Allentown (PA) Morning Call*, April 2, 1942.

74. *Honolulu Advertiser*, April 3, 1942.

75. *Owensboro Messenger*, July 17, 1942. See also Molly Kent, *The USS Arizona's Last Band: The History of U.S. Navy Band Number 22* (Kansas City, KS: Silent Song, 1966), 204–5.

76. Kent, *The USS Arizona's Last Band*, 299.

77. *Louisville Courier-Journal*, December 7, 2017. Georgetown College still awards a scholarship named for him. It is given to a needy student annually.

78. "USS Oklahoma (Battleship # 37, later BB-37), 1916–1946," Naval History and Heritage Command, n.d., https://www.history.navy.mil/our -collections/photography/us-navy-ships/battleships/oklahoma-bb-37.html.

79. *Paducah Sun*, December 7, 1991.

80. Martinez interview.

81. Allison Family Scrapbook, in possession of David Heathcott, Mayfield, KY. See also *Paducah Sun-Democrat*, December 7, 1975.

82. *Louisville Courier-Journal*, February 11, 1942.

83. *Madisonville Messenger*, December 16, 1941.

84. *Madisonville Messenger*, December 16, 1941.

85. *Madisonville Messenger*, December 16, 1941.

86. *Madisonville Messenger*, December 16, 1941.

87. *Louisville Courier-Journal*, December 17, 1941.

88. "Military IDs 100 Killed on USS Oklahoma in Pearl Harbor," Voice of America, December 1, 2017, https://www.voanews.com/a/military-identifies -one-hundred-marines-sailors-killed-uss-oklahoma-pearl-harbor/4146298 .html; *Madisonville Messenger*, June 19, 2016.

89. *Madisonville Messenger*, June 19, 2016.

90. *Madisonville Messenger*, June 19, 2016.

91. *Madisonville Messenger*, June 19, 2016.

92. Rebecca Reynolds Yonker, "Burial in Kentucky for Newly Identified Pearl Harbor Victim," *Seattle Times*, December 8, 2017, https://www.seattletimes.com /nation-world/burial-in-kentucky-for-newly-identified-pearl-harbor-victim; *Louisville Courier-Journal*, April 26, 2019, October 6, 2019.

93. *Owensboro Messenger-Inquirer*, December 5, 1991.

94. *Owensboro Messenger-Inquirer*, December 24, 2000.

95. *Louisville Courier-Journal*, December 8, 1941.

96. *Louisville Courier-Journal*, December 8, 1941.

97. *Louisville Courier-Journal*, December 8, 1941; Pearl Harbor National Memorial Hawai'i, "U.S. Navy Casualties."

4. Elsewhere on Battleship Row

1. "USS West Virginia and USS Tennessee," Naval History and Heritage Command, n.d., https://www.history.navy.mil/our-collections/photography

/wars-and-events/world-war-ii/pearl-harbor-raid/battleship-row-during-the
-pearl-harbor-attack/uss-west-virginia-and-uss-tennessee-during-the-pearl
-harbor-atta.html.

2. *Owensboro Messenger,* November 1, 1942.

3. Lord, *Day of Infamy,* 101–2.

4. *Owensboro Messenger,* December 17, 26, 1941, November 1, 1942.

5. *Owensboro Messenger,* November 1, 1942. See also "USS *West Virginia,* Report of Pearl Harbor Attack," December 11, 1941, Naval History and Heritage Command, https://www.history.navy.mil/research/archives/digitized-collections /action-reports/wwii-pearl-harbor-attack/ships-s-z/uss-west-virginia-bb -48-action-report.html.

6. *Owensboro Messenger,* November 1, 1942.

7. *Owensboro Messenger,* November 1, 1942.

8. *Owensboro Messenger,* November 1, 1942.

9. "USS *West Virginia,* Report of Pearl Harbor Attack." See also *Louisville Courier-Journal,* October 9, 1941, December 8, 1941, February 8, 1966. Beattie graduated from Louisville Male High School in 1917 and the naval academy in 1922. He was tapped for promotion to lieutenant commander in October 1941.

10. "USS *West Virginia,* Report of Pearl Harbor Attack."

11. "USS *West Virginia,* Report of Pearl Harbor Attack."

12. "USS *West Virginia,* Report of Pearl Harbor Attack."

13. Nelson, *Pearl Harbor,* 428. Doris Miller died aboard the escort carrier *Liscome Bay* when it was torpedoed and sunk in 1943.

14. "USS *West Virginia,* Report of Pearl Harbor Attack."

15. "USS *West Virginia,* Report of Pearl Harbor Attack."

16. Lee Philip Ebner, interview by Dennis Fritz, April 28, 2003, Oldham County Historical Society: Oldham County Veterans Oral History Project, Louie B. Nunn Center for Oral History, University of Kentucky Libraries, Lexington.

17. Ebner interview.

18. Ebner interview.

19. Ebner interview. Ebner died in 2014 at age ninety-four.

20. *Kentucky Post,* December 17, 1941.

21. *Kentucky Post,* December 17, 1941.

22. *Kentucky Post,* December 8, 1941.

23. *Kentucky Post,* December 18, 20, 1941.

24. *Kentucky Post,* December 20, 1941.

25. *Kentucky Post,* December 20, 1941.

26. *Ashland Daily Independent,* December 18, 1941.

27. *Owensboro Messenger,* December 17, 23, 1941. Cobb survived World War II and died in Miller, Missouri, in 2003 at eighty-four. *Springfield News-Leader,* November 24, 2003.

28. *Paducah Sun,* November 23, 1991.

29. *Paducah Sun,* November 23, 1991.

30. *Paducah Sun,* November 23, 1991.

31. *Paducah Sun,* November 23, 1991.

32. "USS West Virginia and USS Tennessee."

33. *Owensboro Messenger-Inquirer,* December 8, 1996.

34. *Owensboro Messenger-Inquirer,* December 7, 1999.

35. *Owensboro Messenger-Inquirer,* December 7, 1999.

36. *Owensboro Messenger-Inquirer,* December 7, 1999. See also *Owensboro Messenger-Inquirer,* December 8, 1996; and "USS *Tennessee,* Report of Pearl Harbor Attack," December 11, 1941, Naval History and Heritage Command, https://www.history.navy.mil/research/archives/digitized-collections/action -reports/wwii-pearl-harbor-attack/ships-s-z/uss-tennessee-bb-43-action -report.html; "USS West Virginia and USS Tennessee."

37. "USS California during the Attack," Naval History and Heritage Command, n.d., https://www.history.navy.mil/our-collections/photography /wars-and-events/world-war-ii/pearl-harbor-raid/battleship-row-during-the -pearl-harbor-attack/uss-california-during-the-pearl-harbor-attack.html.

38. Clipping (*Harlan Enterprise,* [December 31, 1941?]) in possession of Stan Hamlin, James Hamlin's son. Green Hamlin's residence is sometimes listed as Wallins Creek. See also Hamlin interview; and *Paducah Sun-Democrat,* December 7, 1977.

39. *Harlan Enterprise* clipping.

40. *Harlan Enterprise* clipping.

41. Hamlin interview; *Paducah Sun-Democrat,* December 7, 1977.

42. Hamlin interview; *Paducah Sun-Democrat,* December 7, 1977; Lord, *Day of Infamy,* 61.

43. Hamlin interview; *Paducah Sun-Democrat,* December 7, 1977.

44. Hamlin interview; *Paducah Sun-Democrat,* December 7, 1977.

45. "USS *California,* Reports of Pearl Harbor Attack," December 13, 22, 1941, Naval History and Heritage Command, https://www.history.navy.mil /research/archives/digitized-collections/action-reports/wwii-pearl-harbor -attack/ships-a-c/uss-california-bb-44-action-report.html. See also Hamlin interview; *Paducah Sun-Democrat,* December 7, 1977.

46. Hamlin interview; *Paducah Sun-Democrat,* December 7, 1977.

47. Hamlin interview; *Paducah Sun-Democrat,* December 7, 1977. "'Geedunk' is a slang term with origins dating to the 1920s, adopted by Navy sailors and seagoing Marines to refer to ice cream, candy and other assorted snacks, or to the place aboard ship where those items could be purchased," according to a sign aboard the USS *Missouri* in Pearl Harbor. "The term origi- nates with the popular 'Harold Teen' comic strip first published in 1919, featur- ing Pop Jenks' 'Sugar Bowl' soda shop and his special 'Geedunk sundaes'

described as a concoction of ice cream eaten by 'geedunking' a large ladyfinger cookie."

48. Hamlin interview; *Paducah Sun-Democrat,* December 7, 1977.

49. Hamlin interview; *Paducah Sun-Democrat,* December 7, 1977.

50. Hamlin interview; *Paducah Sun-Democrat,* December 7, 1977.

51. *Indianapolis News,* December 19, 1941.

52. "USS *California,* Reports of Pearl Harbor Attack."

53. *Indianapolis News,* December 12, 1942.

54. *Indianapolis News,* December 12, 1942.

55. *Louisville Courier-Journal,* December 30, 1941.

56. *Louisville Courier-Journal,* December 30, 1941.

57. *Louisville Courier-Journal,* February 8, 1943.

58. *Louisville Courier-Journal,* February 8, 1943.

59. *Louisville Courier-Journal,* February 8, 1943.

60. *Louisville Courier-Journal,* February 8, 1943.

61. "USS Oklahoma and USS Maryland," Naval History and Heritage Command, n.d., https://www.history.navy.mil/our-collections/photography/wars-and-events/world-war-ii/pearl-harbor-raid/battleship-row-during-the-pearl-harbor-attack/uss-oklahoma-and-uss-maryland-during-the-pearl-harbor-attack.html.

62. William Joe Roberts Collection (AFC/2001/001/64990), Veterans History Project, American Folklife Center, Library of Congress, https://memory.loc.gov/diglib/vhp/bib/loc.natlib.afc2001001.64990.

63. William Joe Roberts Collection.

64. William Joe Roberts Collection.

65. William Joe Roberts Collection.

66. William Joe Roberts Collection. Though damaged, the *Maryland* was repaired and fought in several battles in the Pacific theater.

67. "Stan Van Hoose," Harlem Veteran Project, YouTube, January 7, 2018, https://www.youtube.com/watch?v=qv-Tqt6U0FE.

68. "Stan Van Hoose." See also "USS *Maryland,* Report of Pearl Harbor Attack," Naval History and Heritage Command, n.d., https://www.history.navy.mil/research/archives/digitized-collections/action-reports/wwii-pearl-harbor-attack/ships-m-r/uss-maryland-bb-46-action-report.html.

69. "USS Nevada during the Attack," Naval History and Heritage Command, n.d., https://www.history.navy.mil/our-collections/photography/wars-and-events/world-war-ii/pearl-harbor-raid/battleship-row-during-the-pearl-harbor-attack/uss-nevada-during-the-pearl-harbor-attack.html.

70. *Danville Advocate-Messenger,* November 11, 2005.

71. *Danville Advocate-Messenger,* November 11, 2005. See also "USS *Nevada,* Report of Pearl Harbor Attack," December 15, 1941, Naval History and Heritage Command, https://www.history.navy.mil/research/archives/digitized

-collections/action-reports/wwii-pearl-harbor-attack/ships-m-r/uss-nevada
-bb-36-action-report.html.

72. *Danville Advocate-Messenger,* November 11, 2005. See also "USS *Nevada,* Report of Pearl Harbor Attack."

73. *Danville Advocate-Messenger,* November 11, 2005; "USS *Nevada,* Report of Pearl Harbor Attack"; Lord, *Day of Infamy,* 133–36.

74. Lord, *Day of Infamy,* 136. See also "USS Nevada during the Attack."

75. *Danville Advocate-Messenger,* November 1, 2005.

76. *Danville Advocate-Messenger,* November 1, 2005.

77. Earl Emery Davis Collection (AFC/2001/001/09174), Veterans History Project, https://memory.loc.gov/diglib/vhp/bib/loc.natlib.afc2001001.9174.

78. Earl Emery Davis Collection.

79. Earl Emery Davis Collection.

80. Earl Emery Davis Collection.

81. Earl Emery Davis Collection. See also USS *Nevada,* "Report of Pearl Harbor Attack."

82. Earl Emery Davis Collection.

83. Earl Emery Davis Collection.

84. Earl Emery Davis Collection.

85. The *Nevada* earned seven battle stars, five for operations in the Pacific theater and two for the European theater, including for covering the Allied landing in Normandy on June 6, 1944.

5. Cruisers, Tin Cans, Friendly Fire, a Cutter, and Marines

1. Howell M. Forgy, *". . . And Pass the Ammunition,"* ed. Jack S. McDowell (New York: D. Appleton–Century, 1944), ix–x. See also Marion Belote O'Rourke, *Women's Association College Church, Murray* (Murray, KY: First Presbyterian Church, 2018); and *Paducah Sun-Democrat,* August 17, 1939; *Paducah Sun-Democrat,* January 24, 1972.

2. *Life,* November 2, 1942.

3. *Life,* November 2, 1942.

4. *Rochester (NY) Democrat and Chronicle,* November 1, 1942.

5. *Rochester (NY) Democrat and Chronicle,* November 1, 1942. See also Forgy, *". . . And Pass the Ammunition,"* 5–6.

6. *Vancouver (BC) Sun,* November 5, 1942.

7. *Vancouver (BC) Sun,* November 5, 1942.

8. Kathleen E. R. Smith, *God Bless America: Tin Pan Alley Goes to War* (Lexington: University Press of Kentucky, 2003), 17.

9. *New York Daily News,* November 19, 1942.

10. *New York Daily News,* November 19, 1942; Smith, *God Bless America,* 121.

11. *Louisville Courier-Journal,* September 17, 1943.

12. *New York Times,* September 17, 1943. See also *Madisonville Messenger,* January 6, 1943.

13. *Murray Ledger and Times,* October 7, 1943.

14. Forgy, "*. . . And Pass the Ammunition,*" 1.

15. Forgy, "*. . . And Pass the Ammunition,*" 1–2. See also *Louisville Courier-Journal,* September 17, 1943; and *Owensboro Messenger,* January 6, 1943.

16. Forgy, "*. . . And Pass the Ammunition,*" 2.

17. Forgy, "*. . . And Pass the Ammunition,*" 2.

18. Forgy, "*. . . And Pass the Ammunition,*" 3.

19. Forgy, "*. . . And Pass the Ammunition,*" 3.

20. Forgy, "*. . . And Pass the Ammunition,*" 4.

21. Forgy, "*. . . And Pass the Ammunition,*" 5.

22. Forgy, "*. . . And Pass the Ammunition,*" 5–6.

23. Forgy, "*. . . And Pass the Ammunition,*" 6.

24. Forgy, "*. . . And Pass the Ammunition,*" 6–7.

25. Forgy, "*. . . And Pass the Ammunition,*" 7.

26. "USS *New Orleans,* Report of Pearl Harbor Attack," December 13, 1941, Naval History and Heritage Command, https://www.history.navy.mil/research/archives/digitized-collections/action-reports/wwii-pearl-harbor-attack/ships-m-r/uss-new-orleans-ca-32-action-report.html.

27. Forgy, "*. . . And Pass the Ammunition,*" 8–9.

28. Forgy, "*. . . And Pass the Ammunition,*" 9.

29. Forgy, "*. . . And Pass the Ammunition,*" 10.

30. Forgy, "*. . . And Pass the Ammunition,*" 10–11.

31. Forgy, "*. . . And Pass the Ammunition,*" 11.

32. Forgy, "*. . . And Pass the Ammunition,*" 12–13.

33. Forgy, "*. . . And Pass the Ammunition,*" 14.

34. Forgy, "*. . . And Pass the Ammunition,*" 15–16.

35. Forgy, "*. . . And Pass the Ammunition,*" 16–17.

36. Forgy, "*. . . And Pass the Ammunition,*" 19–20.

37. James Gilbert Edwards Collection (AFC/2001/001/22875), Veterans History Project, https://memory.loc.gov/diglib/vhp/bib/loc.natlib.afc2001001.107611.

38. *Louisville Courier-Journal,* November 5, 2008.

39. James Gilbert Edwards Collection.

40. James Gilbert Edwards Collection; *Louisville Courier-Journal,* November 5, 2008.

41. James Gilbert Edwards Collection.

42. *Louisville Courier-Journal,* November 5, 2008.

43. James Gilbert Edwards Collection. See also "USS *New Orleans,* Report of Pearl Harbor Attack."

44. James Gilbert Edwards Collection. See also "USS *New Orleans,* Report of Pearl Harbor Attack."

45. James Gilbert Edwards Collection. See also "USS *New Orleans,* Report of Pearl Harbor Attack."

46. James Gilbert Edwards Collection. See also "USS New Orleans, Report of Pearl Harbor Attack."

47. James Gilbert Edwards Collection. See also "USS New Orleans, Report of Pearl Harbor Attack."

48. James Gilbert Edwards Collection. See also "USS New Orleans, Report of Pearl Harbor Attack"; and Lord, *Day of Infamy,* 144.

49. John Locker, interview by the author, December 2, 1986, Paducah, KY; *Paducah Sun,* December 7, 1986.

50. Locker interview; *Paducah Sun,* December 7, 1986.

51. Locker interview; *Paducah Sun,* December 7, 1986.

52. Locker interview; *Paducah Sun,* December 7, 1986.

53. Locker interview; *Paducah Sun,* December 7, 1986; "USS *San Francisco,* Report of Pearl Harbor Attack," December 10, 1941, Naval History and Heritage Command, https://www.history.navy.mil/research/archives/digitized-collections/action-reports/wwii-pearl-harbor-attack/ships-s-z/uss-san-francisco-ca-38-action-report.html.

54. Locker interview; *Paducah Sun,* December 7, 1986.

55. Locker interview; *Paducah Sun,* December 7, 1986.

56. "USS *San Francisco,* Report of Pearl Harbor Attack."

57. *Paducah Sun,* December 7, 1986.

58. Locker interview; *Paducah Sun,* December 7, 1986. The *San Francisco* earned seventeen battle stars before the war ended.

59. Sanders interview; *Paducah Sun,* December 7, 1978.

60. *Paducah Sun,* December 7, 1978.

61. "USS *St. Louis,* Reports of Pearl Harbor Attack," December 10, 25, 1941, Naval History and Heritage Command, https://www.history.navy.mil/research/archives/digitized-collections/action-reports/wwii-pearl-harbor-attack/ships-s-z/uss-st-louis-cl-49-action-report.html.

62. *Paducah Sun,* December 7, 1978.

63. *Paducah Sun,* December 7, 1978; "USS *St. Louis,* Reports of Pearl Harbor Attack."

64. Sanders interview; *Paducah Sun,* December 7, 1978. See also "USS St. Louis, Reports of Pearl Harbor Attack"; and Lord, *Day of Infamy,* 105.

65. Sanders interview; *Paducah Sun,* December 7, 1978. See also Lord, *Day of Infamy,* 144; and "USS *St. Louis,* Reports of Pearl Harbor Attack."

66. "USS *St. Louis,* Reports of Pearl Harbor Attack."

67. *Mayfield Messenger,* December 17, 1941.

68. *Paducah Sun,* December 7, 1978. The *St. Louis* was in most of the major naval battles of the Pacific theater and earned eleven battle stars. Sanders left the *St. Louis* after a Japanese torpedo hit the ship in the 1943 Battle of Kolombangara. The torpedo smashed the bow, but casualties were light.

69. Clarence Meece, Hopkinsville, KY, telephone interview by the author, December 1, 1981. See also Lord, *Day of Infamy,* 69; and *Paducah Sun,* December 6, 1981.

70. "USS *Raleigh,* Report of Pearl Harbor Attack," December 13, 1941, Naval History and Heritage Command, https://www.history.navy.mil/research/archives/digitized-collections/action-reports/wwii-pearl-harbor-attack/ships-m-r/uss-raleigh-cl-7-action-report.html.

71. *Paducah Sun,* December 6, 1981. See also Lord, *Day of Infamy,* 104.

72. Lord, *Day of Infamy,* 104, 141.

73. *Paducah Sun,* December 6, 1981. See also "USS *Raleigh,* Report of Pearl Harbor Attack." The *Raleigh* was repaired and saw action in the Aleutian Islands and elsewhere.

74. *Owensboro Messenger-Inquirer,* December 4, 1991.

75. *Owensboro Messenger-Inquirer,* December 4, 1991. See also "USS *Detroit,* Report of Pearl Harbor Attack," December 10, 1941, Naval History and Heritage Command, https://www.history.navy.mil/research/archives/digitized-collections/action-reports/wwii-pearl-harbor-attack/ships-d-l/uss-detroit-cl-8-action-report.html.

76. V. C. Kidd, interview by the author, December 5, 1983, Mayfield, KY; *Paducah Sun,* December 7, 1983.

77. Kidd interview; *Paducah Sun,* December 7, 1983.

78. Kidd interview; *Paducah Sun,* December 7, 1983.

79. Kidd interview; *Paducah Sun,* December 7, 1983.

80. Kidd interview; *Paducah Sun,* December 7, 1983. See also "USS *Tucker,* Report of Pearl Harbor Attack," December 15, 1941, Naval History and Heritage Command, https://www.history.navy.mil/research/archives/digitized-collections/action-reports/wwii-pearl-harbor-attack/ships-s-z/uss-tucker-dd-374-action-report.html. Kidd, who made chief petty officer before he left the navy after the war, died in 1998 at age seventy-six. See *Mayfield Messenger,* December 7, 2018.

81. Clarence Gunther interview, September 21, 1987, Louie B. Nunn Center for Oral History.

82. Gunther interview. See also "USS *Farragut,* Report of Pearl Harbor Attack," December 13, 1941, Naval History and Heritage Command, https://www.history.navy.mil/research/archives/digitized-collections/action-reports/wwii-pearl-harbor-attack/ships-d-l/uss-farragut-dd-348-action-report.html.

83. Gunther interview.

84. Gunther interview.

85. Gunther interview.

86. Gunther interview.

87. Gunther interview.

88. Gunther interview.

89. Gunther interview.

90. Gunther interview.

91. Riley interview; *Paducah Sun,* December 7, 1979.

92. Riley interview; *Paducah Sun,* December 7, 1979.

93. Riley interview; *Paducah Sun,* December 7, 1979.

94. Riley interview; *Paducah Sun,* December 7, 1979.

95. Riley interview; *Paducah Sun,* December 7, 1979.

96. Riley interview; *Paducah Sun,* December 7, 1979.

97. Riley interview; *Paducah Sun,* December 7, 1979. See also "USS *Case,* Report of Pearl Harbor Attack," January 2, 1942, Naval History and Heritage Command, https://www.history.navy.mil/research/archives/digitized-collections /action-reports/wwii-pearl-harbor-attack/ships-a-c/uss-case-dd-370-action -report.html.

98. Riley interview; *Paducah Sun,* December 7, 1979.

99. *Madisonville Messenger,* December 7, 1976, December 7, 2003. The grisly fate of the *Indianapolis* is one of the best-known stories of the Pacific war. In July 1945, the cruiser was sent from San Francisco to Tinian to deliver parts of the atomic bomb that was dropped on Hiroshima. After completing its top-secret mission, the ship headed for the Philippines. Shortly after midnight on July 30, a Japanese submarine torpedoed the unsuspecting *Indianapolis,* which sank in twelve minutes. About three hundred of its twelve-hundred-man crew died. The rest were marooned in mid-ocean, many in the water because there were not enough lifeboats. Also, food and water were in short supply. As a result, the survivors suffered exposure, dehydration, seawater poisoning, and endured terrifying shark attacks. The navy did not know the *Indianapolis* was lost until August 2, when the men happened to be sighted by the crew of a plane on routine patrol. Only 316 crewmen survived to be rescued in what is still the worst-ever loss of life on a navy ship at sea.

100. Prange, Goldstein, and Dillon, *At Dawn We Slept,* 561.

101. *Madisonville Messenger,* December 7, 2003.

102. *Madisonville Messenger,* December 7, 2003.

103. Martinez to Craig, May 4, 2020. See also Lord, *Day of Infamy,* 126–27.

104. Robert J. Cressman, J. Michael Wenger, and John F. Divirgilio, *Steady Nerves and Stout Hearts: The USS Enterprise Air Group and Pearl Harbor* (Rockville, MD: Pacific War History Associates, 2010), 80–81. See also Lord, *Day of Infamy,* 206.

105. Cressman, Wenger, and Divirgilio, *Steady Nerves and Stout Hearts,* 83–84.

106. Cressman, Wenger, and Divirgilio, *Steady Nerves and Stout Hearts,* 83–86.

107. Cressman, Wenger, and Divirgilio, *Steady Nerves and Stout Hearts,* 84–86; Martinez interview. Today, a grove of trees stands on or near the site of the Palm Lodge.

108. *Honolulu Star-Bulletin,* December 8, 1941.

109. *Honolulu Star-Bulletin,* December 8, 1941.

110. *Louisville Courier-Journal,* December 24, 1941, June 9, 1943, October 11, 31, 1947.

111. *Owensboro Messenger-Inquirer,* December 4, 1991.

112. *Owensboro Messenger-Inquirer,* December 4, 1991.

113. *Owensboro Messenger-Inquirer,* December 4, 1991. The *Taney* is preserved as a floating museum in Baltimore's Inner Harbor.

114. *Louisville Courier-Journal,* December 7, 2006.

115. *Louisville Courier-Journal,* July 10, 2014.

116. *Louisville Courier-Journal,* December 7, 2006.

117. *Louisville Courier-Journal,* December 7, 2006.

118. *Paducah Sun,* December 8, 1989.

119. *Paducah Sun,* December 8, 1989.

120. *Paducah Sun,* December 8, 1989.

121. *Franklin Favorite,* November 22, 2012.

122. John Edwards Wood, interview by Julie Anne Williams (WCLU Radio, Glasgow), 2006, https://www.youtube.com/watch?v=Ci2esE9yll0. The video was posted November 19, 2013, but the soundtrack was created in 2006.

123. *Franklin Favorite,* November 22, 2012. See also Wood interview.

124. Wood interview.

125. Wood interview.

126. *Franklin Favorite,* November 22, 2012.

127. *Louisville Courier-Journal,* December 7, 1991.

128. "US Marines at Pearl Harbor, 7 December 1941," Naval History and Heritage Command, November 17, 2016, https://www.history.navy.mil/research/library/online-reading-room/title-list-alphabetically/u/us-marines-at-pearl-harbor.html.

129. "US Marines at Pearl Harbor, 7 December 1941."

130. *Louisville Courier-Journal,* December 7, 1991.

131. *Louisville Courier-Journal,* December 7, 1991.

132. *Louisville Courier-Journal,* December 7, 1991.

133. *Louisville Courier-Journal,* December 7, 1991; "US Marines at Pearl Harbor, 7 December 1941"; Martinez to Craig, May 4, 2020.

6. The Dungaree Navy

1. Eugene B. Hayden and Julia Hayden, interview by Betty Turnell, 1976, World War II Veterans of Kentucky Oral History Project, Kentucky Historical Society, Frankfort; "USS *Curtiss,* Report of Pearl Harbor," December 16, 1941, Naval History and Heritage Command, https://www.history.navy.mil/research /archives/digitized-collections/action-reports/wwii-pearl-harbor-attack/ships -a-c/uss-curtiss-av-4-action-report.html.

2. Hayden and Hayden interview.

3. Hayden and Hayden interview.

4. Hayden and Hayden interview.

5. Hayden and Hayden interview.

6. Hayden and Hayden interview.

7. Hayden and Hayden interview.

8. Hayden and Hayden interview.

9. Hayden and Hayden interview.

10. Hayden and Hayden interview.

11. Hayden and Hayden interview.

12. Hayden and Hayden interview.

13. Hayden and Hayden interview.

14. Hayden and Hayden interview.

15. Hayden and Hayden interview.

16. Hayden and Hayden interview.

17. "USS Curtiss, Report of Pearl Harbor."

18. Hayden and Hayden interview. The term *Kentucky windage* dates to frontier days when shooters would aim and fire their rifles at a point where they anticipated a fast-moving target would be rather than stopping to adjust their rifle sights.

19. Hayden and Hayden interview.

20. Hayden and Hayden interview.

21. Hayden and Hayden interview.

22. Hayden and Hayden interview. See also Pearl Harbor National Memorial Hawai'i, "U.S. Navy Casualties."

23. Hayden and Hayden interview.

24. Hayden and Hayden interview.

25. Hayden and Hayden interview. Hayden made a career of the navy, retired as a commander, and died in 1993 at age eighty-two.

26. "USS *Curtiss,* Report of Pearl Harbor."

27. H. S. Reeves, interview by the author, December 2, 1981, Paducah, KY; *Paducah Sun,* December 6, 1981.

28. Reeves interview; *Paducah Sun,* December 6, 1981.

29. Reeves interview; *Paducah Sun,* December 6, 1981.

30. "USS *Medusa,* Report of Pearl Harbor Attack," December 16, 1941, Naval History and Heritage Command, https://www.history.navy.mil/research /archives/digitized-collections/action-reports/wwii-pearl-harbor-attack/ships -m-r/uss-medusa-ar-1-action-report.html.

31. Reeves interview; *Paducah Sun,* December 6, 1981.

32. Vance Leneave, interview by the author, December 3, 1980, Cadiz, KY; *Paducah Sun,* December 7, 1980.

33. Leneave interview; *Paducah Sun,* December 7, 1980.

34. Reeves interview, December 2, 1981; *Paducah Sun,* December 6, 1981.

35. Leneave interview; *Paducah Sun,* December 7, 1980.

36. "USS Medusa, Report of Pearl Harbor Attack."

37. Leneave interview; *Paducah Sun,* December 7, 1980.

38. "USS Medusa, Report of Pearl Harbor Attack."

39. Leneave interview; *Paducah Sun,* December 7, 1980.

40. Leneave interview; *Paducah Sun,* December 7, 1980.

41. Leneave interview; *Paducah Sun,* December 7, 1980.

42. *Louisville Courier-Journal,* December 7, 1991.

43. "USS *Argonne,* Report for Pearl Harbor Attack," January 28, 1942, Naval History and Heritage Command, https://www.history.navy.mil/research /archives/digitized-collections/action-reports/wwii-pearl-harbor-attack/ships -a-c/uss-argonne-ag-31-action-report.html. See also Lord, *Day of Infamy,* 124.

44. *Louisville Courier-Journal,* December 7, 1991.

45. *Louisville Courier-Journal,* December 7, 1991.

46. Calhoun interview; *Paducah Sun,* December 6, 1981.

47. Calhoun interview; *Paducah Sun,* December 6, 1981.

7. The Army

1. "Hickam Field," National Park Service, n.d., https://www.nps.gov /articles/hickam-field.htm.

2. "Hickam Field."

3. *Louisville Courier-Journal,* January 17, 1943.

4. *Louisville Courier-Journal,* January 17, 1943.

5. *Louisville Courier-Journal,* January 17, 1943. See also Lord, *Day of Infamy,* 117.

6. *Louisville Courier-Journal,* January 17, 1943.

7. *Louisville Courier-Journal,* December 7, 1991.

8. *Louisville Courier-Journal,* December 7, 1991.

9. *Louisville Courier-Journal,* December 7, 1991.

10. *Louisville Courier-Journal,* December 7, 1991. See also "Hickam Field."

11. *Louisville Courier-Journal,* December 7, 1991; *Gaffney (SC) Ledger,* March 3, 1942.

12. *Owensboro Messenger,* October 3, 1943; "The Purple Heart," Celebrating America's Freedoms, US Department of Veterans Affairs, n.d., https://www.va.gov/opa/publications/celebrate/purple-heart.pdf.

13. *Owensboro Messenger,* October 3, 1943.

14. *Owensboro Messenger,* October 3, 1943.

15. *Owensboro Messenger,* October 3, 1943.

16. *Paducah Sun,* December 7, 1991.

17. *Paducah Sun,* December 7, 1991.

18. *Louisville Courier-Journal,* October 3, 1943.

19. *Louisville Courier-Journal,* October 3, 1943.

20. "George T. Ingram," Hall of Valor Project, n.d., https://valor.militarytimes.com/hero/47823. See also *Louisville Courier-Journal,* October 3, 1943.

21. *Louisville Courier-Journal,* October 3, 1943.

22. *Louisville Courier-Journal,* October 3, 1943. See also *Lexington Herald-Leader,* December 7, 2011.

23. *Owensboro Messenger-Inquirer,* December 4, 1991.

24. *Owensboro Messenger-Inquirer,* December 4, 1991.

25. *Owensboro Messenger-Inquirer,* December 4, 1991.

26. *Louisville Courier-Journal,* December 13, 1959.

27. *Louisville Courier-Journal,* December 13, 1959.

28. *Louisville Courier-Journal,* December 13, 1959.

29. *Louisville Courier-Journal,* December 13, 1959.

30. *Louisville Courier-Journal,* December 13, 1959. It is doubtful that the Japanese knew about the empty hangars.

31. *Louisville Courier-Journal,* December 13, 1959.

32. *Louisville Courier-Journal,* December 13, 1959.

33. *Louisville Courier-Journal,* December 13, 1959.

34. *Louisville Courier-Journal,* December 13, 1959.

35. *Louisville Courier-Journal,* December 13, 1959.

36. *Louisville Courier-Journal,* December 13, 1959.

37. *Louisville Courier-Journal,* December 13, 1959.

38. *Louisville Courier-Journal,* December 13, 1959.

39. *Louisville Courier-Journal,* December 13, 1959.

40. *Louisville Courier-Journal,* December 13, 1959.

41. P. R. Davis, interview with Janice Miller, November 18, 2017, Worthington, KY. A version of Miller's interview was published in the *Ashland Daily Independent* on December 8, 2017. The original typescript is in Miller's possession.

42. Davis interview.

43. Davis interview.

44. Davis interview.

45. "Wheeler Field."

46. "Wheeler Field." In 1939, the army, which had shared air operations with the navy on Ford Island, closed Luke Airfield, named for Second Lieutenant Frank Luke. Dubbed the "Balloon Buster" for shooting down German observation balloons, Luke was the second-ranking US air ace in World War I and the posthumous recipient of the Medal of Honor in 1918. Luke Air Force Base in his native Arizona is named for him; Martinez to Craig, text message, May 14, 2020.

47. Raymond Turley, interview by Sarah Milligan, February 23, 2008, World War II Veterans of Kentucky Oral History Project.

48. Turley interview.

49. Turley interview.

50. Turley interview.

51. Turley interview.

52. Turley interview.

53. Turley interview.

54. *Madisonville Messenger,* May 13, 1944.

55. *Madisonville Messenger,* May 13, 1944.

56. *Madisonville Messenger,* May 13, 1944.

57. *Louisville Courier-Journal,* December 10, 1941.

58. *Louisville Courier-Journal,* December 10, 1941.

59. *Louisville Courier-Journal,* December 10, 1941.

60. *Louisville Courier-Journal,* December 7, 1960.

61. *Louisville Courier-Journal,* December 7, 1960.

62. "The 25th Infantry Division on December 7, 1941," 25th Infantry Division Association, Tropic Lightning, n.d., https://www.25thida.org/division/pearl-harbor.

63. Taira McAfee, interview by the author, November 14, 2019, Mayfield, KY. Saxon died in 1986. McAfee is Saxon's great-nephew.

64. *Owensboro Messenger-Inquirer,* December 7, 2011. See also *Owensboro Messenger-Inquirer,* April 7, 2012.

65. *Owensboro Messenger-Inquirer,* April 7, 2012. See also *Owensboro Messenger-Inquirer,* December 7, 1999. Quotes are from the April 7 paper.

66. Tommy Lewis, interview by the author, December 5, 1982, Mayfield, KY; *Paducah Sun,* December 7, 1982.

67. Lewis interview; *Paducah Sun,* December 7, 1982.

68. Lewis interview; *Paducah Sun,* December 7, 1982.

69. *Owensboro Messenger,* December 7, 1942.

70. *Owensboro Messenger,* December 7, 1942.

71. *Owensboro Messenger,* December 7, 1942.

72. *Owensboro Messenger,* December 7, 1942.

73. *Owensboro Messenger,* December 7, 1942.

74. *Owensboro Messenger,* December 7, 1942.

75. *Louisville Courier-Journal*, December 4, 2016.

76. *Louisville Courier-Journal*, December 4, 2016.

77. *Louisville Courier-Journal*, December 4, 2016.

78. McWilliams, *Sunday in Hell*, 252.

79. McWilliams, *Sunday in Hell*, 252–53.

80. McWilliams, *Sunday in Hell*, 253.

81. McWilliams, *Sunday in Hell*, 253.

82. McWilliams, *Sunday in Hell*, 547. McWilliams said that the absence of gangrene cases was "a tribute to a new, simple life-saving procedure begun by Dr. Heaton and later recognized and used throughout the Army." Ibid.

83. McWilliams, *Sunday in Hell*, 253.

84. *Louisville Courier-Journal*, August 8, 1943.

85. Sam Dick, "Pearl Harbor Survivor Remembers Attack on 75th Anniversary," WKYT.com, updated December 6, 2016, https://www.wkyt.com/content/news/PearlHarborSurvivorRemembers-404831736.html.

86. Dick, "Pearl Harbor Survivor Remembers Attack." See also *Louisville Courier-Journal*, May 12, 2018.

87. Dick, "Pearl Harbor Survivor Remembers Attack." See also *Louisville Courier-Journal*, May 12, 2018.

88. *Louisville Courier-Journal*, December 7, 1983.

89. *Louisville Courier-Journal*, December 7, 1983.

90. *Louisville Courier-Journal*, December 7, 1983.

91. *Louisville Courier-Journal*, December 7, 1983.

92. *Owensboro Messenger*, September 16, 1942.

93. *Owensboro Messenger*, September 16, 1942.

94. *Owensboro Messenger*, September 16, 1942.

95. *Owensboro Messenger*, September 16, 1942.

96. *Owensboro Messenger*, September 16, 1942.

97. *Owensboro Messenger*, September 16, 1942.

98. *Owensboro Messenger*, September 16, 1942.

99. *Louisville Courier-Journal*, December 27, 1941.

100. *Louisville Courier-Journal*, December 7, 1953.

101. *Louisville Courier-Journal*, December 27, 1941. Goebel died in 1974 at age fifty-one.

102. *Georgetown Times*, December 17, 1941.

103. Morison, *The Two Ocean War*, 41.

104. *Louisville Courier-Journal*, December 24, 1941.

105. John Trowbridge, "'Neither riches or poverty, neither creed or race . . .' —the Story of Pvt. Robert H. Brooks," Kentuckyguard, February 14, 2014, https://kentuckyguard.dodlive.mil/2014/02/14/neither-riches-or-poverty -neither-creed-or-race-the-story-of-pvt-robert-h-brooks.

106. *Georgetown Times,* December 17, 1941; *Louisville Courier-Journal,* December 24, 1941.

107. *Louisville Courier-Journal,* December 24, 1941.

108. *Louisville Courier-Journal,* December 24, 1941.

109. *Louisville Courier-Journal,* December 24, 1941.

110. Trowbridge, "'Neither riches or poverty, neither creed or race . . .'"

111. Trowbridge, "'Neither riches or poverty, neither creed or race . . .'"

112. Trowbridge, "'Neither riches or poverty, neither creed or race . . .'"

113. Trowbridge, "'Neither riches or poverty, neither creed or race . . .'"

114. "Kaneohe Naval Air Station," National Historic Landmarks Program, n.d., https://web.archive.org/web/20070301174131/http://tps.cr.nps.gov/nhl/detail.cfm?ResourceId=2003&ResourceType=District; Lord, *Day of Infamy,* 84, 117.

115. *Lexington Herald-Leader,* December 6, 2016.

116. *Lexington Herald-Leader,* December 6, 2016.

117. *Lexington Herald-Leader,* December 6, 2016.

118. *Lexington Herald-Leader,* December 6, 2016.

119. "Interview with Mr. & Mrs. David Neal," February 3, 1981, William H. Berge Oral History Center, Eastern Kentucky University, https://oralhistory.eku.edu/items/show/421.

120. "Interview with Mr. & Mrs. David Neal."

121. "Interview with Mr. & Mrs. David Neal."

122. *Honolulu Star-Bulletin,* July 25, 2004; *Honolulu Advertiser,* April 22, 2009. Bolstered later in the war, the fort housed Hawaii National Guard Nike antiaircraft missiles in the 1960s and 1970s. The Honolulu Department of Parks and Recreation took ownership of the property in 1972. Now fenced off, the old fort is next to Kapolei Regional Park.

123. *Lexington Herald-Leader,* December 7, 2011, December 6, 2016.

124. *Lexington Herald-Leader,* December 7, 2011, December 6, 2016.

125. Jack D. Ellis, *Patriots and Heroes: Eastern Kentucky Soldiers of WWII* (Ashland, KY: Jesse Stuart Foundation, 2003), 250–51.

126. Ellis, *Patriots and Heroes,* 251.

127. Ellis, *Patriots and Heroes,* 251–52.

8. Civvy Street, Hawaii

1. *Georgetown Times,* January 7, 1942. The letter was reprinted from the *Cynthiana Democrat.* Cynthiana is the Harrison County seat.

2. *Georgetown Times,* January 7, 1942; "Footlocker: Seeing Red at Pearl Harbor," History Net, n.d., https://www.historynet.com/footlocker-seeing-red-at-pearl-harbor.htm.

3. *Georgetown Times,* January 7, 1942.

4. *Georgetown Times,* January 7, 1942.

5. *Georgetown Times,* January 7, 1942.

6. *Georgetown Times,* January 7, 1942.

7. *Georgetown Times,* January 7, 1942.

8. *Georgetown Times,* January 7, 1942.

9. *Georgetown Times,* January 7, 1942.

10. *Georgetown Times,* January 7, 1942.

11. *Georgetown Times,* January 7, 1942.

12. *Honolulu Star-Bulletin,* May 21, 1942. See also "Footlocker: Seeing Red at Pearl Harbor."

13. Toni Stahl, untitled and unpublished handwritten account of December 7, 1941. The account remains in Stahl's possession at her home in Butler County.

14. Stahl handwritten account.

15. Toni Stahl, telephone interview by the author, March 4, 2019.

16. Stahl telephone interview.

17. Stahl telephone interview.

18. Stahl telephone interview.

19. *Madisonville Messenger,* May 23, 1942.

20. *Louisville Courier-Journal,* January 9, 1942.

21. *Louisville Courier-Journal,* January 9, 1942.

22. *Louisville Courier-Journal,* January 9, 1942.

23. *Louisville Courier-Journal,* January 9, 1942.

24. *Louisville Courier-Journal,* October 28, 1943.

25. *Louisville Courier-Journal,* October 28, 1943.

26. *Louisville Courier-Journal,* October 28, 1943. See also *Louisville Courier-Journal,* November 4, 1943.

27. *Louisville Courier-Journal,* October 28, 1943.

28. *Louisville Courier-Journal,* October 28, 1943.

29. *Louisville Courier-Journal,* January 10, 1942.

30. *Louisville Courier-Journal,* January 10, 1942.

31. *Louisville Courier-Journal,* January 10, 1942.

32. *Louisville Courier-Journal,* January 10, 1942.

33. *Louisville Courier-Journal,* January 10, 1942.

34. *Louisville Courier-Journal,* January 8, 1942.

35. *Louisville Courier-Journal,* January 8, 1942.

36. *Louisville Courier-Journal,* January 8, 1942.

37. *Louisville Courier-Journal,* January 8, 1942.

38. *Louisville Courier-Journal,* January 8, 1942.

39. *Louisville Courier-Journal,* January 8, 1942.

40. *Louisville Courier-Journal,* January 8, 1942.

41. *Louisville Courier-Journal,* January 8, 1942. Major Cords became a fighter pilot and was killed on April 20, 1944. Soon afterward, his widow joined the new Women's Army Corps.

42. *Kentucky Standard,* March 19, 1942. The story was copied from the *Ohio Chronicle.* Braly graduated from the Kentucky school in 1935, Huff five years later. The latter's wife, Anna Huff, also taught at the Honolulu school. Rawsor Moore, who graduated with Huff, was on leave from the faculty and in the army in Hawaii.

43. *Kentucky Standard,* March 19, 1942.

44. *Kentucky Standard,* March 19, 1942.

45. *Kentucky Standard,* March 19, 1942.

46. *Kentucky Standard,* March 19, 1942.

47. *Kentucky Standard,* March 19, 1942.

48. *Kentucky Standard,* March 19, 1942.

49. *Kentucky Standard,* March 19, 1942.

50. Hayden and Hayden interview.

51. Hayden and Hayden interview.

52. Hayden and Hayden interview.

53. Hayden and Hayden interview.

54. Hayden and Hayden interview.

55. Hayden and Hayden interview.

56. Hayden and Hayden interview.

57. Hayden and Hayden interview.

58. Hayden and Hayden interview.

59. Hayden and Hayden interview.

60. Hayden and Hayden interview.

61. Hayden and Hayden interview.

62. Hayden and Hayden interview.

63. Hayden and Hayden interview.

64. Hayden and Hayden interview.

65. Hayden and Hayden interview.

66. Hayden and Hayden interview.

67. Hayden and Hayden interview.

68. *Louisville Courier-Journal,* May 18, 1942.

69. *Louisville Courier-Journal,* May 18, 1942.

70. *Louisville Courier-Journal,* May 18, 1942.

71. *Louisville Courier-Journal,* May 18, 1942.

72. *Danville Advocate-Messenger,* February 11, 1942.

73. *Danville Advocate-Messenger,* February 11, 1942.

74. *Danville Advocate-Messenger,* February 11, 1942.

75. *Danville Advocate-Messenger,* February 11, 1942.

9. Keeping the Home Fires Ablaze

1. Harrison and Klotter, *A New History of Kentucky*, 370, 372.

2. James C. Klotter, *Kentucky: Portrait in Paradox, 1900–1950* (Frankfort: Kentucky Historical Society, 1996), 256; *Owensboro Messenger*, December 7, 1941.

3. *Owensboro Messenger*, December 9, 1941.

4. Richard E. Holl, *Committed to Victory: The Kentucky Home Front during World War II* (Lexington: University Press of Kentucky, 2015), 3.

5. Holl, *Committed to Victory*, 4.

6. Harrison and Klotter, *A New History of Kentucky*, 370, 372. See also Holl, *Committed to Victory*, 1.

7. *Paducah Sun*, December 11, 1981.

8. *Paducah Sun*, December 11, 1981.

9. *Paducah Sun*, December 11, 1981.

10. *Paducah Sun*, December 7, 1991.

11. *Paducah Sun*, December 7, 1991.

12. *Paducah Sun*, December 7, 1991.

13. *Paducah Sun*, December 7, 1991.

14. *Paducah Sun*, December 7, 1991.

15. *Paducah Sun*, December 7, 1991.

16. *Paducah Sun*, December 7, 1991.

17. *Paducah Sun*, December 7, 1991.

18. *Paducah Sun*, December 7, 1991.

19. Robert Coleman, interview by the author, November 3, 2019, Paducah, KY.

20. *Louisville Courier-Journal*, December 8, 1941.

21. Prange, Goldstein, and Dillon, *Pearl Harbor*, 346.

22. Prange, Goldstein, and Dillon, *At Dawn We Slept*, 583.

23. *Cincinnati Enquirer*, December 8, 1941, Kentucky edition.

24. *Lexington Herald*, December 8, 1941.

25. *Frankfort State Journal*, December 9, 1941.

26. *Lexington Leader*, December 8, 1941.

27. *Lexington Leader*, December 8, 1941.

28. *Somerset Journal*, December 11, 1941.

29. *Paducah Sun-Democrat*, December 8, 1941.

30. *Kentucky Post*, December 9, 1941.

31. *Mayfield Messenger*, December 8, 11, 1941.

32. *Franklin Favorite*, December 11, 1941. Charles A. Lindbergh became a hero to millions worldwide when, in 1927, he became the first pilot to fly solo and nonstop across the Atlantic. Accused of being anti-Semitic and a Nazi sympathizer, he joined the antiwar America First Committee and claimed that

FDR, the Jews, and the British were colluding to drag the United States into the war.

33. *Madisonville Messenger,* December 8, 1941.

34. *Middlesboro Daily News,* December 8, 1941.

35. *Ashland Daily Independent,* December 11, 1941.

36. *Ashland Daily Independent,* December 11, 1941.

37. *Owensboro Messenger,* December 8, 1941.

38. *Owensboro Messenger,* December 8, 1941.

39. *Owensboro Messenger,* December 8, 1941.

40. *Danville Advocate-Messenger,* December 8, 1941.

41. *Danville Advocate-Messenger,* December 8, 1941.

42. *Pike County News,* December 11, 1941.

43. *Trail Blazer,* December 13, 1941.

44. *Trail Blazer,* December 13, 1941.

45. *Kentucky Kernel,* December 9, 1941.

46. *Kentucky Kernel,* December 9, 1941.

47. *Madisonville Messenger,* December 9, 1941.

48. *Owensboro Messenger,* December 14, 1941; *Danville Advocate-Messenger,* December 10, 1941.

49. *Somerset Journal,* December 11, 1941.

50. *Kentucky Post,* December 20, 1941.

51. *Kentucky Post,* December 20, 1941.

52. *Somerset Journal,* December 18, 1941, January 2, 1942. See also *Twentieth Century War Veterans: Pulaski County, Kentucky* (Paducah, KY: Turner, 1999), 12–13.

53. *Owensboro Messenger,* December 21, 24, 1941; *Paducah Sun-Democrat,* December 12, 19, 1941; *Louisville Courier-Journal,* December 17, 1941; *Franklin Favorite,* January 15, 1942.

54. *Paducah Sun-Democrat,* February 8, 1942.

55. *Paducah Sun-Democrat,* December 8, 1941.

56. *Paducah Sun-Democrat,* December 8, 1941.

57. *Louisville Courier-Journal,* December 16, 1941.

58. *Louisville Courier-Journal,* December 16, 1941.

59. *Louisville Courier-Journal,* December 16, 1941.

60. *Cincinnati Enquirer,* December 10, 1941, Kentucky edition.

61. *Louisville Courier-Journal,* December 9, 1941.

62. *Louisville Courier-Journal,* December 9, 1941.

63. *Louisville Courier-Journal,* December 16, 1941.

64. *Louisville Courier-Journal,* December 16, 1941.

65. *Louisville Courier-Journal,* December 16, 1941.

66. *Louisville Courier-Journal,* December 16, 1941.

67. *Louisville Courier-Journal,* December 16, 1941.

68. *Cincinnati Enquirer,* December 24, 1941, Kentucky edition.

69. *Cincinnati Enquirer,* December 24, 1941, Kentucky edition.

70. *Frankfort State Journal,* December 10, 1941.

71. *Frankfort State Journal,* December 10, 1941.

72. *Frankfort State Journal,* December 10, 1941.

73. *Louisville Courier-Journal,* December 9, 1941.

74. *Louisville Courier-Journal,* December 9, 1941.

75. *Louisville Courier-Journal,* December 13, 1941.

76. *Louisville Courier-Journal,* December 9, 1941. See also *Louisville Courier-Journal,* December 17, 1941, for Hunter quotes.

77. *Kentucky Post,* December 29, 31, 1941. Quotes are from the December 29 paper.

78. *Louisville Courier-Journal,* December 9, 1941. See also *Kentucky Post,* December 29, 31, 1941; *Somerset Journal,* December 11, 1941.

79. *Louisville Courier-Journal,* December 9, 1941; *Cincinnati Enquirer,* December 11, 1941, Kentucky edition.

80. *Louisville Courier-Journal,* December 9, 1941.

81. *Louisville Courier-Journal,* December 9, 1941.

82. *Cincinnati Enquirer,* December 13, 1941, Kentucky edition.

83. *Louisville Courier-Journal,* December 18, 1941.

84. *Franklin Favorite,* December 18, 1941, January 29, 1942.

85. *Franklin Favorite,* June 11, 1942.

86. *Kentucky Post,* December 25, 1941.

87. *Cincinnati Enquirer,* December 15, 1941, Kentucky edition.

88. *Ashland Daily Independent,* December 12, 1941.

89. *Ashland Daily Independent,* December 12, 1941.

90. *Madisonville Messenger,* December 31, 1941.

91. *Madisonville Messenger,* December 31, 1941.

92. *Louisville Courier-Journal,* December 9, 1941.

93. *Louisville Courier-Journal,* December 17, 1941.

94. *Louisville Courier-Journal,* December 17, 1941.

95. *Louisville Courier-Journal,* December 17, 1941.

96. Harrison and Klotter, *A New History of Kentucky,* 290–91.

97. Dixon, *African Americans and the Pacific War,* 33–34.

98. *Louisville Leader,* December 20, 1941.

99. *Louisville Leader,* December 20, 1941.

100. *Louisville Leader,* December 20, 1941.

101. *Louisville Leader,* December 20, 1941. The writer Pearl S. Buck was the first American woman to receive a Nobel Prize. Though she was white, Buck championed racial, gender, and ethnic equality.

102. *Owensboro Messenger,* December 8, 1941.

103. *Owensboro Messenger,* December 8, 1941.

104. *Owensboro Messenger,* December 8, 1941.

105. *Owensboro Messenger,* December 8, 1941.

106. Lord, *Day of Infamy,* 219; John Ewing Roberts, interview by the author, August 24, 2019, Baltimore, MD.

107. Roberts interview.

108. Roberts interview.

109. Mildred Schofield, interview by the author, November 18, 2019, Mayfield, KY.

110. *Lexington Herald-Leader,* December 5, 2011.

111. *Lexington Herald-Leader,* December 5, 2011.

112. *Lexington Herald-Leader,* December 7, 2011.

113. *Lexington Herald-Leader,* December 7, 2011.

114. *Lexington Herald-Leader,* December 7, 2011.

115. *Lexington Herald-Leader,* December 7, 2011.

116. *Lexington Herald-Leader,* December 7, 2011.

117. *Owensboro Messenger-Inquirer,* December 7, 2016.

118. "Interview with Gradie Jackson," William H. Berge Oral History Center, Eastern Kentucky University, https://oralhistory.eku.edu/items/show/313.

119. *Danville Advocate-Messenger,* December 7, 2011.

120. *Danville Advocate-Messenger,* December 7, 2011.

121. "Interview with Mary Richards," William H. Berge Oral History Center, Eastern Kentucky University, https://oralhistory.eku.edu/items/show/3288.

122. *Paducah Sun,* December 11, 1991.

123. *Paducah Sun,* December 11, 1991.

124. *Paducah Sun,* December 11, 1991.

125. *Paducah Sun,* December 11, 1991.

126. *Owensboro Messenger-Inquirer,* December 7, 2016.

127. *Owensboro Messenger-Inquirer,* December 7, 2016.

128. *Kentucky Post,* December 10, 1941.

129. *Kentucky Post,* December 10, 1941.

130. *Louisville Courier-Journal,* December 18, 1941.

131. *Cincinnati Enquirer,* December 31, 1941, Kentucky edition.

132. *Louisville Courier-Journal,* December 27, 1941.

133. *Louisville Courier-Journal,* December 27, 1941.

134. *Louisville Courier-Journal,* December 27, 1941.

135. *Owensboro Messenger,* March 21, 1942.

136. *Lexington Leader,* December 14, 1941.

137. *Danville Advocate-Messenger,* December 8, 1941.

138. *Mayfield Messenger,* January 2, 1941.

139. *Honolulu Star-Bulletin,* June 22, 1998.

140. Transcription of a shortwave radio broadcast from Tokyo on January 2, 1942, part of a display at the US Army Museum of Hawaii, Honolulu.

141. *Danville Advocate-Messenger,* December 7, 2011.
142. *Danville Advocate-Messenger,* December 7, 2011.
143. *Danville Advocate-Messenger,* December 7, 2011.

Epilogue

1. Lord, *Day of Infamy,* 219.
2. James Vessels interview (December 3, 1976); *Paducah Sun-Democrat,* December 7, 1976; *Paducah Sun,* January 16, 1981.
3. Kenneth Vessels, interview by the author, November 19, 2019, Paducah, KY.
4. Kenneth Vessels interview.
5. Kenneth Vessels interview.
6. Mike Vessels, interview by the author, November 19, 2019, Paducah, KY.
7. Mike Vessels interview.
8. James Vessels interview (1975); Mike Vessels interview.
9. *Louisville Courier-Journal,* March 5, 6, 2002. See also *Honolulu Star-Bulletin,* December 7, 1991.
10. Hamlin interview; *Paducah Sun-Democrat,* December 7, 1977.
11. Hamlin interview; *Paducah Sun-Democrat,* December 7, 1977; *Paducah Sun,* October 11, 1999.
12. Kidd interview; *Paducah Sun,* December 7, 1983; *Mayfield Messenger,* December 7, 2018; *Paducah Sun,* May 23, 1998; "19-N-100503 USS Nelson," Naval History and Heritage Command, https://www.history.navy.mil/our -collections/photography/numerical-list-of-images/nara-series/19-n/19-N -100000/19-N-100503.html.
13. *Paducah Sun,* May 26, 2001. See also Collier Funeral Home, "Obituary for Mr. Riley," https://www.collierfuneralhome.com/obituaries/Mr-Riley-33395 /#!/Obituary.
14. Sanders interview; *Paducah Sun,* December 7, 1978. See also *Paducah Sun,* December 23, 1992.
15. *Madisonville Messenger,* January 6, 1943.
16. Forgy, ". . . *And Pass the Ammunition,"* 242.
17. *Paducah Sun-Democrat,* October 1, 1943, January 24, 1972; *Pomona Progress Bulletin,* January 23, 1972; Forgy, ". . . *And Pass the Ammunition,"* 2.
18. *Kentucky New Era* (Hopkinsville), September 20, 1993; *Paducah Sun,* September 10, 1993.
19. Russ Hatter to Berry Craig, email, September 24, 2019.
20. *Louisville Courier-Journal,* August 1, 1995; "Perry Thomas Calhoun," Find a Grave, n.d., https://www.findagrave.com/memorial/88397226/perry -thomas-calhoun.

21. *Owensboro Messenger-Inquirer,* May 15, 1993; *Paducah Sun,* December 7, 1986, November 1, 1993.

22. *Owensboro Messenger-Inquirer,* May 23, 2006.

23. *Louisville Courier-Journal,* January 24, 2014.

24. *Bowling Green Daily News,* April 29, 2015.

25. *Danville Advocate-Messenger,* November 24, 2015.

26. *Owensboro Messenger-Inquirer,* June 28, 2017.

27. *Louisville Courier-Journal,* July 10, 2014.

28. "John Edwards Wood," Find a Grave, n.d., https://www.findagrave.com/memorial/155801956; *Glasgow Daily Times,* December 7, 2015.

29. *Louisville Courier-Journal,* September 11, 1983.

30. *Paducah Sun,* March 14, 1992.

31. *Louisville Courier-Journal,* December 7, 1991; *Louisville Courier-Journal,* February 23, 2014.

32. "Raymond Clay Turley," Find a Grave, n.d., https://www.findagrave.com/memorial/75273845/raymond-clay-turley.

33. Taylor Upchurch, "Local Vet Celebrates 100th Birthday with Students," November 16, 2018, WYMT.com, https://www.wymt.com/content/news/Local-vet-celebrates-100th-birthday-with-students—500714601.html.

34. "Richard Don Lay," Find a Grave, n.d., https://www.findagrave.com/memorial/53305613.

35. *Louisville Courier-Journal,* November 11, 1977; *Owensboro Messenger-Inquirer,* March 1, 1944.

36. Ellis, *Patriots and Heroes,* 254.

37. Coleman interview.

38. "Who We Are," Alliance of Baptists, n.d., https://www.allianceofbaptists.org/about.

39. "Ben Conrad Fritz," Find a Grave, n.d., https://www.findagrave.com/memorial/36864820/ben-conrad-fritz.

40. Kenneth F. Huff, staff card, Kentucky School for the Deaf, Danville.

41. "Naunearle Brinton Shea," Find a Grave, n.d., https://www.findagrave.com/memorial/112505940/naunearle-brinton-shea.

42. Tom Brokaw, *The Greatest Generation* (New York: Random House, 1998), xix.

43. Studs Terkel, *The Good War: An Oral History of World War II* (New York: Pantheon, 1984). *The Good War* won Terkel a Pulitzer Prize.

44. Nelson, *Pearl Harbor,* 346.

45. *Louisville Courier Journal,* December 7, 1991.

46. *Louisville Courier Journal,* December 7, 2016.

47. Brokaw, *The Greatest Generation,* xxx.

Index